The Secular Spectacle

The Secular Spectacle

Performing Religion in a Southern Town

CHAD E. SEALES

OXFORD
UNIVERSITY PRESS

OXFORD
UNIVERSITY PRESS

Oxford University Press is a department of the University of Oxford.
It furthers the University's objective of excellence in research, scholarship,
and education by publishing worldwide.

Oxford   New York
Auckland   Cape Town   Dar es Salaam   Hong Kong   Karachi
Kuala Lumpur   Madrid   Melbourne   Mexico City   Nairobi
New Delhi   Shanghai   Taipei   Toronto

With offices in
Argentina   Austria   Brazil   Chile   Czech Republic   France   Greece
Guatemala   Hungary   Italy   Japan   Poland   Portugal   Singapore
South Korea   Switzerland   Thailand   Turkey   Ukraine   Vietnam

Oxford is a registered trademark of Oxford University Press
in the UK and certain other countries.

Published in the United States of America by
Oxford University Press
198 Madison Avenue, New York, NY 10016

Library of Congress Cataloging-in-Publication Data
Seales, Chad E.
The secular spectacle : performing religion in a southern town / Chad E. Seales.
pages cm
Includes bibliographical references and index.
ISBN 978–0–19–986028–9
1. Siler City (N.C.)—Religion—20th century.   2. Siler City (N.C.)—History—20th century.
3. Secularism—North Carolina—Siler City—History—20th century.   4. Hispanic American
Catholics—North Carolina—Siler City—History—20th century.   5. Material culture—Religious
aspects—Christianity.   6. Catholic Church—North Carolina—Siler City—History—20th
century.   I. Title.
BL2527.S55S43 2013
305.6'75659—dc23
2013019922

1 3 5 7 9 8 6 4 2
Printed in the United States of America
on acid-free paper

To Emily

Contents

Acknowledgments

THIS BOOK WOULD not have been possible without the help and support of numerous people. I am grateful to the residents of Siler City, North Carolina, who invited me into their homes and their churches and answered my questions about their community and its history. Milo Holt was exceptionally giving of his time and his memories. He passed away in September 2011, seven years after we first met. I am glad to have known him and am thankful for his help during the earliest stages of my research. I also am appreciative of the conversations with members and ministers of Corinth AME Zion Church, First Baptist Church, First United Methodist Church, Rocky River Baptist Church, and Saint Julia Catholic Church. Jane Pyle at the Chatham County Historical Association clarified questions about local sources and records. And the staff at the Wren Memorial Library kindly helped with my requests.

I am thankful for the institutional support that facilitated my research and writing. The Religious Studies department at the University of North Carolina at Chapel Hill was my home for graduate studies. This project began with a suggestion from my advisor Thomas A. Tweed, that I consider Latino migrant arrival to Siler City as a dissertation topic. This is not the book he imagined, I am sure, when he offered his advice over coffee in 2004. Rather than examining how Latinos viewed their new destination, I ended up telling a story about the town itself and how its longtime residents reacted to new migrants. The directional shift was my own doing, and it was neither immediate nor resolute. I changed course several times as I pursued my own history in the history of this southern town. I kept looking for something else—a something that I thought must be hidden in the past. Tom was patient throughout, listening to my reports from the field and the archive and offering a response to each that kept me going. He encouraged me to keep writing. It took many drafts to reach this book. And he has read them all, from proposal to postscript. For his endurance as a mentor and his commitment to his students, I am thankful.

My dissertation committee members gave their time and offered their care to improve my scholarship. Laurie Maffly-Kipp made me a better historian. Randall Styers, a better theorist. Lauren Leve, a better ethnographer. To my other two members, I am fortunate you were willing and able. Samuel S. Hill was an intellectual exemplar of critical conversation. And Donald G. Mathews was a moral force of historical argument. Both modeled the academic vocation for me, and I am thankful to have met them when I did.

During my time at UNC, Ruel Tyson mentored me in the art of writing fieldnotes and the skill of the long pause. Peter Kaufman, Janet Lopez, and the students in the Hispanic Initiative offered comments on my research and allowed me to participate with them in their program meetings. The staff at the North Carolina Collection and the Southern Historical Collection helped me locate materials. And a Research Travel Award from the Perry Fellowship in Religious Studies and a Graduate Summer Research Grant from the Center for the Study of the American South helped fund part of my research.

After leaving Chapel Hill, colleagues in the religion program at New College of Florida and those in the Religious Studies Department at George Mason University offered new sets of questions that sparked new ideas. I am especially grateful to Susan Marks and Randi Rashkover for their collegiality during my time at those institutions. My colleagues in the Religious Studies Department at the University of Texas at Austin have gone above and beyond with their encouragement and support of this project during its final stage of revision. Joel Brereton, Alison Frazier, Oliver Freiberger, Steve Friesen, Virginia Garrard-Burnett, Jen Graber, Jo Ann Hacket, Howard Miller, Patrick Olivelle, John Traphagan, and L. Michael White all read at least one chapter of the manuscript. Martha Newman read an entire draft, an unwarranted act of generosity. Her insightful suggestions helped transform the manuscript into a book.

I previously published related materials in *Numen: International Review for the History of Religions* and the *North Carolina Historical Review*. I am thankful to Gustavo Benavides and Anne Miller for their editorial advice and the journal reviewers for their helpful comments. I presented related papers at the annual and regional meetings of the American Academy of Religion, the International Congress of the Latin American Studies Association, the Chesapeake American Studies Annual Conference, the annual conference of the Southern Historical Association, the Navigating the Global American

South Conference, and the Interdisciplinary Conference for Graduate Research on the American South. I am thankful for comments from respondents, panelists, and other interlocutors in those venues, particularly Courtney Bender, Richard Callahan, William Ferris, Kathleen Garces-Foley, Glenda Gilmore, Jennifer Scheper Hughes, Jalane Schmidt, Harry Watson, and Julie Weise.

I am grateful to my editor Cynthia Read, and the reviewers and staff at Oxford University Press. The text benefited from the careful reading of Betsy Flowers and Manuel Vásquez. Kathryn Lofton voluntarily reviewed the entire manuscript and offered the penultimate comments that inspired the final argument. I am thankful to her and those I know from both UNC and Duke University who offered a critical eye at some point throughout the process: Julie Byrne, Mary Ellen Davis, Jill DeTemple, Shanny Luft, Mary Ellen O'Donnell, David Shefferman, Charlie Thompson, Jeff Wilson, and Isaac Weiner.

Family and friends provided hospitable company and cheerful spurring on: Leslie Babinski and Steve Knotek, Linda Benua, Evan and Gina Berry, Robin Langdon and Chuck Snell, Kyle and Laura Lossen, Mimi McNamee, Mike O'Donnell, Mike and Carol Major, Madison and Sara Major, Lucy B. Seales, Eunice Thompson, and Al and LeaAnne Williams.

To those who knew me on Sundays and Wednesdays in Pensacola, Florida: the religious history I shared with you enabled me to encounter the histories of a small town in North Carolina. For instilling within me the shared vernacular of Landmark Missionary Baptist Church on the west side, First Missionary Baptist Church in Brownsville, and First Baptist Church downtown, I am forever grateful to my parents, Gene and Faye Seales. To my brother Josh, who learned to speak it with me, thanks for making it fun.

Finally, this book is for the person who has known about Siler City almost as long as she has known me. She has heard, "It is almost finished" for several years now. She has listened to three completely different arguments with at least five different titles. And for some reason, she is still smiling. With love, this is for my wife Emily Major Seales and our sons, Adlai and Emmett, who arrived right on time.

The Secular Spectacle

Introduction: Secularism

> This is a brave spectacle, to see how death is destroyed,
> not by another's work, but by its own; is stabbed with
> its own weapon, and, like Goliath, is beheaded with its
> own sword.
>
> MARTIN LUTHER[1]

SOUTHERN SECULARISM IS a greasy pig. This book attempts to catch the greasy pig in a particular place, to tangle it in themes and contain it with chronology. But the subject is elusive, and easily slips the grasp.

On July 4th 1907, a crowd gathered in a field near downtown Siler City, North Carolina, to watch five men prepare the pig for the greasy pig race. They were several rows deep, a few hundred figures in dark coats, light shirts,

FIGURE 0.1 Greasing the Pig for the "Greasy Pig Race" at Siler City, N.C. Fourth of July Celebration, 1907. Credit: North Carolina Collection, University of North Carolina Library at Chapel Hill.

and black ties. Silhouettes in white, of two boys, one smaller than the other, and two girls, one carrying a parasol, dotted the front row. A woman stood at the center. In front of them, at a reasonable distance, the men held the pig by its front legs, turned on its side, atop a wooden crate. The local newspaper issued postcards of the scene, "compliments of *The Siler City Grit*."

The pig race was a tradition—along with a downtown parade, public speeches, Protestant prayer, and a baseball game and other athletic contests—during the annual Siler City Fourth of July celebration, inaugurated in 1901. As part of that tradition, the men set the pig loose, once they finished greasing it. Then the daring chased after it. If someone caught the pig, he got to keep it. But no one cared so much to see the catch. The fun was watching the boys miss, again and again, seeing them kick up dust and eat dirt. Everyone rooted for the pig.

The contest ended when someone captured the prize. Sometimes, though, it was too much for that individual to solely possess the greasy pig. Sometimes he wanted to keep the game going. In 1911, Charles Jones caught the pig after it ran through the crowd. Later the same day, he "turned the pig loose" during a baseball game. The ball players could not pitch or hit, steal second or round third—not with a greasy pig on the field. The spectators loved it. But after a good chase, the pig broke containment, escaping the ball field to find "refuge in a swamp nearby."[2] Out of sight, it was back to business as usual, making outs and counting innings.

Like the greasy pig race, the ritual performances of southern secularism were difficult to contain. They often began in clearly demarcated spaces, but they seldom remained there. They traversed shifting territories. Yet, despite the perpetual motion, local sponsors of secular rites offered a willing audience an impressive feeling of spatial stability, even as they continually relocated their scenic boundaries. With each movement and migration, they declared their social distinctions verifiable facts, and maintained, using in some cases scientific method, that the newly defined was indeed historical record.

In Siler City, the principle performance of southern secularism, the downtown Fourth of July parade, originated in the white business district, crossed over the railroad tracks, and ended at a town park on the edge of an upper-class white neighborhood. By the early twentieth century, the parishioners and pastors of the First Methodist Episcopal Church, South, and the Methodist Protestant Church occupied the homes of that neighborhood, which residents labeled "Palestine" because "the aspect of the area suggested the Holy Land to the minds of some observers."[3] In contrast, residents used the term "Hell's Half Acre" to describe an industrial area that included at least

FIGURE 0.2 First Methodist Episcopal Church, South of Siler City, dedicated 1887, located at 121 South Chatham Avenue. Source: Wade Hampton Hadley, *The Town of Siler City* (Siler City, NC: Caviness Printing Service, Inc., 1986).

FIGURE 0.3 Methodist Protestant Church of Siler City, built around 1895. Source: Hadley, *The Town of Siler City.*

three mills and a factory just across the railroad tracks. The *Grit* even reported the distinction. Offering his commentary, editor Isaac London wrote in 1914, "Angel food and deviled ham—what a mixture; as bad as the names of two sections of Siler City. One section, the eastern, is known as Hell's Half Acre, and the western part is known as Palestine."[4] A century later, no one referred to those parts of town by their religious place-names. But the neighborhood patterns that once evoked biblical comparisons persisted upon the landscape. Stately older homes with green yards and large trees lined South Dogwood Avenue and West Dolphin Street, the streets of former Palestine. Across the tracks, the area once known as Hell's Half Acre remained an industrial parcel, with a dilapidated warehouse, cement plant, and poultry plant.

Milo Holt, a Siler resident since the late 1920s, did not remember the earlier terms "Palestine" and "Hell's Half Acre" ever being used. He did tell me, however, that many of the members and all of the preachers from the two downtown Methodist churches "lived on 'The Hill.'" His family attended the Methodist Protestant Church, and they lived on The Hill as well. He also remembered that when he was a kid, they all walked together with their neighbors through the street down the hill to church for Sunday services.[5]

After World War II, Milo recalled, some of The Hill's earliest residents relocated to other parts of town to avoid an encroaching working class. Offering me a driving tour, he explained that when lower-class white residents earned enough money to buy into the neighborhood, its higher-class white citizens built homes in a more removed area. Eventually, a few among those upwardly mobile could afford a home in that neighborhood. So in the late 1950s and early 1960s, the upper class moved again, this time to the Pine Forest neighborhood, built around the Siler City Country Club.[6]

FIGURE 0.4 Street in Neighborhood Formerly Known as Palestine, 2004. Photo by Author.

FIGURE 0.5 Dilapidated Building in Industrial Area Formerly Known as Hell's Half Acre, 2004. Photo by Author.

Opening in 1957, the Club and surrounding neighborhood was an enclave for a racial class, limited to whites who could afford the membership dues and house payments. Both the Club and the neighborhood remained de facto segregated spaces, after racial integration in the 1970s. Based on 1990 census data, 100 percent of Pine Forest residents were white.[7] When I visited the Club in 2004 for lunch with a First United Methodist Church minister, all of the patrons were white, an African American woman waited the table, and Latinos worked in the kitchen.

Siler City always has been a small town. In 1900, there were 2,222 residents in Matthews Township, the designation for the Siler area.[8] In 1950, there were 2,501 residents within the city limits.[9] And in 1990, there were 4,995 residents.[10] Throughout those years, the racial demographics remained somewhere near 30 percent black and 70 percent white, according to US census records. That all changed, though, with the arrival of new migrants in the last decade of the twentieth century. From 1990 to 2000, the number of Hispanic residents increased from 3 percent (147 persons) to nearly 40 percent (2,740 persons) of the town's total population.[11] Suddenly, for some longtime residents, Siler was no longer a southern town. Almost overnight, it seemed to them, their town had been remade into something else. "You know what they call Siler City now?" asked a local of an out-of-town visitor. "Little Mexico!" the local declared, answering his own question.[12]

In 2006, I attended a panel discussion at the local Jordan-Matthews High School on how the rapid demographic shift had impacted the school and the community. There, I heard an African American teacher describe a moment in which she felt her students shared an experience across racial and ethnic lines. Ms. Price, as she is called at school, explained that the students typically self-segregated. She said this was evident during lunch, when white students gathered at tables with whites, blacks with blacks, and Latinos with Latinos. The last group subdivided themselves by nationalist affiliations and even further by region and hometown within their sending countries. One day in class, Ms. Price saw a Latina student arranging pencils on her desk. Intrigued by the sight, she asked the student what she was doing. The student answered, "This is how we do it at the Club." She explained to the teacher that she worked at the Siler City Country Club and as part of her job she set tables. She was setting her desk as she had learned to set those tables, using pencils instead of cutlery. With a laugh, Ms. Price recalled that she "told the rest of the students that they could act like they were at the Club." Following the student's lead, she said, "We pretended that we went to the Club."[13]

The historical arc that connects The Hill to the Club traces a local story of the rise and run of public religion in America. Religious historians have structured that broader story using narratives of secularization or secularism, recounting the institutional transformation of the sacred into the profane or the institutional diffusion of a religious spirit into a secular ethos. In 1968, historian William A. Clebsch considered the "aspirations of Americans sacred in origin and their achievements profane in fruition," arguing that "religion in America sought ceaselessly to call into being the City of God, and with striking consistency found itself having built instead the cities of man."[14] Surveying the same landscape, but with a narrower focus, the contributors to William R. Hutchison's 1989 edited collection, *Between the Times: The Travail of the Protestant Establishment in America*, detailed the public demise of liberal Protestantism, which peaked in the 1950s and subsequently declined as it succumbed to the challenges of secularization, religious pluralism, and conservative evangelicalism.[15] Voicing a prevailing sentiment, Dorothy Bass argued in her contribution to that volume that those Protestants hastened their own decline, as they promoted the secularization of civic life (particularly in public schools, because they did not want to use government funds for Catholic education), which eroded their cultural authority.[16]

In accounts such as those cited above, secularization is an associative pattern signifying the transformation of religion from sacred to profane and from public to private. Disestablishment was the catalyst of that transformation, as the state displaced church authority in civil matters, inaugurating a political cleansing of sectarian demands from civic space.[17] Outlining the boundaries of civil society, the state permitted that which it relegated to the private domain—religion—to reenter the public sphere. In the United States, a public form of liberal Protestantism underwrote the terms of the removal and reentry of religion as a universal category from civil society, dictating the social policies and political workings of secularism.[18]

American secularism, then, was the proliferative process that offered institutional life for public Protestantism after its political death, providing techniques for the rebirth of Protestant beliefs and practices as immanent within the categories of Christianity and, more generally, religion.[19] Tracy Fessenden describes secularism as "the ability of a Protestantized conception of religion to control the meanings of both the religious *and* the secular."[20] Secularism in the United States identified what Talal Asad has described as "new concepts" of "religion" in relation to the "epistemic category" of "the secular." A "political doctrine" that attempted to purify the public sphere of exclusivist particularity, secularism posited the modern state as the principal vehicle to "transcend the different identities built on class, gender, and religion, replacing conflicting perspectives by unifying experience." Secularism "*is*," Asad contends, that "transcendent mediation."[21]

The case of Palestine and Hell's Half Acre fits within these frames of secularization and secularism, presenting a regionalized portrait for comparison with other views of American religions. When institutional boundaries and social hierarchies were taking shape in the early twentieth century, a group of white southerners—those who attended the First Methodist Episcopal Church, South and the Methodist Protestant Church—used religious language to designate their neighborhood as sacred, as set apart from the rest of the town. If they were uncertain where they stood in the social order, they looked down to the east, toward Hell's Half Acre. If other residents were uncertain, they looked up to the west, toward the neighborhood of Palestine. By the 1930s, the religious particularity of place-names faded into a generic designation. As Clebsch claimed on a larger scale, religion moved from sacred to profane. The term "Palestine" was no longer necessary because everyone knew that those Methodists lived on that hill. They saw them walk the streets together on Sunday mornings, a pilgrimage from brick houses to steepled churches that connected sacred space to sacred place. At mid-century, though, as those who aspired to upper-class status moved in, the Hill became known as "Mortgage Hill."[22] Newcomers challenged taken-for-granted associations between congregational affiliation and social status, and the neighborhood natives worried about their class distinctiveness. To them, the newcomers polluted the purity of that place. If all were allowed entrance, they believed, then their Hill would lose its sacred status. It no longer would be like their church—that is, set apart. Unable to maintain that conflation of congregation and neighborhood, they forsook one for the other. They settled in Palestine and ended up in Pine Forest, moving from a particularly religious to a ubiquitously secular place.

That movement from sacred to profane was not necessarily desacralizing, even if by definition it should have been. The secular club was known by its absent religiosity, by its lack of expressive Methodism, of preacher delivering a sermon, choir sounding the hymns, and laity sharing their concerns. But it was not defined by the absence of the sacred, of powerful things set apart.[23] Rather, the social desire to protect the exclusionary status of their religious place, of an essential difference based on sacred appearance, motivated the migration. The secular project of the Siler City Country Club offered an opportunity to protect the social purity of upper-class white bodies, even if it meant losing their religious particularity. As they left their promised land, those Protestants found another way to ritually perform segregated space using the table manners of the secular club. When the Latina student showed the class "how we do it at the Club," she did not set place in the image of Palestine, as residents of the Hill had done. Nor did she set place in the image of spiritual inwardness, as Separate Baptists in eighteenth-century Virginia had done before, when they gave up common wares for individual utensils.[24] Rather, when she arranged her pencils as forks, knives, and spoons, she performed a place setting, a ritual ordering of differentiated space, in the image of a secular display.

The historical formation of the Siler City Country Club began with the ritual performance of religion. To know that the country club was secular was to recognize it as not a church, and that recognition required a visible classification of the church as religious. Once that relationship was established, the secular could operate as if it were autonomous, as if it were free from religion, if not free of it. Unlike the church, down the hill, the Club was not Methodist property. It transcended a sectarian religious identity, in order to maintain the immanence of its class prestige. The Club also was not an official governmental body. Yet, it functioned as a local apparatus for governmentality and a vehicle for the secular transcendence of religious particularity.[25] The secular club operated as if it were an independent body, unfettered by denominational rulings and federal interventions. But as it declared independence, the secular simultaneously conspired with religion to maintain its social patterns of spatial segregation. In the historical movements of religion and secularity traced from Palestine to the Club, southern whites did not displace or replace religion with the secular. Instead, they added another social list for class ranking, supplementing the First Methodist Episcopal Church, South and the Methodist Protestant Church rolls with the nonreligious membership of the Siler City Country Club. When the Latina student carried the ritual practices of the Club to the classroom, she further complicated that historical relationship and reconfigured its secularizing habits. As with the greasy pig contest, when it looked like the game was over, it began again somewhere else.

Counter to declension narratives of secularization, the secular in this case did not cause religion to lose its social status or significance.[26] Upper-class residents were members of both the church *and* the club. Nor was the secular, contrary to diffusion narratives of secularism, merely religion by another name.[27] The ritual performances of Methodist affiliation that set the neighborhood apart did, like Hutchison's account of Protestant establishment, die a public death. No one ever remembered the exact cause. One day, once upon a time, the pilgrimages down the Hill just stopped. At some point, people moved. Yet, even after they left the neighborhood behind and stopped the Sunday parades, the members of those Methodist churches, former residents of Palestine, haunted the landscape.[28] They persisted in another religious form, not solely in secular likeness. They reconvened as a more private congregational body, meeting within the downtown church of First United Methodist, rather than on the streets that led to its door. Hidden within plain sight, they continued their self-presentation of class privilege. Except now, the building spoke for them, rather than they for the building. The congregation that emerged from the 1940 unification of the First Methodist Episcopal Church, South and the Methodist Protestant Church wielded disproportionate social and cultural capital in the early twenty-first century. As depicted in Table 0.1, the congregation's educational level was well above the national average, and its average annual household income was slightly below the national average. In comparison, both the educational and economic level of the general Siler City community, which included FUMC members, was well below the national average. With regard to education and income, the contrast between FUMC congregants and the rest of the community is striking. FUMC congregants were over four times more likely to graduate from college than members of the community as a whole. Also, they earned on average $12,000 more per household than other members of the community.[29] Economically and educationally privileged, FUMC members banked the social capital necessary for persistent political success.[30] These Methodists were not among the wealthiest in the nation, but they were among the elite of their locale. Congregational life concealed that secular advantage, performing

**Table 0.1 First United Methodist Church of Siler City Educational and
Income Levels, 2003[1]**

	Less Than High School	High School	Some College	College Graduate	Post Graduate	Annual Household Income
FUMC-Siler City	3%	18%	35%	30%	14%	$63,929
Siler City Community	31%	34%	24%	7%	3%	$51,662
U.S. Average	20%	29%	27%	16%	9%	$64,338

[1]Adapted from *Revision Context 2003: First United Methodist Church Siler City, North Carolina*
(Rancho Santa Margarita, California: Percept, 2003), 5–6, 10–11. Reprinted with permission
from Percept Group, Inc. © 2003.

its collectivity behind church doors rather than in city streets. Their religious
affiliation still meant something, even in its more private form. At the end
of the long century, the descendants of Palestine still used the church to set
themselves apart. Along the way, they added the country club as another site
to do the same. And at the turn of a new century, Latino migrants set their
own places within those local genealogies of differentiated space.

Argument

Tracing a twentieth-century path of secularization in a southern town, this
book argues that Siler City residents participated in performances of religion
and projects of secularism; their participation revealed social interests as it
displayed social status, and the relationship between their performances of
religion and their projects of secularism changed over time. Moving roughly
chronologically, I suggest that the relationship transitioned from collaborative, to consonant, to contested during the Incorporation (1890s to 1920s),
Establishment (1930s to 1960s), and Restructuring (1970s to 2000s), respectively, of social institutions. Those shifting relations describe the dominant
mode of public presentation in each historical period, the "mood and motivation" expressed by the upper-class whites that defined and regulated it.[31]

Other residents—upper-class blacks, working-class and middle-class whites and blacks, as well as later arriving Latinos, who composed the bulk of the working class at the end of the twentieth century—also participated in performances of religion and projects of secularism. Their participation, though, was subject to the gaze of a paternalistic minority. From the symbolic vantage point of the Hill, upper-class whites set the discursive terms of civil society by naming and locating the sacred *and* the profane, while simultaneously prescribing the rules of engagement for the ritual interaction of both in public space.

Plotting that path, I reconsider a prevailing assumption that secularism substituted a new form of control for a previous religious one, and that substitution ultimately led to the demise of its predecessor. Max Weber formulated the template for that argument in *The Protestant Ethic and the Spirit of Capitalism* (1905), when he set forth the history of capitalistic economies as the sociology of religious ideas. He maintained that "religious tradition" continued to play a significant role in modern capitalism. But it persisted not as religious tradition, but rather as fiscal discipline, what he called "a regulation of the whole of conduct," which penetrated to "all departments of private and public life."[32] Protestantism was Weber's historical switchman for that ritual innovation. It carried within itself the ideational mechanism that enabled the industrialist to convert Catholic control of self into capitalist self-control, redirecting it down another track that moved away from the religious and toward the economic. Theorists of secularism later reclassified that endpoint as the secular. For those working out Weber's thesis, Protestantism's "emancipation" from Catholicism, as Fessenden phrases it, set the "blueprint" for "secularism's emancipation from 'religion' itself."[33] That reframed assessment assumes, as Weber did, that Protestantism set in motion a historical process that ultimately led to its own death. It diffused its mechanism of control, the pervasive self-regulation of the priesthood of the believer, into the nooks and crannies of everyday life, as the "Reformation," Fessenden writes, "generated its presence 'everywhere,' not least in secular guise."[34] Each individual was, in that Protestant world, forever after responsible for his or her salvation. No longer could anyone rely on the priest to keep watch over the sacrament. That burden now followed each person wherever they went, as they struggled to keep warm the heart inside their hearts. In little time, though, their spiritual striving transformed itself into a secular exercise, its self-discipline no longer in the service of the church but of the factory.[35] Protestantism offered secularism its sword. Upon receiving it, the new science promptly beheaded the religious beast.

That argument fits certain brands of American Christianity that historians and sociologists cite as the starting point for narratives of secularization and secularism in the United States.[36] Emancipation was a cornerstone
of liberal Protestantism and its political liberalism, expressed in the ideals of
self-determination, conscious choice, and the individual freedom to identify
and practice "true religion." Those ingredients, though, do not match the
regional label of evangelical Protestantism that is the central subject of this
book. Tempering traits of personal submission, obedience, and sacrifice in the
name of providential order more accurately describe southern evangelicals and
their sense of collective duty to God and responsibility for family. Those traits
translated to a political disposition of contrasting conservatism and a differing secularism that sought starker divisions between the City of God and the
Secular City. And that secularism did not just appear in the 1970s, as some
have argued.[37] Rather, it was readily institutionalized in the region across the
twentieth century. That may seem counterintuitive, given that southern evangelicals individuated their religious personalities and sacralized their secular
spaces. But even as they evoked heaven below by transforming the world in the
image of their hearts, one person and one space at a time, they never considered
their God the same as their government. That mistake, southern evangelicals
believed, was what made northern liberals godless.[38] At the same time, though,
evangelicals did not neglect governmentality. If anything, they were fiercer in
its exercise. They used *their* government to protect the sanctity of *their* God.
Resisting divine immanence, even as they welcomed divine sanction, southern evangelicals were in, but not of, the world. They imagined themselves as
using secularism without becoming secular, just as they used religion without
becoming religious. On the first account, they distinguished themselves from
their northern counterparts, and on the second, from their Catholic neighbors. Their secularism strove not to fully emancipate itself from religion, but
rather yearned for just enough proximal distance to work as its silent partner.[39]

The revision I propose is a subtle but significant shift in how scholars view
the relational differences between religion and secularity. I emphasize what
Fessenden and others already have posited, that there are "different religions
and different secularisms" and suggest that along with regional varieties of
religion, there are regional variants of secularism in American history.[40] But
I intend more than that. Regional variants of secularism are not just descriptive differences; they are themselves competing descriptions of thinking
about difference.[41] Using the extended case of southern secularism in Siler
City, I supplement the dominant model of thinking about secular and religious difference—a religious-secular continuum—with an alternative model

of locative naming that positions the religious and the secular not along the same line or shared plane, but in spatial relationship with one another, with the secular mutually dependent and constitutively defined (or named) against the religious, as it is performed in a particular place. In contrast to a continuum model, a model of locative naming emphasizes spatial difference over imperceptible similitude.[42] Linear or planar models of a religious-secular continuum track a wide spectrum of secular bandwidth, and the frequency of their usage suggests that they are useful for their task. But I do not consider a continuum the *sine qua non* of secularism in all its varieties, as John Lardas Modern suggests in *Secularism in Antebellum America* (2011), which affirms Fessenden's use of a "Protestant-secular continuum" as an apt descriptor for the "invisible consensus of American Protestantism."[43] Southern secularism was not defined by a religious-secular continuum, but was identified in its local politics of spatial relationships. To be clear, I am not arguing that Fessenden and Modern are wrong in applying a continuum model, as it suits their subjects.[44] A Protestant-secular continuum depicts a grammatical longing within certain strands of American Protestantism, abundantly evidenced in textual mediums and literary loomings, to convert visible religious essence into invisible secular spirituality, often through religious death.[45] But that invisibility did not define an American Protestant consensus that encompassed southerners in its "convenient fiction."[46] For Siler residents, secularism wove not a seamless garment by which they cast their lot with northern Protestants. Rather, in this postbellum town, white residents understood religious and secular difference in much the same way that they imagined racial difference. Their persistently differentiating social knowledge, a hallmark of secularism in numerous accounts, was formed in relation to categorical binaries of spatial segregation, which they regulated using both persuasive and coercive means. Their social knowledge, their way of thinking about the world, did not move along a line, or within a sliding scale, in which the religious could fade into the secular or the secular could replace the religious. A religious-secular continuum was to southerners like a racial continuum; it was institutionally impossible, and the machinations of their secularism enforced that notion.

Religion and Secularism: A Sighting

"Theories," Thomas Tweed writes, "are *sightings* from sites. They are positioned representations of a changing terrain by an itinerant cartographer."[47] This book is a sighting from a southern town, a positioned representation of religion and secularism in Siler City, North Carolina.[48] Tweed notes that the

"Greek term *theōria* is a somewhat redundant compound that combines *theā* (seeing, but also that which is seen, therefore a sight or spectacle) and *horān* (the action of seeing, from the Greek verb "to see").[49] Theory, then, is literally the seeing of a sight from a site. Redundancy is useful in this case, as I account for the ways in which this southern town might be seen from somewhere else, from the historiographical sightings of secularization and secularism in the United States. But the book also reads the satellite surveillance in the local reflection of its looking glass. Placement is important; locality matters. Secularization and secularism look different on the ground than how they look from above. No one view is necessarily more realistic than the other, but multiple views are needed to get a better sense of how we understand what the naming of religious difference did in particular places, why it mattered, and what it meant and still means.

From the perspective of liberal Protestantism and northern liberalism, southern religion *was* the secular spectacle. In southern performances of religion, liberal Protestants located a primitive religiosity and used it to justify national expansion of their secularism. Examples filled northern print media, permeated Works Progress Administration projects, and circulated in coverage of the Scopes Trial.[50] Observers and commentators of the American South viewed its residents as *homo religiosus*, as a people defined by an inherent religiousness. They were the museum display for evangelicals, stuck in time and possessed by the Holy Spirit, by experiential piety, by powerful feelings and simple emotions. Incapable of reason and rationality, these captives of superstition lacked the political skills needed to enter civil society.

Those spectators were blind, however, to the public manner in which southerners strategically wielded secularism with magnificent effect. The boys who chased the pig put on the show—but the men who greased the pig were the ones to watch. Even in the most spectacular case, evangelicals actually won their secular trial, regardless of the national shaming of William Jennings Bryan in 1925. The Scopes conviction was overturned on a technicality, but the Butler Act prohibiting the teaching of evolution in public schools stood in Tennessee until the state repealed it in 1967, the year before the US Supreme Court ruled against such prohibitions.[51] During that period, southern evangelicals used an institutional instrument of governmental authority—the court system—to defend what their opponents described as an antimodern theological position. Northern critics complained that the Tennessee courthouse was no court of law. It was a religious mockery. That legal exercise, they maintained, was not in the image of their secularism. On this last account, they were right. What the Scopes Trial proved, more so than the good fun it made for H. L. Mencken and the cultured gawkers, was that southern secularism was equal to the political task of northern secularism. Southerners would win some and lose some on the national stage. But foreshadowing later victories, their secularism could show itself to be a formidable opponent, disarmingly adept at the modern politics of locative naming.

The view *from* Siler City does not match the theoretical sightings *of* the southern town. What the history of Siler City shows is that secularism in the American South located ancillary *sites* and *sights* of social power, which residents used alongside their principally religious site of sights—the congregation—for the ritual performance and observation of moral community.[52] In this book, secular sites include the factory, bank, street, retail store, courtroom, city hall, neighborhood, hospital, railroad, and automobile.

Residents determined those sites were secular—that they were not religious—by a commonsense understanding that religion was what happened in the congregation, inside the hearts of believers when they gathered together as one body.[53] Everything outside that spatial experience was a secular happening; it was "of the world."[54] But religious feeling was portable. Believers could take it with them into the world, into its secular sites, as did members of the First Methodist Episcopal Church, South and the Methodist Protestant Church when they carried it from their congregation into their community. Secularism sanitized those sites, making it possible for southern evangelicalism to enter and exit secular spaces without leaving behind visible signs of religious presence.

The proliferation of secular sites in Siler City enumerated the possible sights of social power from and of those spaces. Discriminating secular from religious spaces depended upon a way of seeing the world in relation to the performance of religion in those spaces. Working out their self-revelatory common sense, residents saw their local bank, for example, as different from their local church, even though they performed similar rites in both spaces. In the church, they held finance meetings, and in the bank, they translated biblical scripture for fiscal application. But those in need of salvation or renewal did not attend a church finance meeting in hopes of hearing a powerful sermon. Nor did a crowd gather in front of a bank teller for a Sunday school lesson (for one thing, the bank was closed on Sundays). Finance was by commonsense appearance and temporal accounting a secular matter, even when it involved Kingdom business. The secular difference depended upon an observable distinction made visible in the public performance of contrasting religion at a specific time and in a particular place. The "secular" and the "religious" were interrelated sites of power for the social performance and ritual classification of collective associations based on exclusionary difference. And categorical distinctions between the religious and the secular and spatial purifications of the sacred from the profane were made—not revealed—through the spectacle of collective life, in its observable ritual performances, visual displays, and illocutionary acts.[55]

Southerners viewed religious and secular spaces as distinct, as each set apart from the other, even though they were part of the same system, part of the same social body. L. L. Wren, for example, was a founding member of the Methodist Protestant Church and later the Chatham Bank. He balanced the church budget, anonymously contributing to his congregation when tithes fell short, and also kept the bank ledger. Wren had a stake in both institutions, but he never considered them the same type of place. He wrote a history for his religious congregation, "My Church," and another of his financial institution, "A History of the Chatham Bank." His distinct histories suggest that those "sites of power" did not share the same origin. One was of heaven, the other of earth.

With Wren, the religious and the secular were "divided inside himself," as Michel Foucault declared of the modern subject.[56] Such bifurcations were antagonistic. But southerners were ritually adept at smoothing over striated spaces, as they did with logical contradictions of spiritual equality and racial segregation, secular universality and religious particularity. They spoke as if movements across those spaces were fluid and harmonious. With political savvy, they promoted a type of civic contestation that strongly discouraged public argument, and they called it consensus.[57] They imagined shared spirituality that necessitated racial distinction, and they constructed spaces absent of religion that invited Christian missionizing. Democracy was to them not the striving for equality, but the protection of divinely sanctioned difference. The idea that all bodies were the same, that all persons were equal, was to those "who love their white skin," as one North Carolina commentator put it in 1900, blasphemous and unbiblical.[58]

Southern promoters of democratic progress distilled secular difference using techniques of purification that were inseparable from institutional mechanisms of racial segregation. Their ways of seeing the world as secular entailed the sighting of whiteness and blackness within it.[59] Southerners attributed racial difference to biological essence. They assumed it was naturalized, yet they recognized it as performative. And the performative contingency of racial sightings betrayed their commonsense logic that appearances were stable. They refused to admit it, but whites could not keep blackness out of white-only spaces solely based on personal looks, traits, or habits.[60] In moments of unfamiliarity, when white observers did not recognize the person in front of them and could not place them within relational networks of family and church, blacks with lighter skin tones "passed" through the porous boundaries of segregated society, as Homer Plessy did in New Orleans.[61] A longtime resident of the Siler City area described her experience growing up during segregation by saying, "I am from the black community, but everyone says, 'You're not black.'" She explained that "because of the complexion of my skin—I'm light skinned—I was able to get away with a lot." To illustrate what she meant, she recalled a moment when she was eight or nine years old and her "mama told her to go to the drugstore and get a milkshake from the whites-only counter." She said they were shopping on "Main Street," and she would go in and get a milkshake and bring it back out.[62] In her recounting, she moved through spaces of whiteness, but she could not remain there; her family lived outside its boundaries. That was the ultimate institutional leverage that southern whites wielded to enforce racial segregation. They fixed and located individuals by a racial binary not solely on the basis of personal appearance, but in reference to collective associations—their families and the churches they attended.[63]

Southern secularism worked to confine blackness, delimiting its associative secularity, while emphasizing its expressive religiosity. This was both a locative strategy to discern racial difference and a political tool to perpetuate institutional dependence. As part of their attempts at definitional control, southern whites constrained the ability of black citizens to organize and maintain their own secular sites, allowing classrooms but not courtrooms, private services but not public works. Even then, whites perpetuated the perception that black businesses were prone to religious influence in order to justify their secular oversight of those businesses.[64] Whites refused to see or recognize any possibility that religiosities associated with blackness could withstand the secular light.[65] Yet, when those same whites brought religion into their workplace, as Wren did when he used scripture to instruct his bank employees, they considered it ethereal enough to pass for secularity.

Even in their conflating performances, those southerners did not consider that it could work the other way around: that the secular could pass for religion or that whiteness could pass for blackness.[66] They inverted the perceived sacred order by assuming that they always were self-aware, that they knew when the inversion began and when it ended.[67] They conflated religion and secularity in liminal moments, such as the inclusion of Baptist prayer in Fourth of July celebrations, conducting them as public performances akin to blackface minstrelsy. They masked one as the other in those brief performances to reinforce the spatial distance between them.[68] The religious minister stepped away from the church pulpit once a year on Independence Day to sanctify the Christian nation on its secular stage. But only whites, southerners believed, could in the briefest of moments sheet their secularity with religion, holding its cloak in one hand, or paint themselves as blacks, holding that face with the other. Only they could play that game with dead seriousness and retain their secular transcendence, as they retained their racial whiteness. To them, their own "passing" was inconceivable, because that would mean a lack of awareness, a misrecognition of their secularity as religion, or their whiteness as blackness, that would suggest the inherent naïveté of possessed primitives. Yet they, professed white progressive men, were by their own account moderns, justifying public control by self-recognition. Their definition of progressivism differed from its radical articulations.[69] It meant not the striving for equality, but the protection of order. With that premise, southern secularism named and located religion in much the same way that its racial segregation named and located black bodies.

Modern projects of civic cleansing, including those of American democracy, cannot do without dirty spaces and profaned temples.[70] In nineteenth-century pretensions of a US nation-state, Anglo Americans, who happened to be Protestant, named and located the profanation of political danger in the perceived filth of Catholic immigrants, removed to urban ghettos. In twentieth-century affectations of a white republic, American southerners, who also were Protestant, named and located their political danger in the imagined vulgarity of black bodies, removed to segregated neighborhoods.[71] Until the end of the twentieth century, Catholic presence was seldom an imminent threat, though they were no less fearful. Instead, southern whites were preoccupied with a particular type of racial impurity—of blackness ever present, always at the back door. American Protestantism in its major forms of liberalism and evangelicalism may have promised a radical democratic impulse, an "incarnational democracy," to use Nathan Hatch's interpretive term.[72] It may have offered the political potentiality of spiritual equality as eternally present within its projected essence. But the realization of that equality was always postponed. In the southern town, the political deceit of the unattainable horizon was punctuated with a progressive mystique, the historical construction William Chafe has used to describe an "etiquette of race relations" that promoted civility over discord and maintained racial difference, even as it diffused racial conflict.[73]

This was the very definition of secularism in the American South, to give (or take) with the left hand without acknowledging what the right hand was doing. Mill owners in the South frequently gave to Protestant churches in secret, not letting others laud their charitable deeds in public. Or when they did give in full view, their stated intentions were to serve the habits of heart and not the motives of profit. Yet their gifts were never free. They came with a demand that the pastor of the mill church preach a message that served the interest of the shopkeeper, a message of peace, obedience, and work rewarded in the next life.[74] On the one hand, they clothed the material interest of making money in the ideal interest of saving souls. On the other hand, that gift-giver, the mill owner, justified his relationship between church and shop as a necessary component of his secular mission. He was the paternalistic protector of his own city-state, of factory, church, and town. He provided jobs, housing, and education. In his seersucker civility, he was a vessel of civilization.[75] Wherever he went, there he was. Civility was his charisma.

In Siler City, an upwardly mobile class of southern whites used the same strategies as the mill owner. They symbolically masked their social power—an ability to construct moral communities using the coercive techniques of persuasive friendship—in liminal performances in order to gain psychological and economic advantage over southern blacks and secure their social location.[76] Through the 1950s, in gymnasiums, churches, and streets, leading white citizens wore blackface to display control over black bodies. White Protestant men attempted similar feats of gender control when they paraded as blackface mammies on the Fourth of July or cross-dressed for mock matrimony as part of church fund-raisers. In their performances of the racial primitive and the gendered innocent, they publicly displayed a belief that only white men could pull the levers of secular transcendence. Those men possessed the ethereal spirit, which they romanticized as embodied in the feminine purity of white ladies. They imagined themselves protectors of that spirit, guarding its vulnerable body against all perceived threats while declaring themselves the only rightful suitors for her fair hand. In contrast, the principal promoters of secularism imagined black men possessed by bodily instinct and black women by earthly spirituality. They positioned blacks as placeholders of the primitive, closer to nature, and therefore nearer to the origins of creation and creativity, but also closer to its sources of destruction and danger. Donald G. Mathews writes that after Reconstruction "white people became obsessed with blacks" and "crazed by a fascination with purity and profanation that cloaked political designs and made sacred whites' aspirations to supremacy."[77] Whites revered and feared black bodies, marking them as both sacred *and* profane using the religious and secular rites of Jim Crow, including lynching and law, and projected onto them an inherent naïveté that rendered them in one moment spiritual mediums and in the next sexual animals—both qualities that called for the restraining arms of a civilizing Christianity and its requisite projects of secularism.[78]

Sources and Methods

Sources for the book were compiled from fieldwork materials, archival documents, and print media.[79] I conducted semistructured interviews with current and former Siler City residents, and I produced fieldnotes from selected multisite participant observation, which included congregational site visits, Fourth of July celebrations, Good Friday processions, and other community events.[80] Ethnographic techniques enabled me to extend the range of my textual sources, which included church records and organizational documents, local and regional newspapers, town and congregational histories, school annuals, city directories, and denominational records.[81] I also used printed photographs as another source of textual production.[82] To trace the historical development of the downtown parades, for example, I used coverage from the *Chatham News*. Back issues during the 1970s were important, since residents offered fragmented accounts of the racial desegregation of parade participation during that period.

Access to that crucial source posed a challenge, however, because issues dating from 1945 to 1988 were not available to the public. The paper holds them in bound volumes at its office and will not allow them to be microfilmed, citing concerns about the bindings. During my initial stage of research in 2006, I contacted the managing editor, Randall Rigsbee, and was allowed to see a volume covering one year.[83] I later learned that Alan Resch, owner and publisher, infrequently granted individual requests to see particular issues in the volumes on a limited basis. Local historian Wade Hadley, to my knowledge, was the only person Resch ever granted unrestricted access to the bound issues.[84] While Hadley briefly discussed the Fourth of July parade in his history of Siler City, his coverage stopped at 1932. Beyond that, he only mentioned that the parade resumed after 1945.[85] In 2011, I spoke directly to Resch and explained that I needed to consult those issues to better account for the history of the parades for those missing years. After explaining the situation, he agreed to allow me access to the volumes for one workday. Given the dearth of public records on the parades after 1945, I am grateful to Resch for allowing me to see those back issues.[86]

Organization

The book is organized into five chapters that address key themes theorists have used to trace formations of the secular: industry, nationalism, civility, privatization, and migration.[87] Each chapter details local performances of religion in relation to one of these themes, while showing how relationships between performances of religion and projects of secularism changed over time in Siler City. The chapters focus on local sources from one of three periods. The bulk of the sources consulted for the first two chapters are from the period of Incorporation, those for the middle chapter from the period of Establishment, and those for the last two chapters from the period of Restructuring. But chapters themselves are not contained by that periodization. As the book chases its subject thematically in each, it telescopes out from Siler City, to other times and places, and then returns to the southern town from another angle. In the strictest sense, it does not compile a local history; instead, it employs multiple methods to construct a conceptual genealogy of localized secularism in relation to the study of southern religious history and histories of religion and race.

Throughout the book, I use approaches typically filed under the headings of social history, ritual studies, institutional analysis, critical theory, and migration studies. Each chapter highlights one of those approaches in that order, using the others as they are relevant, and the authorial tone shifts stylistically as it takes on differing methodological personas.

In Chapter One, I argue that elite whites in Siler City used industry to resurrect what they considered the divinely sanctioned racial order of the antebellum South. In effect, they democratized that order, distributing it to an expanding middle class of upwardly mobile white Protestants. Southern industrialization in the early twentieth century tore down the plantation structure and made it possible for all white men to achieve the status of head of household. Each middle-class house, or domestic space, had the potential to be transformed into a Christian home, one that aspired to the racial and class order of the plantation, an order in which the idealized husband provided food, clothing, and shelter for his wife and children, and protected them from external danger. With the ever-increasing supply of consumer products, middle-class southern whites created their own domestic kingdoms. Converting the world in their image of the Christian home, they transformed mundane space into social place using mass-produced fashions and styles. Evangelical women and men played a significant role in this transformation, as they worked to bring domestic cleanliness into local churches, streets, and businesses. Drawing on industrial metaphors, I show how Siler City was incorporated as a New South town in the early twentieth century. I employ the term *incorporation* in two senses: referring to the "union in or into one body" and to the "action of forming into a community or corporation."[88] In the first sense: persons, congregations, and corporations located in a specific geographic area (within the "city limits") were "united into one body," the town of Siler City. In the second sense, the "action of forming a community or corporation" manufactured these social actors. I emphasize the first meaning of the term in this chapter, describing the historical formation of Siler City, while tracing the organizational development of congregations and corporations, and treating them as social bodies and mediating institutions for residents.

In Chapter Two, I give more attention to the latter use of incorporation, focusing on the "action of forming" a place and a community through the ritual performances of Fourth of July parades. Citing changes to the downtown parades, I argue that southerners used religious symbols associated with the Lost Cause (what historian Charles Reagan Wilson defined as "a mythic construction that helped white southerners define a cultural identity in the aftermath of Confederate defeat") as a locative placeholder for their own secularism.[89] In the inaugural parade performance of 1901, white residents sanctified an increasingly industrialized and explicitly racialized spatial order with the bodily performance of the Confederate soldier, the symbolic presence of personal sacrifice for Christian homes. They used Lost Cause symbolism to project regional values onto their nationalist rites, trumpeting southern masculine sacrifice as the universal Christian essence of American patriotism. Once they publicly displayed their religious location, they let loose their southern secularism. Retiring their Confederate Colonel, they used their twentieth-century secular parade to reclaim an American tradition of racial minstrelsy that nineteenth-century northern immigrants had conjured in the very image of the antebellum plantation.

In Chapter Three, I examine how city officials used progressive civility, an institutional mechanism of southern secularism, to maintain public power. In the early twentieth century, elite whites in the region proclaimed themselves carriers of civility, a disciplining practice they defined against the religious performance of primitive emotion in mob lynching. By mid-century, elite whites in Siler City had established that practice in their legal institutions, requiring all residents, white and black, to play by implicit rules of etiquette within civic life. Chafe described those rules as a set of "good manners," which included "abhorrence of personal conflict, courtesy toward new ideas, and a generosity toward those less fortunate than oneself."[90] He argued that there were two sides of civility: the side that presented itself as harmonious and peaceful and another side that blacks knew very well, "the chilling power of consensus to crush efforts to raise issues of racial justice."[91] Using a local case study of the 1962 shooting of a black resident by a white police officer, I juxtapose those two sides of civility, showing how white city officials used the restraining techniques of public consensus to perpetuate injustice, diffuse protests from black residents, and distance themselves from acts of violence against those residents. Even though it was clear that the officer shot and killed the resident—and he admitted to the shooting—city officials went to great lengths, using scientific methods of ballistic testing, to argue that the death was accidental. That defense, though, ultimately rested on the social power of progressive civility. In the trial, leading officials testified to the facts of the case and to the officer's inherent goodness. They used their science to prove the shooting accidental. And they used their civic standing to argue that the officer may have acted irresponsibly, but he was not a bad man, and therefore he could not have intentionally shot the resident. But they never acknowledged the racialized methods of their civic science, which they used to produce the evidential knowledge submitted in a court of law. Instead, they performed their science and enforced their laws as if it they were universal. At the midpoint of the book, the court trial renders hollow the secular proclamations of sacred order, democratic process, and civil liberty that white residents annually celebrated in their Fourth of July festivities.

In Chapter Four, I return to the ritual performance of the downtown parades, showing how white southerners privatized that public display to counter the contested racial integration of parade participation. This was not, however, the stated intent of the county commissioner who initiated an invitation-only celebration in the 1970s. Nor did the Jaycees, who organized the downtown parade during its contested years, attribute its decline to the racial integration of parade participation. Dismissing race as a factor, residents instead explained the decline as resulting from economic hardship, lack of public interest, or changes in the participation of women. Evaluating those explanations, I offer a critical interpretation of the social sources of ritual reorganization.[92] Triangulating sources, I argue that the spatial disruption of forced integration contributed to public decline and private renewal. In its reorganized performance, white residents reproduced the ritual traditions and gendered order of the old-time parades of the 1950s, expressing a desire to resurrect the communal body they remembered as vibrant before the local impact of the 1964 Civil Rights Act. In this exercise, they privatized a secular rite to counter the public arrival of another formation of secularism that developed in relationship to the religious performances of African American churches. The institutional changes mandated by federal legislation—its legal authority to forcibly reorganize segregated space and challenge gender inequality—confronted the very core of southern secularism. Contesting its local arrival, white residents recovered a historical past that preceded racial integration and projected it onto their present experience. In that private renewal, they sanctified the sacred order of segregated space—as they had done in earlier parades—with the religious performance of a Baptist minister.

Chapter Five includes a description of the arrival of Latino migrants to Siler City at the end of the twentieth century, emphasizing the public response to the religious performances of Good Friday processions by members of St. Julia Catholic Church. White observers, Protestants and Catholics alike, associated Good Friday displays with what they described as a Hispanic culture of suffering. They considered themselves removed from the daily pain and personal hardship that characterized migrant experience. White observers also reasoned in theological terms that their detachment from suffering explained why they, unlike migrants, emphasized resurrection over crucifixion. Observing the processions, whites viewed Latino Catholic performances of Christian suffering as a religious marker of secular difference, using it to identify migrants as essentially different from other Americans.

I

Industry

IF THE SOUTH was crucified in the Civil War and buried by Reconstruction, as many southern white Protestants believed, then industrialization was the hand that raised it to walk in newness of life. With factories and railroads, southerners resurrected dead cities and christened newborn towns. In an 1880 Thanksgiving sermon, "The New South," delivered at Emory College in Atlanta, Methodist minister Atticus Haygood instructed white Protestants to "cultivate industry and economy, observe law and order, practice virtue and justice, walk in truth and righteousness, and press on with strong hearts and good hopes [because] the true golden day of the South is yet to dawn."[1] Regional renewal was the religious promise of southern secularism, and Siler City shared its industrial baptism. By the 1920s, Wade Hadley recalled that "the sounds of steam mill whistles were heard morning, noon, and evening. On Sunday the bells of four local churches were heard."[2] Smokestacks and steeples, mill whistles and church bells—these were the sights and sounds of a redeemed southern body.

In this chapter, I argue that elite whites used industry to reestablish southern control of the region, sanctioning it with religious blessing; and the early history of Siler City illustrates a particular emplacement of that regenerate cosmos.[3] As Haygood put it, "I am grateful that slavery no longer exists, because it is better for the white people of the South. It is better for our industries and our business, as proved by the crops that free labor makes."[4] In Siler City, like in Atlanta, southern whites consolidated their social power in religious and secular sites, in newly organized churches, factories, businesses, banks, and shops. But unlike Atlanta, where Haygood preached, Siler City was relatively unaffected by Reconstruction. Past glories of the genteel South were not present there. Only a small number of slave owners lived in that part of central North Carolina. When Siler City was incorporated in 1887, three years after the arrival of the railroad, there were no structural ruins to rebuild or social hierarchies to restore. In its industrial novelty, Siler City was every bit the "new" southern town. Despite that blank slate, white residents, even those who never owned a slave, forged a southern future in the racial image of the region's "lost" institutions. Even in the New South town, antebellum legacies lingered in the organizational forms of industrial production.[5]

White residents of early Siler City proudly proclaimed that *their* ancestors were not slave owners. At the 1903 Gettysburg reunion, Colonel John Randolph Lane, from nearby Brush Creek in Chatham County (the same Confederate veteran who led the first Fourth of July parade in Siler City, which I discuss in the next chapter), reminded those gathered that his soldiers "came of good blood." Thirty-eight years after he served with the 26th Regiment of the North Carolina Troops, Lane remembered that the Chatham Boys came from "honest, American stock." He described their eyes as "not dimmed by vice," their bodies of "magnificent physique," and that "their life between the plow handles and wielding the axe made them strong." For Lane, these physical traits signified a moral character passed from one generation to the next through disciplined habit. The Chatham Boys were noble, but they were not nobility. Their status was earned, not inherited. Lane explained that when he said his soldiers came of good blood, "[He did] not mean that their parents were aristocrats...far from it; many of them never owned a slave." He said, "They were the great middle class that owned small farms in central and western North Carolina; who earned their living with honest sweat and owed not any man."[6] For Lane, slave ownership was a sign of class status. By rejecting the owner, but not necessarily the idea of ownership, Colonel Lane extracted a paternalistic principle from the antebellum world—that of head of household—and translated it for a new order built on self-reliance.[7] In contrast to the aristocrats—the plantation masters or mill owners—he proclaimed a middle class of southern whites, those who protected their households and wore their economic struggle as a badge of pride. In Siler City, that fierce individualism and independent spirit distinguished rural farmers-turned-factory workers.

Despite claims of self-reliance, though, upwardly mobile whites in Siler City held factory jobs created through the reinvested wealth of elite white families. Some of these families did own slaves. For example, Hadley, the local historian who described mill whistles and church steeples in early Siler City, was the grandson of a plantation owner.[8] After the Civil War, his grandfather moved to Siler City and reinvested his surviving capital in a factory. In 1895, he and three other investors incorporated Hadley-Peoples Manufacturing Company in Siler City, which produced yarn and textiles.[9] Wade Hadley's father, who was named after Wade Hampton III, the Confederate colonel who served with Robert E. Lee, inherited part of this industrial wealth, managed its growth, and passed it down to the next generation.

Wade Hampton Hadley, Jr., born in 1909 (two generations removed from the plantation), held a distinct financial advantage in life. Social legacies of financial capital accumulated using slave labor, and then factory workers helped fund Hadley's college education at the University of North Carolina and Cornell University. These social funds ultimately enabled him to pursue a career as a petroleum geologist, during which he worked a stint in Venezuela. Although working-class whites in early Siler City did not share the same advantages as the Hadley family, they benefited from the industrial cultivation of the New South. The antebellum wealth that endured the rapid economic changes of the post–Civil War South, including class prestige that outlasted financial loss, not only helped reestablish southern white elites like the Hadley family; it also facilitated the rise of an upwardly mobile white working class.

During the formative years of industrialization in Siler City, residents differentiated congregations and corporations as distinct bodies. Through their association with those bodies, they were incorporated into the town's material divisions of labor. At the local level, religious congregations played a key role in forming and maintaining social differences, particularly those of race and class. Congregations mediated social status and economic meaning at the local level by providing theological explanations of social order (why some are rich and others poor), while cultivating virtuous Christian citizens. The financial fruits of industry—especially the capital produced by mills and poultry plants, which churches received through direct contributions, tithes, and offerings—supplemented congregations in their religious work. During the early period of incorporation in Siler City, white Protestants championed industrialization, blessing it with theological language and infusing it with soteriological expectation. Focusing on the local level, we see a clearer picture of how industrialization "democratized" a racialized class movement, transferring the economic privilege of the plantation master to the public power of the factory owner, while creating an upwardly mobile, white, Protestant, middle class.[10]

Even though Siler City was incorporated and industrialized after the Civil War, religious justifications of a divinely sanctioned racial order which had hardened in the antebellum South survived the arrival of capitalism in the region. As historian Joel Williamson remarked, the North successfully abolished slavery in the South, but not a southern culture predicated on the peculiar institution.[11] Though market forces collided with the parochial order of the region, white southerners synthesized the cultural values of racial hierarchy with the capitalist ideals of profit and property, producing a paternalistic capitalism. As implied in Haygood's sermon, industry rendered Christian defenses of plantation economies anachronistic. The New South stripped white southerners of a taken-for-granted logic predicated on the racial order of slavery. The free market blurred lines between black and white because, at least in theory, it enabled all workers to sell their labor within a "transparent" market system. When northern troops withdrew from the region in 1877, however, market protections were removed, and white southerners reclaimed civic control of public spaces, starkly dividing the New South along racial lines while performing public control of blackness within "whites-only" spaces. There, as elsewhere in the industrial South, religion played a powerful role in the resurrection of white control.[12]

Religious Bodies

Siler City began as a collection of family farms. In the 1750s, its namesake, the Siler family, settled a western area of Chatham County so sparsely populated that it was referred to as "the desolate meadows."[13] The family built their home at the intersection of two North Carolina roads—one running north and south between Greensboro and Fayetteville and the other running east and west between Raleigh and Salisbury. Later, the family managed a store and post office at the crossroads. Though the Siler house changed ownership over the years, it remained the symbolic center of the town.[14] The current Siler City post office occupies the same lot where the Siler family house

FIGURE 1.1 Siler-Matthews House. Credit: North Carolina Collection, University of North Carolina Library at Chapel Hill.

once stood. Inside the building, a mural commissioned by the Public Works Administration project in 1940 depicts early crossroads settlers chopping logs, driving horses, and constructing buildings. In the late nineteenth century, the town grew around those crossroads, first as a stopover for travelers and later as an outpost for goods and services.[15]

Like many other North Carolina settlers, the Siler family came to Chatham County through Virginia. They attended Rocky River Baptist Church, one of the area's oldest congregations, founded in 1756 as a result of the revival work of Shubal Stearns. A Separate Baptist, Stearns attended the Great Awakening revivals and embraced the outlook of New-Light evangelicals after hearing George Whitefield preach in 1745.[16] Rocky River Baptist Church was the organizational predecessor to the two oldest white Baptist congregations in town: Loves Creek Baptist Church, founded in 1825 and located just outside the city, and First Baptist Church, founded in 1889 and located in the downtown area. Since their founding, all three Baptist congregations have remained members of the Sandy Creek Baptist Association, the oldest Baptist association in North America. Descendants of those Separate Baptists provided the bulk of the town's manufacturing labor force. They might not have brought industry to Siler City, but they were the engines that made it work.[17]

Methodists arrived later and proved adept business managers. M. M. Fox, an early member of the First Methodist Episcopal Church, South, recalled that "prior to the coming of the railroad, this [Siler City area] was not a Methodist Community."[18] Incorporated in 1884, Corinth AME Zion Church was the first Methodist congregation organized in Siler City, the result of missionary efforts by its northern denomination. Even though racial segregation was the primary marker of social differentiation and town growth, denominational and class differences were evident within racial categories.[19] Black residents had fewer opportunities, but they still managed businesses and made money. The majority of black business leaders were members of Corinth. The majority of white business leaders were members of First Methodist Episcopal Church, South (1886), or the Methodist Protestant Church (1894).[20] Mill and factory workers had their own churches. Methodists who worked in the mills and factories of Siler, for example, were members of West End Methodist Church (1913).[21]

Denominational differences were less significant during the earliest years of development, between 1884 and 1920. Similar to the atmosphere in frontier cities, this period was characterized by moments of cooperation and egalitarianism among its new citizens.[22] Before constructing separate church buildings, Baptists and Methodists gathered in a nearby brush arbor or tobacco warehouse.[23] Short on educated ministers, they shared preaching duties. Local Baptist historian Andrew Murray commented that, in these Sunday school gatherings, which began in 1885, "it seemed that there was no class structure and everyone met in the same group." According to Murray:

> The church voted to organize Sabbath School on January 18, 1890. This was an outgrowth of a local interdenominational Sunday School formed as many families were moving in after the completion of the railroad through Matthews Crossroads in 1884…This group met at a brush arbor next to [superintendent J. B.] Guthrie's house, or, in cold weather, the group met in a tobacco warehouse…Often, visiting ministers from various denominations would preach for the Sunday school—at other times, lay people would teach a Sunday school lesson. The Methodists left in 1886 to establish their own church.[24]

Those moments of ecumenical worship when Baptists and Methodists gathered together were short-lived. The three largest white Protestant congregations—First Methodist Episcopal Church, South, First Baptist Church, and the Methodist Protestant Church—broke away from the ecumenical Bible study and worship group the following year. Even though these churches continued to exchange Sunday school teachers, they seldom—except during revivals—met together again as a unified evangelical body.

According to local accounts, an evangelical egalitarian spirit of cooperation pervaded institutional life in Siler City, even after congregational differentiation. In an autobiographical statement titled "My Church," L. L. Wren traced the history of the Methodist Protestant Church in the town back to the Springfield Methodist Protestant Church (organized 1873). Several congregants of Siler City Methodist Protestant Church, including R. C. Siler and Henry Siler, members of the city's founding family, formerly attended the Springfield church, located a few miles west of Siler City. When Springfield members moved to Siler City in the 1890s (Wren moved with his family in 1893), that church faded away. By 1917, it was no longer a Methodist appointment. Many years later Wren wrote, "It made no difference to me that in the membership there were no PHD's no DD's or LLD's as I saw then and as I see it now genuine religion is not dependent upon these things but upon true repentance and forgiveness from our sins."[25] Wren's measure of true religion based on right disposition rather than on educational or social status, as something shared and observable as common sense, suggests that some white Protestants imagined themselves as bound together in a church community, even as they differentiated their religious and secular gatherings by race and class.

That feeling of religious cooperation carried across racial lines for whites, though their exchanges always were uneven. In 1919, African American Baptists accepted materials from the old First Methodist Episcopal Church, South, which was torn down to make way for a newer construction. They used those materials to build their own First Baptist Church.[26] It is unclear, though, whether the building materials were sold or donated. According to Methodist records, the old church building was "sold to a Negro Baptist congregation and moved from the lot."[27] But according to African American Baptists, "Mr. L. L. Wren had the idea and foresight of donating the materials from the torn down church to get the church started."[28] The discrepancy may be attributed in part to the fact that early First Baptist Church records were "destroyed in a house fire" of the church clerk. There were no written records of the congregation's birth story. But, according to its own historical accounting, the details of its birth "never left the memory of Mrs. Annie Fox," the First Baptist Church historian who later wrote that her church "was built on a vision of two people, Mr. L. L. Wren and Sister Mary Siler…to (see) a Black Baptist Church in the city limits of Siler City." According to that account, the first black Baptist congregation in Siler City resulted from the work of Sister Mary Siler, a black Baptist woman who held meetings in her home and donated land for the church building, and L. L. Wren, a white Methodist man who secured the building materials.

Industrial Bodies

From 1870 through the 1890s, white operators like Samuel Siler ran small-scale gristmills in the area. In 1884, the Cape Fear and Yadkin Valley Railway constructed a track from Sanford to Greensboro, North Carolina, and designated Siler Station a stop along the way. Three stores immediately opened, and others soon followed. "By April of 1887," noted Hadley, there were "seven stores, a tobacco warehouse, three livery stables, three hotels, a planing mill, a saw mill, and a cotton gin" in town.[29] Local regulation followed close behind upstart growth. When the community officially incorporated as the town of Siler City in 1887, the local governmental body managed and planned economic growth. It shared public power, however, with newly organized industrial businesses like the Farmers Roller Mill Manufacturing Company, which was incorporated in 1893. Outside industrialists often helped fund those companies. M. J. Boling, from Bonsal, North Carolina (between Siler and

Raleigh), for example, invested in the Siler City Bending Company, which opened in 1901. In 1904, he reorganized it as the High Point Bending and Chair Company. The company mill burned in 1907, and he rebuilt it the following year. It manufactured bent wood chairs until 1968, when the Boling family expanded their business to "make desks, tables, and bookcases" under the name of the Boling Company. Hadley remembered it as "one of the major wood furniture manufacturers in the United States."[30] City officials had close financial ties to those types of companies as stockholders or partners. Mayor L. L. Wren, for example, whose term ran from 1913 to 1915, was a partner of the Siler City Milling Company.[31] Local government was a public enterprise. But it was never free from private dealings, because the very ability to govern depended on the economic dividends of manufacturing corporations.

During the busiest years of the railroad, from 1890 to 1930, the Siler City population increased from 254 to 1,730 inhabitants, a rate of nearly 15 percent a year. Between 1900 and 1930, almost all residents, including those composing the managerial class, arrived from other parts of North Carolina, most of them from surrounding agricultural communities. According to the 1900 US Census, only 20 of the 2,222 residents of Matthews Township, the 68-square-mile area that includes Siler City, were born outside of North Carolina. Of the 1,582 persons listed in the census as white, one was born in England, one in Ireland, eight in Virginia, two in West Virginia, and three in

FIGURE 1.2 Ruins of High Point Bending and Chair Company Destroyed by Fire. 1907 Postcard. Credit: North Carolina Collection, University of North Carolina Library at Chapel Hill.

Georgia. Of the 640 persons listed as black, four were born in South Carolina, and one was born in Virginia.[32]

Mill employers provided housing for new workers; however, they retained ownership of the homes and subtracted rent from workers' pay, common practices throughout the South. Many mills required a minimum number of workers per room rented.[33] Near the railroad depot, wooden structures gave way to brick industrial buildings, while working-class neighborhoods outlined a bustling downtown district. Nearly 70 percent of the downtown business structures were built during those early years, totaling approximately thirty-seven new commercial buildings. While Siler City boomed, the total number of residents in Chatham County declined. That demographic shift suggests that area residents, both black and white, left their family farms and migrated to industrial towns, some to Siler City and others elsewhere beyond the county line.[34]

Industrialization transformed farming patterns in the New South, creating urban pockets of manufacturing cities and railroad towns in the midst of a deeply agrarian society.[35] Industrialization, though, was uneven. It was not as if the entire South stopped growing cotton and tobacco overnight, moved to the nearest town or city, and started working the assembly line. Cities like Durham, Birmingham, and Atlanta were not only sites of industrial production, but also market hubs for rural farmers.[36] Larger towns and cities connected rural areas to wider economies of consumption. As these towns grew, distinct religious and economic classes emerged, with race always a factor in that developmental story. A small New South town, Siler City comprised rural and urban elements, as its railroad connected farm and factory to each other and to the outside world.[37]

Early Siler residents maintained familiar farming practices in and around their city homes. Domestic farming supplemented family income, which was increasingly dependent on factory work. Hadley wrote that "The home place of some early residents [of Siler City in the early 1900s] resembled, on a reduced scale, the family farm from which they had recently migrated. A horse, cow, pigs, and chickens were kept on the premises. There was a barn, hogpen, and chicken house on the backside of the lot to accommodate them. Many homesteads had a kitchen vegetable garden."[38] In the midst of industrialization, those agrarian roots persisted. Farms existed side by side with factories in early Siler City, but it was factory life that gradually dominated the town. Free-ranging homestead chickens, for example, yielded to mass produced single-comb White Leghorns. By 1911, a hatchery for poultry-yard chickens was open near town. Customers from ten different states ordered baby chicks from the hatchery by parcel post.[39]

The arrival of the railroad made all of these industrial changes possible. Trains linked Siler City not only to Sanford and Greensboro but also to Baltimore and New York, as well as the eastern North Carolina coastal resorts that attracted northern vacationers. Connected to larger networks of economic exchange, Siler City was a center for agrarian and industrial production. In the early 1900s, the town shipped chickens, eggs, onions, wool, rabbits, and quail from the county to other parts of North Carolina as well as to destinations throughout the northeast. Rabbits, the most notable Siler City export during this period, were listed on menus in northern restaurants. Between 1904 and 1905, Siler City shipped more than forty thousand rabbits to towns across the state and throughout the northeast; from 1908 to 1916, the town exported 150,000 rabbits.[40] Raleigh banker Charles E. Johnson found the "Chatham rabbit" featured on fine dining establishment menus in Norfolk, Baltimore, and New York City. Much to northerners' surprise, the buying and selling of rabbits from Chatham County was regulated like other agricultural markets. The *Siler City Grit* reported that the "Raleigh man, full of pride, told his New York hosts that Siler City, in Chatham County, was the rabbit center of the world" and that "quotations were sent out just as from the great cotton and grain markets. The New Yorkers laughed and hooted at the idea."[41] The dish sold well enough in the northeast that buyers from as far away as Boston placed advertisements in the *Grit*, requesting large shipments of rabbits.[42] One Boston restaurateur requested "3,000 rabbits shipped in lots of not less than one hundred at each shipment and want them shipped open so they will not spoil. I will pay eight dollars per hundred as is usually prepared for shipment. Cash at your nearest express office as fast as shipped. Address, G. O. Sanders, 89 Gainsboro St., Boston, Mass."[43]

Rabbits had their day at market, but chickens defined Siler City.[44] East Coast resorts, such as those at Wrightsville Beach, were the first major buyers of Siler City poultry. In 1911, farmers shipped chickens whole, feathers and all. Resort personnel complained they could not clean the birds fast enough. The next year, John Aiken, a thirty-year-old black cook at a local hotel, set up a guillotine with cauldrons and cleaning tables behind a house in Siler City. Poultry dealers got involved. As the *Grit* described it, "... the dealers are killing and dressing [the chickens] before shipment and shipping them daily in barrels thoroughly packed with ice, so that when they get to their destination they are ready for the cooks and in excellent condition."[45] From that backyard slaughter, the poultry industry developed into the town's leading employer, one that would later bring laborers from Mexico and Central America to Siler City.

FIGURE 1.3 A Chatham Rabbit. 1906 Postcard. Credit: North Carolina Collection, University of North Carolina Library at Chapel Hill.

In the early twenty-first century, many locals still refer to the town's poultry plants as "farms"—an interesting but apt description. The mechanized production of livestock, of chickens stuffed into crates and shoved onto trucks instead of trains, is far removed from the workings of the family farms of the early twentieth century. But this description captures how industry transformed Siler City from a collection of family farms into a New South town, where livestock were raised for efficient killing, reliably packaged, and shipped for sale. Like livestock, industrialization routinized human labor, formatting residents to an economy of production and consumption while fitting them to a segregated space. Some welcomed those changes in the name of efficiency and progress, even encouraging them, while others adapted as best as they could.

Segregated Bodies

From the arrival of the railroad and its incorporation as a New South town, Siler City was a racially segregated place. Settlers divided first by race and then by class. In the industrial South, segregation replaced slavery—even in places where there were few slaves and fewer slave owners—as a structural mechanism for maintaining racial order and white supremacy.[46] Racially segregated

churches were not the norm in the Old South. From the 1830s until the end
of the Civil War, it was common for whites and blacks to worship together.
Following two pivotal efforts by slaves to gain their freedom by force—the
plot led by Denmark Vesey and the uprising led by Nat Turner in the early
nineteenth century—southern whites increasingly disallowed separate religious gatherings, worrying that they provided a space for slaves to communi-
cate and organize against them.[47] In an effort to quell this fear, slave owners
required blacks to attend services in white congregations and sit in segregated
seating within their sight.[48] In those instances, southern whites maintained
racial difference in the midst of religious inclusion. A marker in the Rocky
River Baptist Church cemetery, for example, honors African American members whose burial sites were unmarked. That material artifact confirms that
the congregation comprised black and white members from the 1830s until
the Civil War.[49] The absence of burial markers for black members further
demonstrates that they did not share the same racial status, even if they shared
the same religious baptism. Those organizational patterns of racial differentiation within shared spaces were transformed during and after Reconstruction
into racial differentiation as segregated church space, as blacks formed independent congregations and white churches removed or excluded blacks from
their church membership rolls.

Clean Bodies

As they segregated congregational bodies, southern whites reconfigured private and public spaces in the name of cleanliness. Like many other Americans
during this period, Siler residents and their governing officials diligently
worked to cleanse their homes and their town of what they considered its
filth and grime. In one of its first acts as an incorporated body in 1887, "town
authorities...built a commodious calaboose or lockup...to confine drunk
or disorderly person arrested on the streets." Clean streets, absent of disor-
derliness, distinguished civil society. The need for a commodious calaboose
suggested that the maintenance of societal order required spatial distinctions between clean and unclean spaces, that is, spaces for those of sober
mind and spaces for the drunken stumblers. To build a respectable city, one
in which business investors might consider opening a factory, leaders tidied
their streets and neighborhoods. This was the civic technology of the day, the
all-encompassing enterprise of domestic cleanliness.

The work of cleanliness was not just a personal habit; it was a professional
occupation. Those who could afford it paid others to keep their spaces clean.

Hadley remembered that each home had "the notorious privy or backhouse," and at his residence the "wash women came one day a week [and] built a fire under an iron pot to wash the clothes with homemade lye soap and scrub them on a washboard."[50] This was true for both domestic denizens and civic magistrates. In 1914, the town designated a "Public Scavenger" to drag "dead horses and cows" to the "local boneyard" and to carry excrement outside the city limits "from all the privies and pigpens" to lessen their overwhelming stench. The scavenger earned fifteen cents per privy or pigpen, and the town encouraged him to clean them out more frequently during hot summer months. Even with an employee assigned to that job, domestic maintenance of privies and pigpens was still considered a personal responsibility. In fact, the civil jobs of public cleanliness were described in domestic terms. William Owen Mann, superintendent of the new municipal water and sewer system in 1925, also held a position of "housekeeping" operations of the town in 1930.[51] Those who neglected its care, whether they were public or private citizens, were subject to the same collective shaming. Sitting on his porch during a summer in the early 1900s, for example, Hadley heard a family member comment, "Our neighbor's pigpen certainly is smelling high tonight."[52]

Evangelical revivals fostered that civic sense of disciplined cleanliness. Purifying souls went hand-in-hand with cleaning the town. To early town residents, the altar call was as familiar as the sound of the mill whistle.[53] In 1894, First Baptist Church hosted "a great revival...and many were converted." In 1912, E. B. Craven, pastor of the First Methodist Episcopal Church, South, noted, "Our church in Siler City has just passed through one of the greatest revivals in the history of the church. Its influence was felt in all churches. Finally 75 back-sliders were reclaimed and possibly more than 75 decided for Christ for the first time."[54] On September 8, 1915, the Reverend J. W. Ham preached to over fifteen hundred people at a tent revival in Siler City, securing an estimated five hundred converts, "including iceberg church members as well as sinners."[55] The year before, approximately four hundred people had converted at a tent revival led by traveling evangelist Raymond Browning. From this revival, a "cleanup" movement started, "looking to improved conditions in the moral, religious and civic life of the town." Members and converts held "cleanup meetings" on Sundays, rotating among white congregations, initially at First Methodist Episcopal Church, South, then at Methodist Protestant Church, then at First Baptist Church, and finally at West End Methodist Church. Among their goals, they hoped to stop the sale of cigarettes and ensure complete observance of the Sabbath, including no business on Sundays.[56]

Evangelical efforts to sanitize bodies, buildings, and streets, including banishing social vices like cigarettes and alcohol, were part of a social movement that swept through towns across North Carolina and the American South. At the state level, evangelicals pushed Prohibition through the North Carolina legislature in 1908, eleven years before it became a national law. New South towns like Siler City were primed for regulation, and white Protestants were highly effective in publicly enforcing evangelical propriety.

In the late nineteenth century, Frances Willard, a leader of the Women's Christian Temperance Union, proposed that "the mission of the ideal woman is to make the whole world homelike."[57] In Siler City, Protestant women pursued that mission. Through their involvement in church and civic groups, white Protestant women cleaned up congregational and public spaces in early Siler City. The Ladies Aid Societies of the white Baptist and Methodist congregations raised money for church improvements. Fundraising activities included bazaars, box suppers, mock weddings, and "a mile of pennies."[58] In his church history, Hadley praised the women's financial management skills. Referring to members of First Methodist Episcopal Church, South, he remarked, "It is gratifying to note that the Ladies Aid Society of this period (1911–1940) was thrifty and prudent in regard to money."[59] Other women's civic organizations that were formed in the early 1900s provided a wide range of services to the community.

Members of those organizations typically attended the more elite white Protestant churches. Mrs. C. N. Bray, president of the Community Club, was an active member of First Baptist Church.[60] The women in these organizations furnished the spaces associated with their class status, their homes, churches, and the stores where they shopped with the new conveniences and furnishings that Haygood listed among the things that made the New South a more civilized place: "better furniture, good mattresses, cook-stoves, sewing machines, lamps that make reading agreeable, [windows that] have not only glass but blinds, carpets, [and] pictures."[61] A chapter of the House Wife's Club (1914–1916) made aesthetic improvements to downtown businesses. Members furnished a restroom and toilet at the Farmers' Alliance Store, adding a rug, curtains, chairs, a couch, a library table, books, a washbasin, a mirror, and a closet; they also planted a bed of flowers at the back of the building. They intended the improvements for women shoppers visiting town.[62] In similar fashion, the Community Club (1915–1918) improved business and residential areas by removing and collecting tin cans, distributing flower and vegetable seeds for free, hanging fly traps, and encouraging boys to put up birdhouses.[63] The Women's Club (1918), the Camp Fire Girls (1919), and the

Round Dozen Book Club (1920) provided additional civic services ranging from child care to book distribution. During this period of industrialization and rapid growth, women's organizations cleaned up the town, making it acceptable according to their standards of Christian decency.[64]

If external cleanliness was a sign of internal order, then evangelical Protestant women demonstrated control of self through their external maintenance of public spaces. White Protestant men exercised their own civilizing restraint by not defiling those spaces and by protecting them from others who might soil their reputation. Take Wren, for example, who in 1901 helped organize the Chatham Bank, where he worked for more than fifty years, acting as president for much of that time. At the end of his career, he left a "Ten Commandments" of banking, in which he promoted cleanliness, advocated "cautious" financial growth, warned against "unholy ambition," and emphasized the economic value of practicing those virtues. Wren instructed bank employees to "never permit dust or 'cobwebs' to accumulate in your bank. It would show careless neglect and leave a bad impression. 'Cleanliness is next to Godliness.' Make your bank the most interesting, attractive and inviting place in your town, and make your customers feel that they have a big stake in The Chatham Bank."[65] In that commandment, Wren invoked a long-standing tenet of American Protestantism (of cleanliness being next to godliness), popularized in the sermons of eighteenth-century Methodist minister John Wesley (though not intensely practiced until the period of heavy industrialization in the late nineteenth century).[66] Wren, however, applied that tenet not solely in pursuit of spiritual perfection but also for the purpose of attracting banking customers.

In his financial prescriptions, Wren carried his religious impulse into his secular space. Translating theological tenets as universal principles of fiscal habit, he wrote, "Never let it be said that The Chatham Bank has become a braggart or a bigot. Only fools are in this class. Remember: 'A fool and his money are soon parted.' Treat every customer with courtesy. Kindness costs so little and is worth so much. Practice these virtues. 'A word fitly spoken is like apples of gold in pictures of silver.' "[67] In that commandment, Wren combined the pastoral common sense of Thomas Tusser, the sixteenth-century English poet who declared that "a fool and his money are soon parted," with the biblical wisdom of Proverbs 25:11 that a "word fitly spoken is like apples of gold in pictures of silver." In his final commandment, Wren reworked another proverb, from the book of Proverbs 18:24, in which Solomon describes a "friend who sticks closer than a brother," by saying that "money sticks closer than a brother."[68] Translating those textual sources for financial application,

Wren refined religion to fit it into the secular space of the bank, using biblical passages as a textual guide for the relational comparisons that linked control of money with control of self. To offer a fitly spoken word required a physical and emotional restraint that distinguished civilized bodies and their secular spaces.

Such habits were profitable. Wren instructed his employees to practice those axioms because it "costs so little and is worth so much." For Wren, the principles he outlined enabled the Chatham Bank to survive the Great Depression without any financial loss to its customers. Tried and tested during a time of crisis, those guidelines were worthy of emulation. In his banking commandments, Wren codified a set of expectations for business behavior that he and other managers modeled in their ritual performances. The commandments were a textual record of his generation's habits, which he felt compelled to write down because for him they marked the path of true progress, a path that led both the individual and community to what he called a "progress that will endure." Cleanliness, in this context, was the art of the clear path.[69]

Emulative Bodies

Wren's "ten commandments" were emblematic of a particular type of pecuniary emulation of civilizing restraint that corresponded with bodily cleanliness. In financial terms, this was expressed as "pay as you go."[70] By not taking a loan, the responsible citizen maintains a spotless reputation. They do not risk sullying their friendships with the insults of late payment. Successful businessmen in Siler City, including black resident and jeweler Tod Edwards, proudly professed such fiscal discipline. When a *State* magazine reporter asked Edwards, the only black businessman in the white business district, if he had to borrow money to pay for his jewelry store, Edwards answered: "No, sir. I waited until I had the money before I started building. I've always stuck to that policy as long as I've earned my own living." The reporter then asked, "How about your home here? Wasn't there a mortgage on that?" Edwards "smiled and shook his head" and said, "I waited until I had the money in the bank...I never have had a mortgage on anything, and I've always paid in full for everything I bought. I don't like to worry about anything. When you owe money, you usually have to worry, and that's something I don't ever want to do. And if *you* don't worry about it, then the man to whom you owe it usually does."[71] This kind of pecuniary practice, expressed as the ability to pay in full and not be burdened by debt, distinguished the business class in Siler City, both white and black.

Against the backdrop of segregated spaces, white residents never considered Tod Edwards "white," even though he operated a store in the white business district and practiced the same kind of pecuniary emulation as other white businessmen, like Wren, who worked on the same street. [72] Edwards was to them a black man working in the white business district. At the same time, white residents in Siler highlighted that very presence – of a black man in the white business district – as a symbol of racial harmony for their town. Their notion of racial harmony depended on the contrast of that difference. Without it, there was nothing exceptional. Bankers and businessmen like Wren used their Protestantism and their whiteness to project their fiscal habits as if they were universal principles. Despite the religious and racial particularity of their own secular projections (defined by its transcendent mediation), those principles were the standards against which all others were measured. White businessmen thus considered black businessmen as merely emulating their secularism, mimicking in their actions a social knowledge that was universal in application but could only be administered by whites. By that understanding, blacks could never possess the universal. Otherwise, Wren would have been just one of several white men working in the black business district with Edwards. That is, of course, a self-obvious statement that betrays common sense. But that also is the point. In the segregated South, ideational possession was racial property.

Consuming Bodies

During the period of incorporation, the town manufactured a variety of products in addition to poultry and lumber production—furniture, hardware, shuttle blocks, oak washboards, plow handles, sashes, doors, and blinds—and shipped them by rail to larger cities. Siler City businesses also imported their own mass-produced goods for sale in downtown shops. The Farmers' Alliance Store, which was organized at Loves Creek Baptist Church, opened downtown on Chatham Avenue in 1888. Evolving from a barter system into a stockholding cooperative limited to farmers of the "Anglo-Saxon race," the store carried farming supplies, clothing, groceries, and hardware.[73] That same year, E. Callie Smith opened the first millinery store, selling "hose, buttons, dress trimmings, lace, collars, ruching, etc." Mrs. J. J. Crutchfield started her own millinery shop in 1892, followed two years later by Kate Vestal. In 1916, Bessye Caviness moved the Caviness Shop to the downtown business district and advertised it as "Chatham County's Shopping Center for the Discriminating and Conservative Buyers of the Authentic and Exclusive in Millinery and

Ladies Ready-to-Wear."[74] With the exception of the Edwards jewelry store, all shops and businesses on Chatham Avenue were owned and operated by white Protestants and spatially segregated to privilege white customers.

Hardware stores, a jewelry store, barbershops, drugstores, and hotels lined downtown streets. Shopping in the white business district was a social activity. When residents wanted to conduct business at the bank, shop at the millinery store, buy groceries, farm equipment, or hardware, get a haircut, pick up medicine, or try a cold, nonalcoholic drink, they went downtown. Businesses displayed their products in storefronts, and buyers purchased national brands and styles. Window displays and newspaper advertisements proved highly successful for many stores, so much so that the Farmers' Alliance, which had relied on a steady clientele, adopted both marketing techniques. In 1921, the directors "ordered the Manager to secure space in the *Grit* for advertising," and in 1927, they asked him to construct a front-window display. Window displays were prominent features in downtown shops during the early twentieth century, and each year, advertisements filled more space in the *Grit*. For example, R. G. Edwards of the Ladies Emporium advertised "Easter slippers and pumps at prices to suit" and advised shoppers that "with only four more days before Easter it will be wise for you to make your selection early for an Easter dress. You will find at The Emporium a variety that will make your Easter shopping easier, and, with the girls' assistance, really a pleasure."[75]

By the 1920s, downtown Siler City was the place to visit with friends and neighbors while shopping for ready-made goods and services. In a few decades, Siler City residents had gone from making their products at home, such as soap, to purchasing manufactured products, including name-brand soaps and perfumes, from a handful of thriving stores.[76] The fashion-conscious could discern between "authentic" and "inauthentic" products, distinguishing themselves as tasteful shoppers.[77] During the period of incorporation, the churches and shops on Chatham Avenue were established as *the* public sites for displaying and observing the consumptive practices of religious and secular goods. By the bustle of their collective activity, of church attendance and shop traffic, locals measured the town's civic strength and economic vitality.

Conclusion

Southern whites in Siler City used industrialization to their religious *and* secular advantage. For elite whites first, and an upwardly mobile middle class second, factory production benefited their churches, businesses, banks, and shops—that is, if we understand benefit as a type of profit, whether of financial and political gain, or social prestige. In the industrial context of secular accumulation—where progressive whites secured public power—southern religion did not struggle to survive. Rather, it flourished. Elite whites leveraged evangelical Protestantism alongside southern secularism to govern the public display of civic status and the uneven distribution of monetary wealth. Upwardly mobile whites, despite assurances of self-reliance, also received an economic advantage from that racial regulation. During this period of incorporation, elite and middle-class whites invested together in the cultural norms of Jim Crow. Bodily purity was a highly valued spiritual habit, but it also had social rewards, both psychologically and fiscally. Revivals made new Christians and reclaimed old ones, while spawning town cleanup efforts. For whites, town cleanup carried multiple meanings, including the regulation of black bodies in defined public spaces. But even as whites racialized the habits of cleanliness that characterized American capitalism and its citizen consumers in the early twentieth century, those habits were never racially defined traits. While white banker L. L. Wren translated religious cleanliness into business axioms, black business owner Tod Edwards performed the same disciplining traits of fiscal responsibility and industrious habit. Despite the ubiquity of practice and a trending towards a universal that characterized a pervasive secularism, southern whites distinguished its presentation, in order to purify its essence. In Siler City, whites placed Wren and Edwards within a racial binary—even as they occupied the same street—that divided one from the other and ranked them accordingly. On their side of the binary, Wren embodied the universal and inhabited the secular. By their ledger, Edwards merely emulated the principles Wren performed. In the southern town, this was the religious limit of secularism, an inability to publicly speak or transact business without the influence of racial difference.

2

Nationalism

JOHN RANDOLPH LANE, son of John Siler Lane, was born on July 4, 1835. By his twenty-ninth birthday, he had seen action as a Confederate soldier and had been promoted to Colonel, after surviving a bullet through the neck at the Battle of Gettysburg.[1] On his sixty-sixth birthday, several years removed from the Civil War, he returned to the place formerly known as Matthews Crossroads, where he had drilled with the Chatham Boys, to lead the town's inaugural Fourth of July parade. Mounted on his horse, the highest-ranking living soldier from the 26th Regiment of the North Carolina Troops ushered in a "procession of mounted ladies and gentlemen, costumed in the national colors" through downtown Siler City.[2]

To his admirers, Colonel Lane was a religious figure. In her graduating speech at the closing exercise of Ore Hill Grade School (near Siler City), around the turn of the century, Lillian White remembered Lane's "frankness

FIGURE 2.1 Colonel John Randolph Lane in Confederate Uniform, date unknown. Courtesy: The 26th North Carolina Regiment Troops Past and Present.

and sincerity[1] as reflecting "a certain openness of soul" and declared to those gathered, "How appropriately the words of Paul—I have fought the good fight, I have finished my course, henceforth there is laid up for me a crown of righteousness—describe such a life!"[3] Concluding her remarks, she asked an audience assumed familiar with the life of Jesus, "Where can we find one so worthy of emulation?"[4] To White, Lane modeled the imitable Christian life.[5]

As southerners reemerged to celebrate the republic, they likewise remembered the Confederate soldier—the regional ideal of patriot martyr—motivated by Christian duty. To defend the southern states was to defend a Christian nation against a godless invader. This was, as historians have noted, the myth of the Lost Cause. Southerners may have lost the war, but they maintained, as a matter of principle, that their bloody crucifixion was the spiritual foundation of American transcendence. When Lane appeared in Siler on the Fourth of July 1901, he visually displayed the bodily presence of that religious sacrifice.

Southerners, though, did not affirm their heroic figure solely through personal testimony, as Lillian White did in her public speech. Despite the individualism of an evangelicalism that conquered the twentieth century, the idea of the Confederate soldier did not persevere solely because southerners believed in *him*. This was the evasive Protestantism of religion in the New South: that belief was a matter of the spirit and not the body, even as southerners, like Jesus with Thomas, invited the rest of the country to feel their flesh wounds. To defend the South meant more than defending the belief of the godly against the unbelief of the atheist. It also meant defending the moral order of divine command, with its earthly incarnation in the antebellum plantation.[6] As Faulkner wrote of Sutpen's Hundred, that command arrived as a spoken word from nowhere, as in "the oldentime *Be Light*."[7] But for the majority of southern whites in the twentieth century, it need not be spoken at all, because those who had collectively experienced God already possessed a fearful knowledge. Once those southerners began their secular parade, they seldom needed to testify to that common sense.

In this chapter, I argue that white residents of the Siler area used the nationalist rite of Fourth of July parades during the early period of incorporation to redeem southern conceptions of religious sacrifice and project them onto the nation-state as the essence of American patriotism. Performing the religious role of southern sacrifice, Lane marked another beginning, a moment from which whites in Siler turned to the projects of secularism in a new American century. Like the street processions from the Palestine neighborhood to the Methodist church, the public ritual of the downtown parade followed a secularizing path. The Lost Cause religious performance of Confederate presence gave way in later parades to the secular displays of blackface minstrelsy, with its assumed secularity proven by it belonging to the realm of popular culture, and not the church (even though, as I note, local congregations often sponsored minstrel shows). Using minstrelsy in later parade activities, southern whites expressed something more and something less than the separatist nationalism symbolized by the resurrected soldier of the Lost Cause. They expressed a desire to transcend their regional particularity, even as they reinforced it, and redeem the American nation. By including the Confederate soldier in their inaugural march, white residents of Siler City sanctified their bodies by his blood, blessing all those who rode after him, preserved the cause in another epoch, localized nationalism and nationalized locality, and used the secular tools of industry and law to rebuild and protect the kingdom.[8]

Southern Shouts of American Liberty

For more than two decades after the Civil War, during a period when African Americans were elected to public office, southern whites did not celebrate the Fourth of July. But at the turn of the century, sufficiently removed from Reconstruction, they reclaimed their parade. In Siler City, white residents dusted off their Confederate clothing, waved the American flag with pride, and sang the national anthem with a southern accent, which in this case proved their central North Carolinian descent. From the overarching perspective of race and religion in American history, it is no coincidence that the memories of the Old South returned to white southerners at the same time that they renewed their Fourth of July celebrations. This was to them the meaning of independence and the song of their South. African Americans had heard that refrain before. In a speech to a northern abolitionist group in 1852, Frederick Douglass gave his thoughts on white celebrations of the Fourth of July. He asked, "What to the American slave is your 4th of July?" And he answered:

> ...a day that reveals to him, more than all other days in the year, the gross injustice and cruelty to which he is the constant victim. To him, your celebration is a sham; your boasted liberty, an unholy license; your national greatness, swelling vanity; your denunciation of tyrants, brass-fronted impudence; your shouts of liberty and equality, hollow mockery; your prayers and hymns, your sermons and thanksgivings, with all your religious parade and solemnity, are, to Him, mere

bombast, fraud, deception, impiety, and hypocrisy—a thin veil to cover up crimes which would disgrace a nation of savages.[9]

In his prophetic pronouncement, Douglass pulled back the veil of American patriotism to uncover the radical incongruity between the democratic egalitarianism celebrated by the nation and the immediate realities of American slaves within its peculiar institution. The return of the parades in Siler City at the dawn of Jim Crow renewed that discordant tradition. There, southern whites celebrated an American nation with a Confederate soul, liberated from what they considered the ignoble experiment of northern Reconstruction.

Reconstruction (1865–1877) was one of the most democratically representative moments for African Americans in United States history.[10] During this period, former slaves celebrated Emancipation Day with their own parades—a tradition that continues today in many southern towns, though not in Siler City.[11] While the patriotism of southern whites was buried under a blanket of dismay for a decade after the Civil War, African Americans asserted themselves into public life in the South, in some places celebrating American Independence on the Fourth of July.[12] This window of possibility closed in 1877, when the United States government removed troops from the South as part of a political compromise with Democrats that gave Republican candidate Rutherford B. Hayes the White House.[13] Without US military protection, African Americans were subject to the legal injustices of constrained freedoms in the Jim Crow South. Historian Noel Ignatiev describes the changes after Reconstruction that reconfigured the racial status of whiteness for economic and psychological advantage, and redirected the solving of freedom away from liberation from slavery and toward equal access to the market:

> If the abolition of slavery called into question the meaning of whiteness, the overthrow of Reconstruction marked the restoration of the color line on a new basis. No longer did it coincide with the distinction between freedom and slavery; it now came to correspond to the distinction between free, wage labor and unfree, semi-feudal labor, and between those who had access to political power and those who did not.[14]

The restructured constraints of freedom as a distinction between free wage labor and unfree semifeudal labor is critical to understanding the renewal of Fourth of July parades in a New South town like Siler City. Similar to the Independence Day celebrations before the Civil War (those events that

Douglas considered festivals of hypocrisy), the Fourth of July celebrations in the New South signaled a return to what many southern whites considered the foundation of social and economic institutions: a divinely sanctioned racial order, which they now used to determine "those who had access to political power and those who did not."

To gain political advantage in the market economy, southern whites pulled themselves up by pulling down on the bootstraps of southern blacks, who had made political gains in parts of the region during Reconstruction. Whites joined together in segregated cooperatives, like the Farmers' Alliance in Siler City. Southern whites in Siler harmonized those types of discriminating economic strategies with their divine callings, moving across religious and secular boundaries as they collaboratively used both types of sites to exercise social power. The Reverend A. H. Perry, a white Baptist minister and president of the Siler City Agriculture Society, organized in 1887 as the predecessor of the Farmers' Alliance, offered a "fitting prayer" at the 1911 Fourth of July festivities.[15] In his festival performance, he blessed the sacred order displayed in the parades, or what Douglass described as that unholy license to conduct segregated business as a providential right. Over time, that relationship between religious and secular labor became increasingly differentiated. In later parade celebrations, the preachers who prayed no longer farmed for their living. They were trade specialists, like the politicians and judges who spoke to the crowds. Those social divisions did not hinder the growth of religious power but only fertilized it in separate fields with the dung of politics. Candidates for office sought pastoral blessing, and preachers clamoring for influence yearned to hear their silent petition. White representatives of religious and secular spheres excluded blacks from their collaborative accumulation of social and financial capital. Despite progressive panegyrics on the common good, the racial cooperatives of religious and secular sites, such as the First Baptist Church and the Farmers' Alliance, served the social interests of an upwardly mobile class of southern whites.

In the late eighteenth and early nineteenth centuries, most white evangelicals were antiestablishment upstarts. Some were abolitionists. By the end of the nineteenth century, they abandoned radical democracy, bounding its egalitarian potential by reformatting racial difference for political, economic, and psychological gain.[16] According to historian Donald G. Mathews, "Rather than distribute the democratic vision of Evangelical worship and recognize all believers, including blacks, as equal under God, Evangelicals recreated the hierarchical world of the elites in Southern fashion." In Mathews's interpretation, "slavery was the basis of this hierarchy" and "standing on the backs of their enslaved brethren, white Evangelicals built their own institutions."[17] In Siler City, southern evangelicals exemplified this pattern. Though they never owned slaves, their economic opportunities depended on the reinvested capital of former slave owners, as I noted in Chapter One. Even when they considered themselves untouched by slavery, as Lane considered his great middle class, those white evangelicals built institutions in the early twentieth century that "created and maintained Southern white esteem and respectability," as Mathews put it, built upon racial distinctions formerly guaranteed by slavery.[18] In the bodily presence of the Confederate soldier, parade observers witnessed that white esteem and respectability. Colonel Lane physically displayed their self-representational genealogical traits, what he described as his soldiers' "good blood" and "honest sweat." Against this backdrop, southerners tied their public ritual of the Fourth of July parade to that religious performance in an effort to once again locate their bodies as white, to reclaim a conflated racial and class status that Ignatiev noted was threatened by Reconstruction.[19]

The southern reclamation of public space, a secular project, began with the religious performance of masculine defense of domestic spirituality. Each to his own home, evangelical men replicated the antebellum role of head of household, protecting the sexual purity of white femininity, one woman to one man. In the late eighteenth and early nineteenth centuries, white evangelical Protestants procured domestic spaces for familial religious practices within the pervasive patriarchal establishment of the Old South. By the mid-nineteenth century, for example, white Methodists domesticated the antebellum "culture of honor," moving its public sacrifices of "place and station," into the family home and individual hearts of Protestant believers.[20] The spread of evangelical Protestant domestic space through individual conversion transformed the totalizing institutions of the Old South, particularly the peculiar institution of slavery, so that it resembled a medieval-like feudal order.[21] Despite this transformation (or perhaps because of it), a fundamental component of patriarchal order, what historian Gregory Schneider describes as the "image of a sacred feminine space to be protected from encroaching, polluting forces," persisted in southern white evangelical practices.[22]

Southern Protestants, particularly Methodists, engaged public spaces in an effort to protect the propriety of private domestic life. Over the course of the nineteenth century, they grew bolder in their attempts, domesticating the unruliest of festivals, the Fourth of July parade. By the 1840s and 1850s, white Methodists changed their attitudes toward parades, now celebrating rather than condemning them. Previously, participating in the intoxicating displays of patriotism on the Fourth of July was grounds for church expulsion. But that changed once the parades were "no longer beset by drunkenness and revelry, Independence Day celebrations [became] times for great Sabbath school jubilees, family gatherings, and pious sociability."[23] In the mid-nineteenth century, Schneider argues, "evangelical churches turned July 4th into the cult day of the Protestant God, American flag, and middle-class domestic circle."[24]

The Civil War halted the public march of white southern evangelical Protestants, but only for a few decades. After Reconstruction, they reemerged with a renewed public vigor, staking claim to a southern landscape scarred by war. Reflecting these historical trends, white Protestants in Siler City embraced Fourth of July celebrations, using them to domesticate public space and transform it in defense of their Christian homes and congregations. Like the nineteenth-century Fourth of July parades that preceded them, the parades in Siler City ritually displayed the domestic habits of the town. With increasingly more public power at their disposal, white Protestants in Siler City regulated Fourth of July activities, using its ritual resources to stake claim to a segregated landscape. They cultivated that landscape in what Schneider referred to as the "image of feminine sacred space," sanctifying it with the blood sacrifice of the southern soldier and blessing it with the prayers of their ministers.

In the first half of the twentieth century, a typical Fourth of July celebration in Siler City opened with the downtown parade, which began in the Chatham Avenue business district and made its way to the town park, just south of downtown on the edge of the Palestine neighborhood.[25] At the park, the crowd gathered in front of an elevated stage, where a music leader directed them in patriotic song, a local pastor led a prayer, public officials offered a few words, and an honored guest delivered his speech. Following the songs and speeches, attendees shared dinner. Afterward, fitness contests and sporting matches concluded the day's events.

The 1911 celebration that included Reverend Perry followed that ritual order. According to Isaac London of the *Grit*, the festivities began at 11 a.m. with the downtown parade, led by "Joe Bray, who is 76 inches tall, and E. A. Bean, who is only 48 inches tall. The former waved a tiny flag while the latter bore aloft a large flag." They were followed by the Franklinville Brass Band, carriages of speakers and guests, a "handsome float with a score of lovely girls all dressed in red, white, and blue," a wagon with a string band, and a "long distance" of "decorated buggies and carriages and horse back riders." London remarked that once they arrived at the park, "the crowd was comfortably seated and they were served with water all during the exercises." The post-parade festivities followed a familiar format of religious prayer, political speech, and musical performance, which London chronicled. He wrote that they

> ...opened with the singing of "My Country Tis of Thee," after which Rev. A. H. Perry offered a fitting prayer. The manager, Mr. I. S. London, then made a few remarks. Mayor Jesse F. Milliken was then introduced and he bade the assemblage a cordial welcome to the town. Major H. A. London, of Pittsboro, responded to this in a most felicitous manner. The assemblage then sang "Carolina." Ex-Sheriff Jenkins made a neat speech in introducing the speaker of the day, Hon. E. J. Justice of Greensboro. The band interspersed the program with music. After dinner the athletic events were pulled off.

The athletic events following the civic displays included a 100-yard dash, a sack race, a three-legged race, and a greased pole contest in which "the band played while a score of fellows made a pass at the greased pole, but all efforts to reach the coveted watch proved futile." There was a potato race on the baseball field and "then the greased pig was turned loose." As noted in the Introduction, Charles Jones caught the pig that year after it ran through the crowd and later "turned the pig loose" during the baseball game. After they resumed, the team from Gulf beat Siler City, six to five, in eight innings. Before sunset, Dan Campbell successfully climbed the greased pole, "thereby securing the watch." After sundown, local white residents performed the play *Fun on the Sunset Limited* in the Town Hall. London reported a record crowd of five thousand for that year's celebration.[26] The liturgical rhythm of early celebrations, of songs, prayer, speeches, food, and games, set the ritual tradition for later parades.

The Visible Presence of Southern Sacrifice

In the inaugural moment of 1901, the bodily presence of Colonel Lane sanctified that ritual order. Those who remembered Lane often described his battle wounds as evidence that he eluded death. They remembered how the enemy shot him through the neck, jaw, and mouth at Gettysburg, after he picked up the regimental flag from a fallen comrade. He was left for dead, but survived, though he did lose part of his tongue. Lane rebounded from other wounds suffered in later battles but was finally forced off the battlefield after sustaining a violent injury sustained at Reame's Station on August 25, 1864. According to an account printed in the *Randolph Tribune* in Asheboro, North Carolina, Lane "was wounded in the left breast, by a shell fracturing two, and breaking one rib and tearing open the flesh to the bone just over the heart." He was "thought mortally wounded." But as before at Gettysburg, he defied death by "his superb vitality" and "returned to duty, November 1864." He struggled to remain with his regiment but was eventually "broken down by exposure and suffering." As his comrades "surrendered at Appomattox," he recovered in "a hospital at Greensboro, North Carolina"[27]

Rather than feeling defeated by war, white southerners considered the essence of southern patriotism, its Christian character of religious sacrifice, to have been purified by its suffering. In their memories, they collected the remaining fragments, their saintly relics, and used them to adorn the new body. After Reconstruction, the industrialization of the South was inevitable. But rather than surrender to its perceived godlessness, or retreat in solitude, southerners like Lane continued to publicly protect their Christian "place" and redeem a South with mechanized righteousness. During this period of national reconciliation, Lane worked to preserve Confederate ideals in an emerging industrial America. He announced in his 1903 Gettysburg Reunion speech that "we lost our cause, but we have won back our place in the American Union."[28] For Lane, winning "our place" meant protecting the moral voice of the South and using it to shape the region and influence the country.[29]

Projecting regional opinion, Lane compared the sacrificial display of Confederate soldiers to that of the Revolutionary heroes who fought for the independence of the American nation. After referring to the "boys" of his own 26th Regiment as "good, honest, American stock" who "loved their country and loved liberty," he recalled that they "had grown up to love and cherish [the] noble deeds [of] their forefathers [who] had fought the British at King's Mountain and Guildford Court House." Lane measured the nobility of the Confederate soldier by his loyalty to family and his willingness to protect them from all enemies, even when the reasons for war were unclear. Lane admitted that "not every man of them was convinced that the cause for which he was fighting was just." He also made it clear that each of his soldiers "believed he owed allegiance first to his home and state." It was this sense of duty—an obligation to defend family and state from an "unjust invader"— that Colonel Lane identified as the distinguishing trait of the Confederate soldier, placing him through his blood sacrifice in a lineage of American patriots.[30]

Even as Lane's descriptions of that sacrifice were compatible with secular banalities of duty to country, he understood it first and foremost in a more particular sense, as a sacrifice on behalf of the sacred white feminine. In his 1903 Gettysburg Reunion speech, Lane reassured his buried brothers that they offered their lives in defense of the Daughters of the Confederacy, those with "the tenderest hearts and fairest hands of our Southland." Speaking to the dead as if they were living, he told them that those daughters "water your graves with tears that rise from hearts full of grateful and loving remembrance of you who suffered death as champions of Southern homes."[31]

The heroic bravery Colonel Lane displayed in defense of southern homes was one of the characteristics, along with his spiritual simplicity, that made him a model of Christian manhood to his admirers. In addition to his "frankness and sincerity," Lillian White celebrated Colonel Lane's chivalry, kindness of heart, and sense of "grand manhood that never failed to make itself felt."[32] Lane's participation in the inaugural Fourth of July parade in Siler City made present that sacrificial strength, attaching Christian manhood to white middle-class status and performing its bodily synthesis in a new southern place.

Confederate Memorial to Blackface Minstrelsy

The 1901 Fourth of July parade was the earliest public recognition of a Confederate soldier in Siler.[33] That performance, though, did not endure; I did not find any record of Colonel Lane participating in later parades. As Methodist processions in Palestine eventually stopped, visible symbols of Confederate presence faded from the Fourth of July. They reappeared much later in the 1971 and 1976 parades, when residents celebrated the bicentennials of their county and nation, respectively. Prior to those appearances, it seemed that Confederate memorializers were content to leave their markings on monuments and in battlefield reenactments.[34] Town officials did observe Confederate Memorial Day, beginning with a service on May 10, 1909, at Oakwood Cemetery. The annual Confederate Reunion and Fourth of July celebration were the two largest public gatherings in early Siler City. Both events attracted roughly the same number of people; however, by the end of the 1920s, the parades surpassed the reunions in size and significance. Approximately 2,500 people attended the 1913 Confederate Reunion in Siler City, where Mayor L. L. Wren presented the Confederate veterans with a key to the city, while two thousand spectators were present at the Fourth of July parade that year. The next year, a reported three thousand attended the parade, and the year after, estimates reached as high as four thousand attendees.[35] This trend continued. As reunions declined, parades boomed. By 1918, the Fourth of July celebration attracted close to six thousand people, nearly five times the town's population.³⁶ Railroad companies added additional trips to Siler City from neighboring towns to accommodate the increasing numbers of passengers. Even then, it was difficult to find room on the train. According to the *Grit*, "The coaches and baggage cars were completely overflowed, with scores of passengers finding room on the top of boxcars."³⁷

Displacing the Confederate Reunion as the town's dominant public ritual, the Fourth of July celebrations retained the Lost Cause ethos that Charles Reagan Wilson described as "paternalistic, moralistic, well ordered, and hierarchical."³⁸ By the early twentieth century, the Spanish-American War galvanized the country, as southern whites reconciled with their northern brothers and sisters and joined in the celebration of the Fourth of July as a national holiday. But they never completely gave up the "southern values" that they considered the essence of American patriotism. In Siler City, white southerners used the national rite of the Fourth of July celebration to reconfirm regionally specific racial and social hierarchies.³⁹

As symbols of American nationalism displaced visible signs of the Confederacy, southern whites reconstituted the manner in which they performed a sacred order predicated on white masculine defense of Christian homes and white women. In the Old South, slavery ensured racial difference. In the New South, absent that institutional referent, southerners had to perform blackness elsewhere, within urban pockets of industrial towns. Only after reestablishing that antebellum order could they relocate white men and white women and pursue the racialized dynamics of gendered protection. To accomplish that task, they included the ritual tradition of blackface minstrelsy—performing racial difference in relation to the imagined southern plantation—in their parade festivities. Northern immigrants set the template for American cultural usage of minstrelsy in the nineteenth century, rendering it a strategic practice to distinguish their bodies as not black, contest nativist claims to the racial status of white American, and gain an economic advantage in a competitive labor market.⁴⁰ Having lost the antebellum institution that offered blessed assurance of racial derma, southerners employed a similar strategy to that earlier used by northern immigrants to once again become white.

In the New South, southern Protestants reconstituted their whiteness, both in terms of its feminine representation and its need for masculine protection, using the ritual tool of blackface minstrelsy. Blackface minstrelsy was, according to Eric Lott, the "most popular entertainment form of the nineteenth century" in the United States, a "theatrical practice, principally of the Urban North."[41] Ignatiev notes that many of the earliest blackface minstrels in the United States were immigrants of Irish descent, whom "native" Anglo-Americans grouped within the same racial category as freed slaves.[42] Upon their arrival, immigrants entered into an American pattern of racial sorting institutionally established through southern slavery, which forced incarcerated West Africans to exchange varied ethnicities for a singular race.[43] Performing blackface minstrelsy, northern immigrants sought to control their own sorting, associating their ethnicity with a nationalized whiteness that they made recognizable in oppositional caricatures of African Americans.[44] Annemarie Bean has argued, "Performed primarily in northern, urban venues to white male audiences, early minstrelsy situated itself in the South, giving a symbolic significance to a contained universe located on the plantation which also allowed a permissible attitude of 'anything goes.'" It was, she writes, "where the plantation culture of the South existed as a performed cultural imaginary of the urban displaced white man."[45] An immigrant tool of racial differentiation, ranging from blackface performances by Irish immigrants in Philadelphia parades to Al Jolson's performance in *The Jazz Singer* as a Jewish immigrant's attempt to resist "nativist pressure that would assign them to the dark side of the racial divide," minstrelsy associated ethnic whites with a racialized nationalism that was defined in relation to the antebellum plantation.[46] From that historical angle, the nationalist projects of the mid-nineteenth century could not do without southern religiosity and its racial performances. So it is not surprising that southern whites swiftly reconciled their regional practices with American nationalism in the early twentieth century by wearing the minstrel mask. Regional reconciliation with the nation-state offered, in the racial terms of performative blackness, merely a path for southerners to find their way back home.

This was the case in Siler City, where southerners staged racial difference in Fourth of July celebrations.[47] According to the *Grit,* the 1912 parade included two clowns, one dressed as a woman and both in "false face." The newspaper editor Isaac London and a member of his staff, "The *Grit*'s devil Brooks Harris," played the clowns. An estimated two thousand or more attendees viewed the spectacle. In the evening, London led a minstrel show with local talent. Later, he reported in the paper that "the 'coons' did their parts splendidly, and the continuous laughter that greeted them indicated the enjoyment of the audience."[48] In the 1918 parade festivities, "all the specials, consisting of quartets, solos, and songs by blackface comedians were decided hits with the pleased audience."[49] Blackface clowns appeared in later parades, as corporations sponsored racially themed floats. In 1913, the Oak Washboard Company

FIGURE 2.2 Fourth of July in downtown Siler City, circa 1910. Credit: North Carolina Collection, University of North Carolina Library at Chapel Hill.

float, which represented one of Siler City's first manufacturing companies, featured a "colored mammy."[50] The public display of blackface performers in daytime parades continued into the more private gatherings of Fourth of July evening activities, which included minstrel shows held in local white churches. In 1920, the *Grit* advertised: "Minstrel at town hall tonight by young ladies of the Methodist Church for the benefit of the Church Building Fund."[51]

By sponsoring, organizing, and participating in the parade and its activities, white businesses and churches controlled Fourth of July celebrations and their racialized performances. Blackface minstrelsy extended that control, signaling not merely a minority view of white supremacists, but a pervasive white supremacy that encompassed southern progressives, industrialists, and business leaders as well. The Fourth of July celebration was performed for the glory of southern whites and intended to reflect their racial and patriotic superiority. Photographs from early parades suggest overwhelmingly white crowds. In addition, newspaper accounts exclude the opinions or participation of African Americans in the parades and other events, or any contestation or protest that may have occurred.[52] Infrequent mentions of black residents in parade reports were condescendingly congratulatory. In 1918, the *Grit* described Milton Foushee, who prepared barbecue pork and mutton for the festivities, as "a good colored citizen who knows well his business."[53]

Blackface performances defined racial difference in early Siler City, and they continued into the mid-twentieth century.[54] A longtime white resident told me that white residents attended minstrel and medicine shows at the

old Siler City High School in the 1920s. He said one show featured a man
with the strongest jaws in the world. Around 1944, that resident and another
boy used soot from a stovepipe to "black up," as he described it, for a talent
show at the local theater. He remembered a white girl accompanied them by
singing an American Indian love song. He also remembered blacks attending
the talent show. But he did not recall blacks ever wearing blackface. He told
me it was common practice in Siler for white residents, including "leading
citizens," to "dress up like 'kuhns' [his spelling] and walk around town on
the Fourth of July." Blackface, he said, was a part of Fourth of July celebrations, in addition to being performed during other holidays. He distinctly
remembered that "prominent" members of the Siler City community walked
the streets in blackface during Halloween as late as the 1950s. After speaking
with that resident, I later found a photo from a 1954 Siler City High School
annual that confirmed his account. It shows two male students in blackface
with two female students dressed as Native Americans. The caption reads,
"Oh, Halloween."[55]

FIGURE 2.3 High School Students in Blackface Halloween Costumes. Source: Siler City
High School Annual (Raleigh, NC: Edwards and Broughton Company, 1954).

Holiday public performances, including the Fourth of July, also included cross-dressing white men. In the parade, white men who performed as black mammies or female clowns painted their faces, wore mid-length skirts, and stuffed their upper shirts. For a Halloween costume, as one resident recalled, boys often wore their sisters' bathing suits. During other parts of the year, churches sponsored mock weddings between young men. An advertisement from the neighboring town of Sanford that ran in a February 23 edition of the local paper in 1917 invited those in the area to a "Mock Wedding of Men at Graded School Auditorium, West Sanford, Tonight." The invitation read:

> If you want to laugh come and see the happy nuptials of this unique and unusual wedding, wherein two pulsing and withered hearts will be welded into one. To the tender strains of the dulcet wedding march the blushing bride, too long a family treasure, Miss Fertil Liza, who for generations has been the reigning belle, and Mr. Corn Graber, also a drag on the social and matrimonial market will be married.

A mock reception followed that ceremony. Attendees were promised the opportunity to "look upon the rare and unique features of the bridal party, and such visions of loveliness will be on display as not often seen." Admission was twenty-five cents for adults and ten cents for children. All money raised by the mock wedding was "given for the benefit of the Methodist Church [of Sanford]."[56]

In their performances of blackface, cross-dressing, and drag performances, southern white evangelicals expressed a desire to control racial and gender identities, while reinforcing their normative status. Advertised as family entertainment, minstrel shows and mock weddings were intentionally absurd. The audience at minstrel and drag shows collectively knew, in cultural terms, that black-faced entertainers were not really black and young men in wedding dresses were not really women, which provided what Clifford Geertz referred to as an "aura of factuality."[57] White male "loveliness" performed in that Protestant church played upon the socially accepted role of white women as the bodily presence of spiritual purity, a depiction of women that met the biblical standards of Ephesians, Chapter Five.[58] Corresponding displays of ideal feminine beauty in Fourth of July parades, which always included a float carrying a white woman as the beauty queen, referenced without citation religious performances of feminine spirituality.[59] The beauty queen must be without wrinkle or blemish, holy and blameless, as Paul instructed the Christian men of Ephesus to keep their wives, to sanctify and cleanse them, in order to present them as he would present to himself a glorious church.[60] Against that divinely sanctioned gendered order, the lovely young men of the Sanford Methodist Church were an absurd display. Members of that Methodist congregation did not consider that display a religious performance, even though it was inside their church. Instead, they called it entertainment. Because it was not serious, they considered it of the secular world. Even the things of that world, though, like financial accounting, could be used for God's purpose, such as raising money for the church. Thus, divine sanction did not necessarily mean religious practice.

Even when southern evangelicals performed blackface minstrelsy and cross-dressing matrimony within sacred space, they did not consider those *church* rites. In the contrasting absurdities, they referenced divine order without proclaiming what they did religious. This is how they made white feminine beauty sacred in the parades. They set her apart by surrounding her with mammies and minstrels, with the tall Joe Bray and his tiny flag and the short E. A. Bean holding the large flag. Collocating those visual contrasts assured observers that they could knowingly laugh, self-consciously aware of the inverted foolishness.[61] The pure whiteness of the parade queen was "true" because everything around her was not. White observers sighted white bodies in blackface knowing they could never really "be" black, just as Christian men whom they witnessed taking hands in marriage could not actually "be" married, just as E. A. Bean would never "be" as tall as Joe Bray, even if he carried the larger flag. For most white observers, racial and gendered status were ontologically predetermined, recognizable as observable physical differences akin to differences in height. To say otherwise was unnatural and outside the bounds of what they considered a divinely sanctioned social order. Otherwise, the joke would not be funny.

State Politics: A Comparative Case

Though highlighted with humorous entertainment, the southern comedy of the Fourth of July was serious politics. The first parade in Siler City came on the heels of a state amendment to the North Carolina constitution to disenfranchise black voters in 1900. The six years leading up to that amendment were among the most consequential in the state's history. In 1894 and 1896, the Fusion Party of Populists and Republicans was on the road to changing state politics, when the disenfranchisement campaigns of Furnifold Simmons reclaimed the electoral map of North Carolina. The Wilmington coup d'état of November 1898 and the election just before, along with the legislative changes beginning in 1899, recast racial politics across the state. Southern white elites like Simmons, who attempted to regain white control of public space after being displaced during Reconstruction, used the 1900 Amendment to throw a racial wedge in populist movements that encompassed black and white voters.[62] They promoted the amendment using propaganda tactics that played on working-class white fears of racial inferiority and economic scarcity, ultimately arguing that if blacks continued to vote, they would seize control of southern towns and steal jobs from whites, humiliating them in the process.[63]

Proposed amendment changes included reading and writing tests for voters, designed to exclude blacks. But some whites also worried that they would be disenfranchised by those changes. One white protestor in Siler City submitted that because the amendment "will disenfranchise the unlettered white man with the unlettered negro I am doubly opposed to it." This protestor, though, like many whites, did not object to the disenfranchisement of blacks. He just did not like the method in which it was executed in the amendment. Other white voters expressed the concern that the amendment might incite civil unrest, since it still taxed black citizens even after disenfranchising them. In the same letter to the editor in Siler, "Another Voter" wrote that he saw no advantage for "us as a government" to allow "the negro to vote." But he felt that the amendment would still require blacks to pay a poll tax, even if denied the right to vote. This, he thought would "create trouble." Another Voter suggested that "the better solution would be to disqualify [blacks] from office by amending our constitution which would not conflict with the constitution of the United States."[64] Responding to that letter, a supporter of the amendment wrote the editor of *The Siler City Leader*, saying, "It will disenfranchise no colored man any longer than he can learn to read and write and establish for himself a good character," and, "It will disenfranchise no white man any longer than he wants to be disenfranchised."[65]

Fusion Party members held varying oppositional views to the amendment. Strongest in the central part of the state, the party helped defeat the amendment in Siler City and surrounding Chatham County, though it garnered enough votes to pass statewide. Across much of the state, the Democratic Party relied on terrorist tactics, such as the Red Shirt Movement, to keep oppositional voters away from the polls, and those efforts swayed the electoral outcome.[66] In total, sixteen counties in central North Carolina opposed the amendment, in contrast to the roughly eighty counties across the state that supported it.[67] That did not necessarily mean, however, that white residents opposed to the bill supported equal voting rights for blacks. As evidenced by Another Voter, they merely opposed the disenfranchisement of illiterate whites.

For a comparative example, take Mount Airy, North Carolina, which residents today consider a sister city to Siler City because of a shared connection to Mayberry, the mythical town of the 1960s television series *The Andy Griffith Show*.[68] In 1900, the editor of the *Mount Airy Times* called the defeat of the amendment in his town, with 2,013 residents for and 2,653 against, "very disappointing." He felt that "the fight being waged against us was bitter and many white men had been deceived by those who claimed to be their friends." He blamed the failure of the Democrats to garner support for the amendment in Mount Airy on Republican use of liquor, but took pleasure in "informing [Republicans of Surry County] that the Amendment carried the State by about fifty thousand majority, and that the Democrats elected the Governor and entire State Ticket."[69]

The return of Fourth of July parades in southern towns like Siler City came directly after the amendment controversy, at a time when elite whites regained control of the state. Given this context, the parades were a ritual tool for standardizing white control of public space in the localized South.[70] Siler City, a desolate meadow without an urban history, served as blank slate for that ritual inscription. As I mentioned in Chapter One, the political contestations of Reconstruction did not directly affect that part of North Carolina. But the performance of Fourth of July parades ritually connected the local town to a broader body politic. In the downtown parades, residents performed a nationalist drama on the local stage. The ritual performance of Fourth of July parades, sponsored by elite whites working to support and strengthen their political and business interests, connected Siler to a larger world of racial contestation.

In towns with a historical African American presence, southern whites used parades to contest black claims to public space, including those involving independent black parades. While reports of Fourth of July festivities in Siler City infrequently cited supervised black participation in related activities, I did not find any evidence of public independent black performances as contested ritual counterparts to white-controlled parades.[71] In contrast to Siler, black residents of Mount Airy sponsored the first Fourth of July parade in their town following the 1900 amendment. In 1901, the *Mount Airy Times* announced that "the colored Odd Fellows will parade the streets July 4th (to-day) and have lots of music, speaking, refreshments, etc., at the Globe Warehouse."[72] A week later, the editor reported that with the parade, "The colored brass band discoursed some good music on our streets."[73] The editor gave no indication that white residents attended the event at the Globe Warehouse. His comments, though, suggest that some whites at least heard the parade music. Other white residents would not have heard the music, though, as they left Mount Airy to attend a Fourth of July celebration at a nearby Battleground. But for most, the editor remarked, the "weather was decidedly too hot for a trip anywhere."[74]

The Odd Fellows' Fourth of July parade in Mount Airy symbolized the perseverance of independent black organizations and the rise of black political leadership in pockets throughout the South. White residents expressed appreciation of black parades as entertainment, without recognizing them as a legitimate performance of political equality. The editor for the *Mount Airy Times*, who supported the amendment to disenfranchise black voters, celebrated their "good music" while maintaining control of public space as "our streets." A year earlier, promoting the upcoming amendment in 1900, he told Mount Airy residents and voters in surrounding Surry County that if those "who love their white skin are still in doubt as to what they should do on August 2nd, they are indeed a dull set of people." He added, referencing towns that had seen black political gains, that "if you are safe and your family is in no danger, it is no reason why you should withhold a helping hand from your less fortunate brother in the counties where the negroes run things in their own way. God pity the people who live in such a community and are unable to move out."[75]

In early Siler City, southern whites used Fourth of July celebrations to gain control of political space and bolster local business. They did the same in Mount Airy, though a few years later, and may have used them to squelch oppositional performances. From 1902 to 1912, there was no formally organized Fourth of July celebration in the sister city. When black residents marched on the Fourth of July during this period, news reports characterized those events as violent and dangerous. A story in the *Mount Airy News* from July 6, 1904, recounted a confrontation at a Fourth of July event in which a woman was shot, a man was stabbed, and another man was put in jail.

> The colored folks in Mt. Airy celebrated the Fourth [with] a cake walk and ice cream supper down on Nedmore Str. And all was going well until one Cora Cox and her "fellow" Joe Jones decided to disagree and all because Cora showed some desire to be with another gentleman of color. This was too much for Joe and he got out his old pistol and shot her in the mouth. John Harris took a hand at this junction and tried to stop the racket and one Pat, brother to Joe Jones, stabbed him in the back with a knife. Cora is not hurt much—she says she swallowed the

bullet but two teeth are missing and Harris is hurt but was able to be at the trial. Pat will go to jail if he does not give bond and Joe is gone and nobody cares—unless it is Cora.

This description of "colored folks" celebrating the Fourth of July in Mount Airy sensationalized black violence, presenting it as an inevitable outcome of personal character ("…this was too much for Joe"). In contrast to the glorification of Colonel Lane's bodily wounds, the news account references black bodily suffering only as minor detail. Cora was shot in the mouth, but "not hurt much." And the outcome of death and prison were treated as just consequence. "Pat will go to jail" and "Joe is gone" but "nobody cares—unless it is Cora." Two weeks later, the paper reported without remorse that Cora was dead.[76]

Characterizing black parades as prone to violence, white business leaders encouraged the town of Mount Airy to sponsor its own white-organized and white-controlled Fourth of July celebrations, arguing they would stimulate the local economy and encourage political consensus as they had in other cities. Their efforts were successful. In 1913, a little over a decade after the "colored" Odd Fellows' parade, the city "celebrated the Fourth of July last week as never before in recent years." Organized by white civic leaders, the parade followed the same format used in Siler City. That year it was reported, "Attorney E. C. Bivens, a bright and wide awake young lawyer, stirred around among the business men and put the movement on foot and under his leadership the city did itself proud." Like Siler City, the Mount Airy parade included automobiles and "beautifully decorated wagons" carrying "displays of merchandise." It moved through "literally packed" streets "with people from all parts of the county." As in Siler City, festivities included contests of all kinds. Participants attempted to climb the "greasy pole" to grab a five-dollar bill at the top. They tried to catch a "pig well saturated in oil." And they played "a ball game in the afternoon." The Daughters of the Confederacy served dinner to Confederate soldiers on the school grounds. J. H. Folger, another attorney, delivered a speech to the crowd of about sixty veterans. He was introduced by still another attorney, who praised Folger as a "product of the South and the spirit represented by the heroes of the late war." The Wood Men Band provided music. Accompanied by "several of our sweet singers" they "rendered a delightful program, singing the old songs of long ago and in recitations recounting the noble deeds of the heroes." A panel of three judges awarded prizes for parade participants: the Best Team of Mules, the Best Team of Draft Horses, and the Best Pony Team. The Women's Christian Temperance Union won the Best

Decorated Automobile award. Miss Mary Sawyers came in first in the Best
Lady Mount. There were athletic contests: a walking contest, a high jump, a
long jump, and a mile-long race. In the boys' foot race, G. Hill placed first. Mr.
Moser won the wheelbarrow race, the bay race, and the barrel race. No one
entered the watermelon eating contest and "no one climbed the greasy pole
but somebody got the pig." The newspaper noted sponsors and their donation amounts under "Popular Subscriptions." The list included First National
Bank, Bank of Mt. Airy, Granite City Bakery, National Furniture Company,
Cook-Badget Barber Shop, Central Hotel, and the Globe Theatre, among
others. Sponsors contributed a total of $95, and the organizers spent $91.57 of
that amount. Special thanks were given to "the people of Mount Airy" along
with the Judges, the Boy Scouts, and specific community members, including
Chief Marshal E. C. Bivens.[77]

Sponsoring the Fourth of July parade, white businessmen in Mount Airy
followed a ritual formula to spur economic progress and develop manufacturing. The parade became a priority for them after hearing the reported success of an "Industrial Parade" on the Fourth of July in nearby Elkin, North
Carolina. For that festivity, an estimated five to ten thousand people gathered to celebrate the "beginning of the track laying on the New Elkin and
Alleghany railroad." Local businesses sponsored a variety of floats. The parade
was "followed by a balloon ascension and parachute leaps. Then the big free
barbecue and band concert. Next the speaking." The Mayor of Elkin addressed
the crowd and recognized representatives of the railroad. At 2:30 p.m., they
ran the "fast engine and car over the quarter mile of completed track." The
running of the train was a popular event, as "every available space on engine,
tender and car on top was crowded with humanity." A band played as the
train pulled out of the station. For the editor of the Mount Airy paper, it
meant "much for industrial development of western North Carolina."[78]

Echoing the faith in progress displayed in Elkin, the Fourth of July of 1913
in Mount Airy was praised as "a great day for this city and section of the state."
In contrast to the characterization of black Fourth of July celebrations, the
white-sponsored event was described as peaceful and without incident. Despite
the estimated thousands of people in attendance, it was said, "Not a thing happened to mar the good feelings of the people and the great throngs returned to
their homes in the afternoon after spending the day with friends and relatives
many of whom they had not seen in months." The only recorded mention of
harm involved an errant bat that flew out of the hands of a baseball player and
struck Mr. Folger, a spectator, in the head. The paper reported that bystanders
heard the bat "fracturing his skull," but noted there were "no bad effects."

Conclusion

Demonstrating a pattern similar to that found in other New South towns like Mount Airy, whites in early-twentieth century Siler City used Fourth of July parades, a secular rite of American nationalism, to reclaim a racial status that referenced the sacred order of antebellum plantations. In the inaugural parade of 1901, they displayed a spatial marker of their southern secularism: Colonel John Randolph Lane. To his admirers, Lane fought not to defend slavery but to protect Protestant Christian homes and the southern white women who kept them warm. As I noted in Chapter One, Lane declared that he and his soldiers were members of a great middle class who earned their way without any aristocratic advantage of slave labor. Issuing such claims, Lane detached a religious understanding of head of household from its totalizing institution. On the antebellum plantation, whites and blacks lived under the same symbolic roof, its racial boundaries defined by the relationship of slaves to master. But in Lane's house, there were no slaves. He claimed a social status of white Christian independent of incarcerated blackness. Yet, the whiteness he performed depended upon that present absence and its accompanying silence. When Lane described the "tenderest hearts and fairest hands" of those he protected, he evoked the sexual danger of the slave plantation without calling it by name.[79] With the Colonel's performance, southern whites in the New South town of Siler City connected their defense of segregated spaces—homes, churches, and streets—to the divinely sanctioned racial hierarchy of the antebellum plantation while disclaiming any notion that they defended slavery. Such racial projects were in their secularizing formulation neither particularly religious, regional, nor restraining, but were natural, nationalist, and progressive. After branding their pig, southerners shook hands with the American nation and took back its minstrel mask because, wrote Ralph Ellison, "the darky act makes brothers of us all."[80]

3

Civility

THE LAST LYNCHING of a Siler City resident occurred in 1924, according
to Chatham County Commissioner Tommy Emerson. We arrived at that
topic after I asked about the Palestine neighborhood. He did not remember
anyone ever calling it that; he knew it as the Hill. He also knew that several
members of the Methodist church had lived in that neighborhood. Tommy
then interjected, "Do you know why Jesus was a Baptist?" "No," I said, "why
was he?" "Because," he said, "there was no John the Methodist in the Bible."
I laughed and told him that I had not heard that one before. Then he told me
about the first black family to move to the Hill, which was not too long, he
implied, before we spoke in February 2006. They were not locals, he said. The
family consisted of a woman from the North, a retired postal employee, and
her grandson, who moved to Siler City in an attempt to get him out of gang
trouble. Though Tommy did not live in that neighborhood, he knew that
their arrival "has caused some turmoil," adding that some of the Hill residents
were afraid that "the boy is going to pillage." Up to that point in the conversation, I had not asked about race. I had asked about the Fourth of July parade,
about the history of Catholics in Siler, the Good Friday processions at Saint
Julia Catholic Church, and about local reactions to the April tenth immigration rally in front of City Hall in 2006. On that last subject, Tommy said
that some of the protestors [immigrant rights supporters] flew the flag upside
down, which upset some people like Richard Vanderford, the local gas station
operator who had invited David Duke to Siler City in 2000. But Vanderford,
Emerson explained, was "a radical with a small minority following, an equal
opportunity hater," who disliked "Jews, Catholics...everybody." Distancing
himself from Vanderford, Tommy let me know that the only two Jews in town
were "upstanding citizens—one is a veteran and the other is a dentist." He
also said Siler City "has always been a blue-collar town, and there is nothing
wrong with that." The problem now was a "lack of economic opportunity,"
People were "looking for someone to blame." But, he said, Hispanics were
"hard workers." They "take jobs people don't want."[1]

This was the sequence of that part of the conversation. I directly asked about local reactions to Latino protestors in downtown Siler City. After that, I asked about the history of the Palestine neighborhood, without directly inquiring about local reactions or racial differences. When Commissioner Emerson answered the second question, about Palestine, he was, in my interpretation, still responding to the one that preceded it. He was positioning his politics within a progressive narrative by locating himself against the racial anxieties on the Hill and the supremacist fears of Richard Vanderford. To set that narrative, he recounted the last lynching of a Siler City resident.

Hen Johnson, according to Commissioner Emerson, was not guilty of any crime. Retelling the circumstances, he explained that Hen arrived at the Moore farmhouse one Saturday evening to meet his girlfriend, who worked as a maid there. He wanted to surprise her, so he hid in her room, waiting for her to return. The farmer's daughter had a date that evening and was looking for the maid, because she had not yet ironed her dress. When the daughter entered the maid's room, Hen mistook her as his girlfriend and embraced and kissed her. Shocked and embarrassed by his error, he fled the house. But as Johnson left, Tommy recounted, someone recognized him and reported him to the authorities. Sheriff Blair came with help, located "the black man" (though Tommy did not say where), arrested him, and took him to jail in Pittsboro. The white girl's uncle, Tommy added, was on the Chatham Board of Commissioners and in the Klan. He put the word out and got the area Klan together. When the sheriff in Pittsboro heard them coming, he left town, leaving the jail unprotected. The mob overtook it, carried Hen Johnson up on a hill, and hung him.

As he finished the story, Tommy got up and walked out of the living room to look for a photograph of the hanging of Hen Johnson, which he said was given to him by another resident. He returned, unable to find the image, but recounted a second story, of an "almost lynching." In the 1960s, Tommy's father, Sheriff John Emerson, along with Chief of Police June Moody, intervened and stopped a crowd of white men "from hanging a black man." Tommy was teaching science and biology at Jordan-Matthews High School at the time. A fellow member of First Baptist Church, who also taught at the school, asked him for a ride to the Livestock Market on Wade-Paschal Road. It was a Friday afternoon. When they arrived, they saw an excited crowd gathered around the hut where they sold hot dogs. Tommy said an "old fella" from the Bennett area, an "old farmer," had gone to the window for a hot dog, when a "black fella" grabbed his wallet. The crowd caught the man in the pines and dragged him back to the livestock market. Unable to find the wallet, they demanded he tell them where the money was. A local white resident, Tommy remembered, pulled a rope out of his truck. The crowd was, he said, "ready to hang the man." At that moment, Chief Moody intervened, stating, "He's mine. I'll take it from here." He and Sheriff Emerson, also on the scene, removed the alleged thief from the situation and took him into custody. According to the commissioner, they later learned that the black man had a white accomplice across the street, that both men were from Durham, and that they worked for a white boss.[2]

Tommy's contrasting stories follow a narrative pattern that sights governmental interventions against mob lynching as a locative placeholder of historical progress in the New South. His first account of an actual lynching delineated the way things were, when white men, overcome with an emotional sense of urgency for swift justice, would act on that impulse if they were not effectively restrained. His second account of an almost-lynching demarcated the way things are, when white men trained in civil manners, steadfast for judicial procedure, prevent the crime. Tacit in that comparison is the political premise of a modern South: if men like Chief Moody and Sheriff Emerson were ever removed from public office, then the citizens of the state would be left unprotected from primitive violence. Haunted by the specter of lynching, the promise of protection was the power of southern civility.

In this chapter, I argue that in the early twentieth century, elite whites cultivated civility as an institutional mechanism of southern secularism, defining it in opposition to the religious rite of mob lynching. I then show how white officials in Siler City later utilized civility within the secular spaces of their city hall and county courtroom to maintain public power in the mid-twentieth century. After outlining the historical context for white progressive condemnation of lynching in the South, I describe the public drama surrounding the shooting of black resident Melvin Vernell White by white officer Joe Kucinic in Siler City. I use this case to show how, by the 1950s, elite whites had established civility as the operating principle of legal institutions in such a way that it no longer needed a religious referent. After locating secular civility against the spectacle of religious lynching in the early twentieth century and then removing that ritual sacrifice from public view by mid-century, progressive southerners made such civility requisite practice for white and black citizens who encountered one another in the asymmetrical spaces of civic institutions. Once established, they used their civility to obfuscate the obvious. They did not stop violence against blacks. Rather, they reconfigured the manner in which it was executed.[3]

The practice of civility in the United States was not limited to the South, just as lynching was not restricted to the region.[4] Civility describes personal habits of democratic citizenship widely promoted throughout the nation, principally as "civics" by liberal Protestants in voluntary organizations, such as the YMCA, and by Roman Catholics in their own ecclesiastical and educational institutions.[5] In the North, white Protestants utilized civility as a tool to acculturate immigrants, and Catholic leadership instilled it in the laity to Americanize the Church. In the South, white Protestants used it to maintain public control of black bodies. This is an oversimplification, of course, since civility was used for both purposes across both regions. But northern cities were more variegated in terms of their ethnic and religious diversity than southern cities in the early twentieth century. The South was never homogenous by any means—for example, see the cities of Charleston and Savannah.[6] But waves of European immigration, such as that in the northeast, did not overwhelm the region. Unlike New York City, in particular, the South was not as directly impacted by late-nineteenth-century and early-twentieth-century immigration.[7] There always is more to the story—for example, see the city of New Orleans. But as a general guideline the southern region did not encounter the same number of arrivals. This does not mean, however, that the South was any less significant to the development of the nation-state during that period. Even if many European immigrants never set foot in its states, the "idea of the South" was inextricably part of their American experience. It was unavoidable, even if it was distant.[8]

Cultivating Southern Civility

Lynching, historian Donald G. Mathews has argued, was a southern religious rite. At the 1899 lynching of Thomas Wilkes, who was burned alive, a white observer among the frenzied crowd screamed, "Glory be to God!" as he jumped up and down to imitate the "writhing of the tortured black man." He continued, shouting, "God bless every man who had a hand in this. Thank God for vengeance."[9] Lynching was more likely to occur in counties with higher church affiliation. And many southerners considered lynch law, as one commentator put it in the *Sparta* [Georgia] *Ishmaelite* in 1901, "part of the religion of our people."[10]

Progressive southerners professed differently. In the early twentieth century, they associated mob lynching with "primitive communities" and defined their progress—their forward movement toward modern civilization, citizenship, and civility—by their protest against its disorderly primitivism.[11]

Lynching was to them part of the religion of "those people," but not a part of theirs. Progressive southerners did not share the same definitions of modern religion or racial progress, but they all sought to purify, restrain, and control that which they considered a primitive religious rite. They disagreed on the efficacy and ethics of lynching, but they all agreed that something must be done to modernize its affect. In the Wilmington Riot of 1898 and the Atlanta Riot of 1906, white men utilized lynching as a tool of economic and political gain for their racial caste.[12] But other white men, southern elites, particularly industrialists in Atlanta, found those methods counterproductive to their goals. Faced with the political threat of public disgrace from within but mostly from outside the region, they concluded that mob lynching undermined their civic reputation and threatened a pecuniary strength that depended upon their good repute.[13]

The Atlanta Riot of 1906, for example, damaged the city's progressive reputation. In response to the violence, elite whites formed a relief committee to assist the victims and their families and held public meetings to improve communication between white and black communities. According to historian Fitzhugh Brundage, those actions demonstrated a genuine remorse—not for the ten blacks who died, or the sixty more wounded, or their neighborhoods burned to the ground, but rather for the political fallout and economic impact from the national and international coverage of that death and destruction.[14] If industrialists, politicians, and civic leaders, including members of the Chamber of Commerce, did not denounce lynching, they risked being labeled violent and associated with its visible acts. For them, the deadly disturbance was bad for business. To that point, W. E. B. Du Bois, who attended the white-led interracial meetings, decided they had been "gotten up primarily for advertising purposes."[15] Working to recover their city's reputation as a place of racial harmony and enlightened commerce, progressive whites distanced themselves from the rioters, calling them murderers, and then pursued a two-year community relations campaign to show that they opposed extralegal violence and would protect citizens from mob lynching.

The concept of southern progressivism, though, could not do without the idea of mob lynching.[16] Elite whites marked the civic progress of the region in the early twentieth century by their reconfigurations and denouncements of lynching. For some, progress meant only halting certain forms of lynching. Methodist bishop Atticus Haygood, for example, defended lynching but denounced burning someone alive because it was "so much of the Dark Ages surviving in modern and civilized life."[17] For others, like lay Methodist Willis D. Weatherford, who was president of both the Blue Ridge Assembly in North Carolina, and the YMCA graduate school in Nashville, as well as a faculty member of Fisk University, progress meant ridding the region of lynching entirely.[18] In his address, "Lynching, Removing Its Causes," delivered before the Southern Sociological Congress in New Orleans on April 14, 1916, a decade after the Atlanta riot, Weatherford declared that "there was not one decent citizen who took part in the initial outbreak on Decatur Street." Proclaiming a new definition of southern citizenship, he argued that "lynch law is just the forgetting that the person of every human being is sacred and should be inviolate."[19]

Scholarly narratives of early-twentieth-century social movements cite progressive denouncements of mob lynching as evidence of a new historical era in the American South. Historians typically classify southern whites like Weatherford as "liberal Protestants."[20] They reinforce that distinction by comparing them to northern liberals who promoted the Social Gospel. Historian Mary Beth Swetnam Mathews, for example, writes that when white Methodist minister John Carlisle Kilgo, who was president of Trinity College in Durham, North Carolina, advocated education as a means to stop lynching, it sounded "like a sermon from Social Gospel leaders Walter Rauschenbusch or Washington Gladden."[21] This designation gestures to the institutional connections, such as the YMCA, and theological engagement, such as the Social Gospel, between northern and southern Protestants. For that purpose, it is helpful. But for the purpose of identifying southern secularism, it is misleading, since it suggests that southerners like Weatherford did not possess their own dialect of secularism and thus depended upon the vocabulary of northern liberals to speak of social causes. Southerners who denounced lynching may have made the same joyful noise as those northerners, as they too promoted education as the solution to social ills; however, in their configuration of secularism, they did not share the same social epistemology.[22] In particular, they did not share what Rauschenbusch and Gladden shared, which was Friedrich Schleiermacher's attitude toward culture.[23] This was the attitude that Karl Barth described as making possible the "theologian's being at the same time entirely a modern man, with a good, and not a divided conscience"—the very attitude that, according to William Hutchison, defined liberal Protestantism.[24]

Contrary to the historiography, southern white denouncements of lynching did not confirm the distributive affects of that liberal attitude in America. Instead, they marked its limits. Weatherford indeed promoted a good, but he also had a divided conscience. His talk of universal principles sounded like liberalism, and it sounded radically different from white defenses of lynching.

Historian Philip Dray, for example, has argued that Weatherford "denounced both lynching and the black rapist myth."²⁵ The very last section of his address may suggest as much, and it was suggestive enough to offer African Americans a rhetorical ally in their struggle to end lynching— prophetic words spoken by a white man to use against white aggressors. The NAACP considered it beneficial to their anti-lynching program and funded the printing and distribution of Weatherford's speech throughout the South.²⁶ But the rest of the address sounded much different. Weatherford promised equality in his final remarks, an equality that could be read as denouncing the black rapist myth. But by that point he had emptied those promises and had recast the myth with his preceding divisions of the very "personality" which, he claimed, "knows no class distinctions, it knows no aristocracy, and it knows no race difference."²⁷

In his speech, Weatherford declared a sacred personality. Yet, unlike proponents of liberalism, he never considered its sacredness immanent in nature or human nature.²⁸ The sacred was to him, as black bodies were to him, set apart. In his reasons for ending lynching, he distinguished "white women," who were members of "womankind," from "colored girls," who were not. He never questioned the "fact" that "Negro brutes" accused of raping white women actually "commit this terrible crime." To those who doubted that fact he said that, "some Negro leaders have denied that there are Negro rapists, and others have failed to condemn it because of certain injustice done the Negro, but no such position is pardonable." He argued that lynching should stop, not because it condemned innocent persons to death, but because it incited "Negro brutes" to rape "white women." He elaborated his point that "lynching does not prevent crime" by saying that "Negroes have been known to assault white women on the way home from a most horrible and revolting lynching scene." The crime, for Weatherford, was not the execution of the lynched, but the lawlessness it brought forth. Its lack of judicial procedure was, to him, what left white women vulnerable to assault. Lynching begat assault, which begat lynching, which begat assault. "Lynching thus seems to be a self-impregnating hermaphrodite of crime," he said, "that both engenders and transforms its own hideous deformity." Against the anarchy of mob violence, Weatherford argued that white men, the "defender[s] of womankind," must insist on "changes in court procedure as will ensure prompt and just punishment of criminals, particularly in cases of criminal assault." Lynching, he concluded, occurs because a verdict is not swiftly administered and "the people" are apprehensive that "justice will be lost."²⁹

The strategies Weatherford offered to halt lynching separated blacks from whites, marking them essentially different. He instructed whites to deal with whites and blacks to deal with blacks. "White men must start a crusade," he said, "against the white vultures who prey on colored girls." That sentence might suggest that Weatherford felt that some white men, the "vultures," committed the same crimes as accused black men. But he qualified the statement, lest there be any doubt, by saying, "Any man who knows the facts knows full well that for every white woman assaulted by a Negro man, there are a number of colored girls who are seduced by white men." Those varying descriptions implied that for Weatherford assault and seduction were not the same act; one was a crime and the other was a mistake, and the difference distinguished differing bodies.[30] To those on the other side of that line, to "the leaders of the Negro race," he asked that they "preach a crusade against those Negro brutes who commit this terrible crime."[31]

Only after marking racial difference did Weatherford speak to whites and blacks in collaborative terms. He encouraged both races to cultivate deference for the law, which was his rhetorical device for enforcing particular difference under the banner of universal principle. To "the white and colored alike," he said, "unite in uncovering every criminal and bringing every offender to justice." And to the "younger generation," he said, "we must inspire new respect for law." Despite the collective call for all to live in accordance with the law, Weatherford never encouraged black participation in its exercise. In that address he never suggested that blacks should legislate and administer civic ordinances, at least not any rules that would govern members of the white race. Ultimately, his argument to abolish lynching rested upon the legal protections ensured by southern whites, those he considered fit to "administer the law."[32] Throughout his address, he made racial difference immanent in law, while universal equality transcended legal order.

The spirit of the law was, to Weatherford, as it was to other southern progressives, manifest in the protection and defense of white women. To this end, he reconfigured the meaning of chivalry. "Furthermore," he said, "we need to help men see that breaking the law in the name of chivalry is an absolute false principle. A real chivalry will not protect its womanhood by destroying law, but [by] building such a respect for law that none will dare violate it."[33] Southern progressives considered anyone who challenged the chivalry of the law, even white women who protested lynching, disrespectful and excluded them from their movements.[34] Jessie Daniel Ames, a white woman from Texas who founded the Association of Southern Women for the Prevention of Lynching in 1930, for example, was considered too radical for close company.[35]

Historian Jacquelyn Dowd Hall observed that "[Ames's] self-conscious femi-nism had become an anomaly within the southern left," and "she found herself increasingly alienated from the thrust of modern liberalism."[36]

Weatherford's address illustrates how southern progressives could pro-mote human equality, a liberal principle, at the same time that they defended racial difference, a southern virtue. This was the dualistic proximity of their secularism. This was its transcendent mediation. The southern insistence on intimate distance and epistemological disjunction confounded northern lib-eralism and its corresponding secularism. This is perhaps why, as historian Ralph Luker notes, Rauschenbusch "hesitated to address race relations and did so publicly only in the second decade of the century."[37] When he did finally speak on the matter, Rauschenbusch said, "For years, the problem of the two races in the South has seemed so tragic, so insoluble that I have never yet ven-tured to discuss it in public."[38] In that admission, Rauschenbusch uttered his own indictment of northern liberalism: it could not comprehend the racial order of the American South. Despite its social science, it could not dissolve race into a comprehensible form. Rauschenbusch dared not try, because he had no answer. In the face of the mysterious, he was silent. Even Gladden, who did have something to say against the disenfranchisement of "people who are thoroughly fitted for good citizenship," and visited the South to say it, preached patience. Like Rauschenbusch, he struggled to fit the binaries of race into a continuum of liberalism. He began with philosophical citations of deontological duty but ended with an eschatological vision, translating the sentences of Immanuel Kant into a racial theodicy: "The stronger race that tries to treat the weaker not as an end, but as a means to its own selfish ends, plucks swift judgment from the skies upon its own head. On such a race there will surely fall the mildew of moral decay, the pestilence of social corruption, the blight of its civilization."[39] The "problem" of race led liberalism away from the secular and back to religion, away from the North and back to the South. But its proponents could not stay there long; race was a sad problem, but it was the South's problem.

The liberalism espoused by Rauschenbusch and Gladden never chal-lenged the entrenched realism of racial difference in the United States. Rauschenbusch and Gladden reluctantly fretted over its persistence and pub-licly expressed their concern, but they left it to others to figure out and mud-dle through. Filling in theological gaps of racial silence, southern progressives bent the Social Gospel to their ear, rather than let it bend theirs. But that too is misleading, because it assumes northern proponents of the Social Gospel encouraged changes that could potentially erode the foundations of racial order in the South, should they ever be applied there. Many of its staunch-est advocates, though, maintained the same racial differences as Weatherford. Take, for example, Lyman Abbott, Social Gospel stalwart and pastor of Plymouth Congregational Church in Brooklyn.[40] In Abbott's review of *The Souls of Black Folks* (1903), he decided that W. E. B. Du Bois was "ashamed of the race," but Booker T. Washington was "proud of it." Of the many dis-paraging comparisons he listed, he said, "One demands for him the right to ride in the white man's car. The other seeks to make the black man's car clean and respectable."[41] Even northern liberals like Abbott preferred to keep their racial distance.

If liberalism carried the sword of universalism, few dared swing it, lest they risk stabbing themselves. Schleiermacher already risked the sacred distinction of divine providence when he wrote, "all belonging to the human race are eventually taken up into living fellowship with Christ."[42] Barth, who would not affirm nor deny a doctrine of universal salvation, later concluded that Schleiermacher led theology down a path that ended in the "death of God."[43] To wield universalism in racial terms further risked all earthly distinctions. Most proponents of liberalism, despite their theological swagger, were not willing to go there. And for southern progressives, to even behold the idea of racial universalism was to suffer the fate of Lot's wife, when she looked back upon Sodom.

That pervasive fear was evident in Weatherford's response to statements that Josiah Royce made to Chicago's Ethical Cultural Society in 1905. When Royce declared that "America's race problem was caused by nothing inherent in the races themselves but by race antipathy," he rankled Weatherford and fellow progressive Edgar Gardner Murphy to no end.[44] On Luker's account, Weatherford dismissed Royce by saying his claims could "hardly be called unbiased or scholarly" and by adding that "few Southern men will accept Professor Royce's statement that race antipathies are on a 'level with a dread of snakes and of mice.'"[45] Murphy, who also protested lynching, felt that Royce "ignored the stubborn realities of racial inequality" and that ignorance led to "a spurious 'Catholicity' of race."[46] He worried that "if the state acted on Royce's false egalitarian 'racial cosmopolitanism' it could do untold damage to the weaker black race, the stronger white race, and the whole society."[47] Those reactions were telling. They suggested that the ultimate threat to south-ern progressives was not the infinite horizon of human equality, but the tem-poral insistence of racial similitude. Murphy considered Royce threatening because he told "the weaker group that it has nothing peculiar to itself, which it must sacredly conserve in the interest of all."[48] To say there was no essential difference between black bodies and white bodies, as Royce had done, denied the divine power of southern religion and its accompanying secularism. Weatherford may have expressed a transcendent sentiment that day in New Orleans, and it may have sounded radical. But he, like Murphy, could not relinquish control over that which southern whites considered sacred: black bodies set apart. This was the distinction that named the divine sanction and located the earthly authority of southern secularism.

From the point of view of southern whites, the dissolution of race was the danger posed by Reconstruction. Most southerners felt that when northern troops forced them to accept the governmental rule of African Americans elected to public office, the federal government was institutionalizing the racial atheism of northern secularism. To resist the perceived unbelief of that secularism, progressive southerners did not use religion alone, as the Klan did.[49] Instead, they configured their own secularism against the performance of religious primitivism, as northern liberals did to them. Then they used their secularism to defend their divinely sanctioned racial order with the legal violence of their southern civility. To show the institutional mechanics of those criminal procedures, I examine a case study in Siler City.

Southern Civility: A Case Study

I first learned of the shooting of Melvin Vernell White during a conversation with a black resident in 2011. After discussing her memories of Fourth of July parades and her experiences at Chatham High School in the late 1960s, that resident, who preferred to remain anonymous, told me that when she was around twelve years old she was afraid for her father. The reason, she said, was that "a gentleman, Vernell White, a black man, [had been] shot in the back of the head and killed by a Siler City policeman." She said it happened at a local carnival when he was running away. The policeman, she said, got out of it by saying that he was only firing a warning shot, which ricocheted off the ground and hit the man in the back of the head. But she did not believe that explanation. It just didn't make sense. She said, "When did you ever hear of someone shooting a warning shot into the ground?"[50]

Everyone I had spoken with up to that point, white and black residents alike, had never mentioned racial conflict. The common sentiment was one of racial harmony. When I asked Elizabeth Edwards, daughter-in-law of Tod Edwards, "What makes Siler City a good place to live?" she responded, "I found that the people are very friendly, both white and black, and easy to get along with."[51] Other residents I spoke with never mentioned the shooting incident when responding to questions about racial integration. They almost always mirrored the statement of Edwards, saying, in effect, "We always have gotten along." But when I later asked directly about the shooting, after hearing about it, the responses of black residents significantly differed from those offered by white residents. Another black resident who had lived in Siler City long enough to recall the incident told me that the police shot White and then "tried to say he was intoxicated." She said she was very young at the time but remembered her parents talking about it at the table. When I asked white residents from that same generation about those events, few remembered them at all. Those who did described the shooting as an unfortunate accident, saying the officer fired a warning shot and the bullet ricocheted off the ground. All the residents who remembered the shooting agreed that the officer fired his gun. But black residents had a different interpretation than white residents of *why* he fired his gun. Motivation meant everything in this case. Straining against their shared profession of racial harmony, blacks and whites disagreed about the officer's intent. If consensus was the standard of civility, then this was an uncivil matter. In what follows, I describe that matter using newspaper reports and NAACP files.

The Incident

At 9:25 p.m. on Saturday, July 14, 1962, white police officers Joe Kucinic and B. B. Raynor arrested black residents Melvin Vernell White and Melvin Alston at the Jaycee Carnival behind the Farmers Mutual Bank in Siler City. They charged White and Alston with "being drunk," and drove them to "the jail at the city hall." In the driveway of City Hall, Officer Kucinic fired two shots from his .38-caliber pistol. One bullet struck Melvin White, who died thirty minutes later at the Chatham Hospital. An hour after White was declared dead, Melvin Alston pleaded guilty to public drunkenness in front of Justice of the Peace J. A. Hunter, who released him after he paid taxing court costs.[52]

Chief of Police June Moody called the death a "tragic accident." He explained that White ran from Kucinic as the officer tried to move him from the car to the jail. They had ridden in Raynor's private car, because Officer Henry Kimball was using the patrol car. Raynor and Kucinic typically covered the 10:00 p.m. shift but reported early that night to patrol the carnival. When the victim fled, Kucinic "called White to stop." When he kept running, the officer fired two warning shots, "aiming at the ground." The bullet that hit White "ricocheted" off the concrete. White fell to the ground, 150 feet from Kucinic, who "thought he stumbled." Hearing gunshots, Raynor ran out of the jail, where he had taken Alston. He remembered hearing Kucinic say, "I've shot him." Raynor called an ambulance.

Melvin White, age twenty-eight, was survived by his wife and three children. The family requested an autopsy, which was performed at Alamance General Hospital in Burlington the following morning. The autopsy "revealed that one bullet entered the head behind the right ear, and that a second hole in the skull was caused by a piece of bone which broke loose from the impact of the bullet. The right brow was lacerated and there were bruises on the arms and legs, apparently caused by the fall to the concrete drive." No tests were conducted to measure "the alcohol content of the dead man's blood." Police Chief Moody and Sheriff John W. Emerson, Jr., sent the bullet recovered from White's body to a crime lab in Raleigh "for testing to determine if it ricocheted." They did not find any "concrete particles" on the bullet.

Kucinic was a "former GI who landed in France on D-Day as a tank driver." He had lived in Siler City for fifteen years but had only served five days as a police officer at the time of the shooting. Prior to joining the police force, he was a self-employed truck driver and a mechanic at a bowling alley. Melvin White was also a truck driver, employed with Clyde Reed Perry of Silk Hope, an area near Siler known for its Klan presence. "[White] was described as a quiet, capable worker."

The Protest

On Thursday, July 26, 1962, "a crowd of approximately 225 Negro residents of Siler City and surrounding area requested and received an audience with Mayor Don Lee Paschal." The county coroner's inquest into the shooting was scheduled for that day, but "was delayed when [the coroner] could not obtain a court stenographer until Friday." Ervis Womble, an "elderly Negro leader of Siler City…opened the meeting with a prayer in which he said that he hoped no one came to the meeting with malice in their heart." Guytanna Horton of Pittsboro, "a first-year student at North Carolina College, Durham," told the mayor that, "if the Town of Siler City is to be redeemed in the eyes of the citizens, officer Joe Kucinic must be fired." Womble then described Kucinic as "unthoughtful" and said he was the type of man to "shoot first and think later." He then said to the mayor:

> We don't want to go down the street and be fearful that if we stub our toe and fall down and get up we might be shot at. [Applause] There is no use of my telling you that this is the fourth such happening and

if it keeps on something can get out of hand. We don't want that to happen, we don't want folks grabbing guns and fighting in our streets. I feel good when I see officers with uniforms on because I know that they are there to protect me and my rights…we ask that the town board and you to screen and so counsel whatever men our police force has that they will be careful what they do when they come down to protecting the rights of other people. We beg the people of Siler City to see that we don't have that man to be afraid of henceforth, now and forevermore.[53]

Mayor Paschal answered Horton and Womble's request to fire Kucinic by saying, "We suspended him within two minutes after we found out what happened that night. We were not in a position to prejudge him and we will not be put in that position." He continued, saying, "It is my personal opinion that Officer Kucinic did violate the law, and I advised him to get a lawyer on the night that he was suspended."

Grady Horton asked the mayor why the city did not hire Negro police officers. Chief Moody responded by saying that he and Sheriff Emerson discussed the possibility of "hiring a Negro policeman for the town and a Negro deputy for the county, with the pair to work together." He stated that they "even went so far as to discuss this with some of the Negro's here today at this meeting."

Guytanna Horton informed the mayor that the town never officially notified Melvin White's widow of her husband's death. Paschal said, "I was not aware of any official statement that should be made, but if that will make her feel better I'll see that she is officially notified." Chief Moody explained, "That is partly my fault. I saw her when she was talking to the hospital authorities. I didn't talk to her. I thought she knew what was going on." The mayor stated that he was with Chief Moody around 10:00 p.m. when he "received a telephone call from the hospital that Melvin White was dead." He said, "When we got to the hospital we asked for White's wife and were told that she was gone. I presumed that Dr. Northington had notified her." Ervin Womble closed the meeting by telling "the mayor that he believed him to be a man of his word and a man who 'would do what he said he would do.'"

On Friday, July 27, 1962, members of the local NAACP chapter marched to City Hall for the coroner's inquest. The courtroom was "two thirds full, with about half of the crowd being Negroes." Jack Moody, the attorney representing Kucinic, offered the only public statement. He said that White "came to his death as a result of a wound from a shot fired by Officer Kucinic." Moody had spoken with District Solicitor Ike F. Andrews and the attorneys for the White family. All agreed to send the case to the grand jury. The coroner's jury heard no evidence. The following Friday the NAACP held a meeting at Corinth AME Zion Church. "Handbills" were distributed throughout town advertising a "protest" meeting. Field secretary Charles McLean led the meeting. He played a recording of a speech by Martin Luther King, Jr., and encouraged residents to "join the NAACP, register for elections and exercise their ballot in order to attain their full citizenship." That same day, the NAACP issued a press release on the shooting, noting that, "Under North Carolina law, it is illegal for the police to shoot in connection with a misdeamenor [sic] such as drunkenness."

The Defense

At a special meeting held on July 28, 1962, the Siler City town commissioners voted in favor of a motion to request the resignation of Joe Kucinic. On Monday, August 6, 1962, Kucinic submitted a formal letter stating that he was resigning, "for the best interest of the town of Siler City." In the letter, he said that his resignation was not an admission to having "committed any violation of the rules of the Police Department or laws of the State of North Carolina." He maintained that for fifteen years, as a resident of the town of Siler City, he "diligently and faithfully complied with the laws of society which constitue good citizenship."

In October 1962, a Chatham County jury indicted Officer Kucinic in the killing of Melvin White. A trial was held in November 1962 at the Chatham County Superior Court. Solicitor Ike Andrews, assisted by Floyd McKessik, a private attorney from Durham, prosecuted the case. Officer Raynor first took the stand. He testified that the "shooting occurred outside [the] city jail" and that "White ran from the patrol car." Sheriff Emerson followed and confirmed "the results of the autopsy and the investigation of the bullet removed from White," stating that it was determined that the bullet ricocheted and struck the victim in the back of the head. Mayor Paschal and former deputy sheriff C. A. Simmons also took the stand. They, along with Emerson, testified to Kucinic's "character." Melvin Alston stated that "to [his] knowledge White had not been drinking." Kucinic did not testify.

Superior Court Judge J. C. Pittman "sentenced Kucinic to 5 to 7 years in jail, suspended for 5 years. He was placed on probation with conditions that he be allowed to follow his occupation out of state, report to a probation officer once a month and pay court costs." The judge explained the sentencing:

Kucinic was put on by the city to handle a job and was given a gun without previous training. It's hard to get capable officers and that's very unfortunate. But no man ought to be given a badge and a gun to go out to enforce the law without training in a school or from other officers. I'm sure the defendant regrets the action and wouldn't have harmed the victim for anything.

The judge stated that he did not personally consider Kucinic a criminal. He added:

Race does not enter into my decision. The colored race gets as fair treatment in my court as does the white race. But this unfortunate incident was due to inexperience.

The judge advised that all law enforcement should know when to use a gun. He quoted the law to that effect. He then emphasized that the sentence handed down to Kucinic would make him "feel the arm of the law around him for a number of years." When later asked his reaction to the sentencing, Floyd McKessik told reporters, "It was an accident and there is suffering on both sides. But we think Mr. Kucinic should serve some portion of an active sentence."

After the verdict, Kucinic told reporter Jim Parker, "A man learns who his friends are when he goes through something like this." He said:

I want you to try to express to the people of Siler City my feelings over this matter. I really wanted that policeman's job and I think I could have been a good policeman. I had no intention of shooting Vernell White. When he ran from me I tried to put him in jail. I fired at the ground. It was a terrible accident.

Kucinic emphasized that he "was given no instruction in when to use the pistol, how to go about making an arrest, or anything else." He was just told to "take your instructions from officer Raynor; he is an experienced officer." Kucinic said that soon after he was suspended from the police force, he was fired by the bowling alley. They told him it was "bad for business" for him to work there. Kucinic also said that he received anonymous telephone calls telling him he was a "murderer." He said that he lost his job, was behind in his house payments, had to pay lawyer fees, and now had to find a new job and start a new life. "Frankly," Kucinic said, "I feel the town let me down. When they forced me to resign, many people took that as a sign that the town offi-cially felt I was guilty of some crime, even though no trial had been held." He said, "A man who joins the police department has no protection whatsoever. If he makes a mistake...he can't count on the town." He continued, saying:

> I didn't mean to shoot Vernell White. It was an accident and could have happened to anyone who joined the police force as I did. But even though I knew it was an accident, it has caused me more grief than I can possibly express to you. I have the deepest sympathy for the fam-ily of Vernell White, I know it is trite to say, 'I wish it had never hap-pened,' but that's about the only way you can say it.

The reporter summarized his final comments, stating that Kucinic "looks back on the entire experience with sadness and regret and he says that he hopes his experiences as a rookie policeman might have done some good in that they might serve as a warning to any other men who find themselves given a gun and a badge and told to go work as a police officer."

Lynch Law to Legal Killing

Based on the available sources and evidence, the judge ruled that the shoot-ing of Melvin Vernell White was accidental due to the officer's inexperience. That decision ultimately rested on the assumption that Joe Kucinic was a man of good character. Testimony offered by white men of higher standing in the community substantiated his inherent goodness. He acted irrespon-sibly in firing his gun, but he meant no harm. He was no criminal. Without those assumptions, the material evidence was at best inconclusive, at worst condemning. Melvin White was charged with public drunkenness, yet there was no evidence of alcohol in his blood. Melvin Alston's admission of public drunkenness discounted his testimony to White's sobriety. Yet that admission was acquired an hour after the shooting. And Alston later testified at the trial that to his knowledge White had not been drinking. Raynor testified that White ran from the car, yet earlier accounts placed him in the jail with Alston at the time of the shooting. The investigation into the shooting concluded that the bullet hitting White ricocheted off the driveway, however, there was no evidence of concrete particles on the bullet. Kucinic was described as untrained in using a pistol. Yet he had served in the US military. The Siler City police department may not have trained him, but he surely knew how to use a weapon.

Without projecting benevolent humor onto the officer, it was reasonable to conclude, as most black residents did, that the shooting of Melvin White was no accident. In the civil discourse of Siler City, though, common sense that favored the opinions of black residents was disregarded as biased emotionalism, while biased emotionalism serving the interests of white residents was projected as common sense. This was the key institutional mechanism of southern secularism exercised by progressive whites in their public defense of Kucinic's intent. They redirected common sense away from the production of knowledge based on the sensorial evidence one accumulates through years of experience, and toward the interpretation of scientific evidence manufactured within a secular space segregated from that experience, in the lab, by those in power who benefited only from a certain outcome.

On August 2, 1962, the editor of the *Chatham News* published an opinion column titled "Justice Results From Orderly Process Not Emotionalism." He stated that during the two weeks since the "shooting to death of a young Negro man seeking to escape from an arresting officer," the people of the Siler City area have "adequately demonstrated" a "common-sense" approach. He described the actions of "Negro citizens" who requested his firing as conducted in an "orderly manner." They had an "appointed spokesmen to speak for them" in an official conference with Mayor Don Lee Paschal. Therefore, the editor argued, the concerns of "Negro citizens" were heard. He further noted that the meeting was free of "outside influence although there may have been some outsiders present." Though the initial request was untenable, he implied, it was delivered in a proper forum. The editor also believed that the city official responded reasonably and acted wisely, following the only available path to justice. By not firing Kucinic, they did not condemn the officer without evidence and proper trial. He stated:

> A man is presumed innocent until he is proven guilty and such proof of either innocence or guilt must stem from courts of law and not from street-corner talk or emotional-packed actions by any group. To bring matters out into the open, by peaceful means, is the best way to dissipate rumor and idle talk. Our people have acted with wisdom and good judgment. And that is good for the community we are trying to build, a community where all people can live in harmony and amid good feeling.

In his statements, the editor outlined two possible courses of actions: "emotional-packed actions" that stemmed from "street-corner talk" and "wise and judicious actions" that yielded to the legitimate authority of "courts of law." The editor's statements did not attribute a racial essence to those actions, but rather suggested that white city officials could more capably control their emotions by thinking and acting rationally. Bringing "rumor" into the "open"—that is, into white-controlled civic space—the editor depicted black residents as handing over their emotional response to white city officials, trusting that the officials would act in a way that would serve the good of the entire community.

Emphasizing the need to protect local order, to avoid outside influence, and to maintain racial harmony and good feeling, the editor legitimated white control of the law in both its physical enforcement and institutional procedure. In his words, "This is as it should be. It is the only way. Emotion has no place nor any pressures." In that discursive context, the editor's argument applied the logic of southern civility only to white male bodies. According to that argument, only white officials could manage the sentiments of personality and submit them to the universal objectivity of the law. The editor's argument found no place for the emotional experiences of black residents or for the deceased Melvin White. It never even mentioned him by name. But it did mention Joe Kucinic and Mayor Don Lee Paschal. Like Weatherford's speech, the argument maintained two standards—one of emotive error for black bodies and one of corrective restraint for white bodies—and reconciled those standards in its proclamations of universal justice. It did not, however, apply the same standards to the victim as it did the officer. It stated a man was innocent until proven guilty, but did not question the charge that White was drunk or the claim that he ran from the car. The argument assumed that black bodies were untrustworthy and white bodies were honest. Otherwise, how could the charge of drunkenness be upheld without toxicological evidence, lest it be done so solely on the officer's word, on the statement of the man who shot the deceased? And why was it "apparent" that White's lacerations and bruises were caused by falling to the ground, and not by blows from the officer, from the man who shot the deceased? Why was it not an equally self-evident possibility that White ran to escape police brutality and was shot because of it? The editor's argument, like the judge's ruling, muted those questions by projecting the virtuous premise of southern civility that white male bodies will always act, even if mistakenly, with good intentions.

When voicing their reactions to the shooting, black residents were constrained by the racialized normativity of public discourse. During the initial protest of the shooting, Ervis Womble questioned Kucinic's character, calling him the type of man to shoot first and think later. But he never at that time questioned the mayor's character. Short of forceful resistance, affirming that the mayor was a man of his word and holding him to his promise for a proper investigation and fair trial was the available recourse. Prior to the trial, white officials could neither confirm nor deny Kucinic's character and his actions without "evidence." At that time, white civic leaders permitted black residents to publicly suggest that Kucinic did intentionally shoot White, even if he did not intend to kill him. But they stipulated that black residents could not demand action based on their judgment of character without submitting to legal procedure. The investigation into the shooting answered doubts about Kucinic's character because, by the standards of white officials, it used scientific method to confirm that the bullet did ricochet off the concrete drive. Once the verdict validated the investigation, questioning the officer's character was no longer acceptable. After the trial, attorney Floyd McKessick quibbled with the enforcement of the sentencing, but he acknowledged the shooting an accident. He could no longer protest, at least in public, that Kucinic intended to shoot White. Ultimately, the principles of legal universality and applicable science used in this case depended on the civility of white officials, which vouchsafed the word of Officer Raynor, the word of Sheriff Emerson, the word of Mayor Paschal, the word of former Deputy Sheriff Simmons, and the word of Judge Pittman, who said race did not factor into his decision. This was the public power of southern civility: to silence any collective revelation beyond its own self-presentation, to segregate racialized memories with its secular science.

Conclusion

In the early twentieth century, elite white men defined civility as an institutional mechanism of southern secularism against the religious performance of mob lynching. They reconfigured the meaning of chivalry such that their public willingness to protect black citizens from primitive violence was a sign of their private strength to protect white women. In both instances, they patrolled secular spaces by detaining those they deemed unable to restrain themselves from extralegal affairs. White officials in New South towns and cities drained secular spaces of an exuberant emotion that they associated with those primitive outbursts. They filled that emptied space with refined etiquette, which they associated with a modern disposition. However, white officials did not seek to rid secular spaces entirely of all religious emotion. Citizens could still bring pious feelings into the secular chambers of government and law. But they had to remake them as modern. Public prayers had to be offered in accordance with the rules of civility. They must be conciliatory, given in the name of transcendent virtues, of love and peace, common to all Christians regardless of race. By that standard, white officials discredited the hysteria of lynching that exceeded the bounds of law and order. But they also used the same standard to discredit any emotional disagreement, including those offered by black residents in pursuit of justice. "Street-corner talk" did not abide by the protocol of civility and its court of law, which whites defined and controlled. Without that secular difference, elite whites would have been subject to the same religious authority as black citizens. Spiritual equality was a dangerous game to white officials in the mid-twentieth century, as it had been to W. D. Weatherford in an earlier period. But they adapted, as he did, reformatting their public rhetoric to protect their civic interests. Promoting civility as if it were a universal practice of their legal institutions, they denied all observable evidence—the plain sight facts, to use their standards of common sense—and hushed protests. Ultimately, they leveraged civility to enforce a religious justification of racial hierarchy. But to say such things was akin to raising your voice. And to be civil was to be quiet and let the law speak for itself.

4

Privatization

THE FOURTH OF July parade of 1976 was a dud. A large crowd gathered—by some estimates, a record crowd. But downtown streets were, according to area reporter Roy Key, "drab as a mid-winter day." There was no bunting, and a lone American flag flew in front of the post office. Parade participation was "pitiful," one observer put it. Area high school bands from Northwood and Chatham Central canceled their scheduled appearances. The Jordan-Matthews High School band from Siler City did perform, though it offered what Key called a "half-hearted appearance, as a dozen or so members, out of uniform, marched as a group." After watching the parade, another observer said she was "embarrassed for Siler City." Don Tarkenton, vice president of the Siler City Jaycees, the organization that sponsored the event, explained, "We asked for people to enter floats in the parade, and all we got was two entries. We lined up bands and they canceled out, one as late as last Friday night. It is obvious to me [that] the people are just not interested in participating in parades anymore; therefore I am hoping the Siler City Jaycees will go along with my suggestion and discontinue the parade."[1]

From the end of the 1920s up until 1976, the Fourth of July celebration had always been the biggest event in town. While numbers varied year to year, the parades were well attended through the 1950s, 1960s, and early 1970s. The *Chatham News* reported that a "crowd of 10,000 packs city for July Fourth celebration" in 1958. The paper estimated twenty-five thousand people in 1965. In 1967, observers "lined up as much as six deep to watch the bands, floats, beauty queens and clowns as they wound their way through downtown Siler City." In 1969, though, only "5,000 spectators lined the streets for the parade."[2] In 1975, the paper offered a playful estimation of "about 9,997 people." And it reported attendance for the 1976 parade in the thousands, citing observers who called it "one of the largest ever to assemble for a Fourth of July parade."[3] The news coverage may have exaggerated attendance, but the estimated numbers gave some sense of crowd size. Those reports suggest that residents were interested in the parade right up until the end. But by that last year, something had changed. It appeared, comparing those estimates with comments by Tarkenton and others, that the change had to do with parade participation more than it did observer interest.

Over the course of the twentieth century, the Fourth of July parades publicly dramatized communal life in Siler City, displaying in the city streets changes to public and civic institutions. Among the changes displayed were those mandated by the Civil Rights Act of 1964 but not enacted at the local level until the 1970s. The parade included its first racially integrated high school band in 1972, two years after Chatham County public schools were fully integrated to the standards of the federal government, and eighteen years after the 1954 *Brown v. Board of Education* ruling. Prior to that entry, blacks participated in the parade in segregated bands. From 1973 to 1976, parade participation was increasingly integrated. In 1977, in the midst of those changes, the Jaycees canceled the downtown Fourth of July parade in Siler City for the first time in three decades.[4] That same year, Tommy Emerson, who was "interested in politics at the time," as one resident described him, organized a private party at his home with the help of his brother-in-law, Dalton Marsh. About fifty to eighty people attended, most of them family. The following year they invited fellow members of First Baptist Church, because as Tommy's wife, Anna, put it, "Church is family, too." Soon others in the community wanted to attend. The Emerson family began sending out invitations, and each year their guest list lengthened. From 1977 to 2009, Tommy and Dalton hosted the annual celebration, rotating between their homes each year. The party recreated the ritual order of the old-time Fourth of July celebrations, as Tommy remembered them, though without a parade. There were games and prizes, a greasy pole, live entertainment, the honoring of veterans, a prayer by the Baptist minister, and barbecue, sweet tea, and desserts. Dalton, who was head chef, according to Tommy, remembered that for many years they welcomed more than five hundred people at each celebration. When the party ended, he said, everyone wanted to keep it going. They had to stop because of Dalton's declining health, not because of the expense, or because of lack of interest. Tommy could have still hosted, but said he would not continue without Dalton.

In this chapter, I argue that privatization was the premise for white-controlled public space in Siler City during the period of restructuring that followed racial desegregation in the 1970s. During its run, the invitation-only Emerson-Marsh celebration was the most consistent Fourth of July celebration in Siler City. It was a white-led function intended for a white audience, though it was never expressly promoted as a segregated event, and later celebrations did include a few black guests. Their participation, however, was akin to the presence of Tod Edwards on Chatham Avenue; it was the exception that proved the rule. The private celebration functioned to protect and perpetuate the racial hierarchy that had been displayed in the downtown parades before integrated participation in 1972, even if that was not the expressed intent of its organizers. Once the social changes mandated by the Civil Rights Act made their local arrival in the 1970s and disrupted that display, a group of southern whites withdrew to their religious community, using the privatized practices of their Protestant congregation to reclaim their secular rite and then publicly display their sectarian stance.

The historical narrative I present in this chapter contests the explanations of parade decline offered by the residents of Siler. Those I spoke with immediately ruled out race as having anything to do with the parade.[5] Nor, to them, did it have anything to do with the Emerson-Marsh celebration. If they gave a direct explanation, they reasoned that the parade declined because of lack of interest, economic changes, or the inclusion of women in civic organizations. Offering as much detail as I could find on parade performances from 1972 to 1976, I evaluate arguments for parade decline as residents presented them to me, and I detail what happened to the parade in the wake of its cancellation. Diverging from residents' explanations, I propose that there is enough evidence to suggest that while race was not necessarily a causal factor in the decline of the parades, it was inextricably linked to the spatial transformations of the 1960s and 1970s that disrupted the divinely sanctioned racial order predicated on the gendered protection of white women, the same enduring order that progressive southerners had established at the local level by mid-century via the mechanisms of their secularism. Prohibitions regarding the discrimination against women enacted by federal legislation in the 1960s struck at the paternalistic core of southern secularism as much as the desegregation of public schools and rules regarding interstate commerce. By the 1980s, white men had abandoned many of their civic organizations, citing the inclusion of women as the cause of their demise. In the wake of the social movements for racial and gender equality that reached public prominence in the 1960s, white Protestant men returned to their congregations and homes to recover lost public power.[6] They never had fully relinquished their leadership roles in those spaces, but they now reclaimed them with renewed vigor and added incentive. Those religious sites offered a refuge from the regional encroachment of federal legislation that resulted from a competing secularism. Within those sites they continued to practice gender discrimination and ignored racial history as they saw fit, strategizing their political reemergence in the public realm.

The privatization of the Fourth of July celebration in Siler City encapsulates broader political strategies employed by muscular evangelicals—those like Pat Robertson who championed physical fitness and flexed political strength—to respond to the social transformations of the 1960s and 1970s, including changes to public policies and civic organizations sparked by feminist movements.[7] The same year that Tommy Emerson organized the private Fourth of July celebration in Siler City, James Dobson, a Christian psychologist, founded the conservative evangelical organization Focus on the Family, with its headquarters in Colorado Springs, Colorado.[8] Two years later, in 1979, Jerry Falwell organized the Moral Majority, which collaborated with political strategists in the Republican Party to reclaim the public power and social influence they perceived as threatened by the federal legislation of the previous two decades.[9] In the ensuing conservative barrage of the 1980s and 1990s, those organizations cast the largest stones. To sling them, they employed the same cataclysmic catapult of religious privatization. Journalist Dan Gilgoff noted that Falwell earlier had "condemned civil rights activists from his Virginia pulpit and opposed the Lyndon Johnson–era civil rights laws as 'a terrible violation of human and private property rights.'" Evangelicals of his stripe were unable to block civil rights legislation that expanded a public sphere historically limited to white men and favorable to those of Protestant faith. In the aftermath of that defeat, a cadre of white evangelicals regrouped and recalculated their position. Feeling pushed aside, they claimed outsider status and declared themselves kindred in spirit to African Americans who had suffered under segregation. Dobson, who spoke with a voice of gentle anger, most clearly articulated that new political directive. Like Falwell, he argued for the private protection of religious freedom as a political strategy to morally discriminate within the public sphere. Dobson lobbied to protect the public expression of private faith, with the intent to exercise it within the shared commons of the courtroom and classroom, and not just within the exclusive and private space of the congregation and home. But differing from the earlier Falwell, he reframed religious freedom as a civil right that was violated in the same way that the civil rights of African Americans were violated when they were disenfranchised. In 2003, Gilgoff reported, Dobson traveled to Montgomery, site of the 1955 bus boycott, to support Chief Justice Roy Moore in his attempt to defy a federal ruling prohibiting the display of the Ten Commandments in the Alabama Supreme Court. Speaking to "more than a thousand Christian demonstrators," Dobson opened with a reference to Rosa Parks and later declared, "We as people of faith are also being sent to the back of the bus."[10] In Dobson's post-1970s America, people of faith were like people of color: they too were victims of discrimination.

The privatization of the Fourth of July in Siler City was not directly related in any way to the overlapping political projects of Dobson and Falwell. To speak of Focus on the Family and the Moral Majority says nothing about Tommy Emerson's local politics—he was a southern Democrat. Nor does it help explain why he wanted to maintain the cherished memories of his childhood. But the manner in which Emerson organized a gathering defined by a "subcultural identity," to borrow a phrase from sociologist Christian Smith, does say much about the secular mechanics of conservative politics after the Civil Rights Act of 1964.[11] When parade participation was desegregated, he and other white Baptists abandoned civic space. They were not forced to the back of the bus. Rather, they were asked to stay on the bus and share seats, as in the parade they were asked to share the same floats and march in the same bands. Rather than observe that new route, they calmly found the emergency exit and excused themselves. But they did not each go to their own house and celebrate the Fourth solely with their immediate families. Privatization was a source of solidarity in this case, not an excuse for individuation. Rather, they gathered together as fictive kin, as a collective "family," and maintained the segregated traditions that marked their distinctive identity, including the religious sanction of a particular evangelical and historically southern gendered hierarchy. Privatization was, like the movement from Palestine to Pine Forest, resettlement, not retreat. It was an attempt to build a new bus without federal oversight. Dr. James Dobson wanted to drive that bus from the white suburbs to the Supreme Court. Commissioner Tommy Emerson was content to park it in his backyard.

The Spirit of '72 to '76

News coverage from 1972 to 1975 suggests that Fourth of July parade participation in Siler was increasingly desegregated leading up to 1976. The 1972 and 1973 parades were likely the first ones affected by "de facto desegregation," as one white resident described it to me, with the participation of at least one integrated high school band. Newspaper accounts and conversations with residents offer no evidence of desegregated parade participation before 1972, the year Northwood High School in Pittsboro was integrated and its school band marched in the parade.[12] In a photo in the *Chatham News* with the caption title "The spirit of '72" band members dressed in white uniforms

led by two white majorettes in front and a white band director to the side.
Examining those photographs, I noticed that the band members near the
front appeared to be white, while members toward the back appeared black,
though it was difficult to tell. That year, what looked like a racially integrated
band was "Chatham County's only band entrant in the parade."¹³

Coverage of the 1974 parade was less descriptive, providing only a reference to a "Kit" Carson appearance in the parade.¹⁴ Photographs from the
1975 parade, though, suggest the presence of an integrated high school band
with white and black cheerleaders. This was a significant change, since that
integrated presence was displayed within the parade itself. That differed from
the typical presence of blacks in athletic contests and in the parade crowd. In
another photo from that year, two boys—one black and one white—competed against each other in a sack race. Additional photographs captured old
cars, wagons, white participants square dancing, and black observers among
the larger white crowd. The *Chatham News* called 1975 "a pretty good Fourth
of July," quoting one observer who said, "It was one of the best behaved crowds
we have ever had as well as one of the largest."¹⁵

Coverage from 1976 suggests continued desegregation of parade participation. The *Chatham News* included a photo of a car in the parade with
"Northwood High" handwritten on poster paper attached to the door and
a ribbon running along the side. Two white cheerleaders were seated on the
hood, another white cheerleader sat on the roof, and a black cheerleader sat
on the trunk. Below that photo, the paper ran the caption, "Cheering in the
Fourth," followed by two consecutive sentences, one clearly descriptive, the
other ambiguously evaluative. The first sentence stated, "The Northwood
High School cheerleaders were among those participating in the Siler City
Jaycees July 4th parade." The second sentence, without transition, stated, "A
poor turnout may bring an end to the annual tradition."¹⁶ When I read those
sentences in the print room of the newspaper office in 2011, I interpreted their
juxtaposition to imply an unspoken connection between integrated participation and poor turnout. Elsewhere in that issue, the paper reported that
the 1976 parade was well attended. So the poor turnout, given that reference,
likely referred to the participants, and not the observers. If that was the case,
then the paper offered a commentary on the racial integration of parade participation without saying anything about race.

Adding to evidence of increased desegregation of parade participation,
the paper included in its 1976 coverage a photo of an integrated Girl Scout
troop riding in the parade on a flatbed trailer. Their participation is significant because four years earlier, two black members of an integrated Girl Scout

troop from nearby Sanford were denied admission to the Rolla-Roma skating rink in that area. According to ACLU North Carolina files.

On or about October 17, 1972 plaintiff's Girl Scout troop consisting of approximately fourteen girls, of whom twelve are white and two are Negro, sought admission to defendant's roller skating rink, and tendered to defendant admission fees for each of the members of the troop. Defendant accepted the membership fees from the white members of the troop and permitted them to use his facilities but defendant refused to accept the admission fee from the Negro members of the troop including plaintiff, and excluded them from the premises.

The plaintiff's attorney, Norman B. Smith, argued that the defendant clearly discriminated against the paying customers based on race. Because the defendant sold food and beverages that "have moved in interstate commerce," he was, argued Smith, violating the 1964 Civil Rights Act. The defendant denied the allegations, saying that "his place of business is open and has been open to members of all races" and that "there is no segregation policy in force or effect and that members of the Negro race, as well as the White race are using the facilities at this time and are doing so on numerous occasions." The US District Court Durham Division ruled on April 30, 1973, in favor of the plaintiff and ordered the defendant to no longer withhold services from the "plaintiff and others of her class."[17]

The participation of an integrated Girl Scout troop in the parade displayed the legal impact of the Civil Rights Act on places of business like the Rolla-Roma skating rink, near Siler City. It was no longer a distant federal law but was now a tangible local reality, visible in the city streets. The social changes symbolized in that parade float contested the 1976 parade's historical theme that year. An integrated Girl Scout troop had never been a part of the old-fashioned parade tradition. It was not *in* those memories. Black participation was part of those memories, but it always had been segregated. Progressive whites tolerated, even celebrated, the inclusion of that kind of racial difference, because it displayed their institutional control of civic space. Integrated participation, though, displayed their failure to maintain that type of spatial control. Faced with a new horizon—a present that carried itself into a different future—most whites in Siler City continued to look back and project their remembered past onto their unforeseen surroundings. In 1976, the Siler City Jaycees promoted the parade as "usual," with the following advertisement:

On Saturday, beginning at 10 a.m. the traditional parade will begin, featuring the usual floats, bands, pretty girls, and politicians. And of course, the wagon train. Everyone is reminded to dress in Bicentennial attire for the occasion, as awards will be given...for best man's, woman's and child's costume portraying a bicentennial theme.

Prior to 1972, the "usual floats, bands, pretty girls, and politicians" were always presented within the familiar boundaries of racial segregation. A "usual" float carried white participants. "Usual" bands were either from white high schools or black high schools. "Usual" pretty girls and usual politicians were always white. Anything otherwise was unusual. "Bicentennial attire" placed participant bodies chronologically backwards, closer to the roots of "usual" order.

In additional photographs from 1976, white residents were dressed in "old-timey" clothing, women wore dresses and bonnets, and men donned fake beards.[18] This was the same attire displayed in the 1971 Fourth of July parade in Siler, when residents celebrated Chatham County's bicentennial. The full schedule for that bicentennial celebration included the "judging of beards and ladies' costumes" at 1:00 p.m. at Bray Park on Saturday July 3rd. The parade was scheduled later that day at 4:00 p.m. in Siler City.[19] Two weeks after the celebration, the *Chatham Record* printed photographs of the festivities with the title, "Beards, old cars, wagons and children star in the parade." A printed photo from that year showed one of the "beards," as they were called and judged accordingly, dressed as a Confederate soldier.[20] While several white men in the photographs from the 1976 parade coverage also wore fake beards, none of them were pictured in uniform. Civil War attire may or may not have been displayed in 1976. But the printed photo from 1971 suggests that Confederate clothing was an acceptable complement to bicentennial beards for at least some white residents.

During the period from 1972 to 1976, the Jaycees promoted the upcoming Fourth of July parade as if nothing had changed. They never mentioned or included photographs of integrated participation in the advertisements that they ran in the local paper, emphasizing instead continuity with earlier segregated parades. Organizers advertised the 1973 parade in the *Chatham Record* as "one of the oldest Independence Day festivals in North Carolina" and the "28th Annual Siler City July 4th celebration plans complete with old fashioned parade." The ad offered a "sneak preview" with photographs of horses and wagons, an old tractor, and a bluegrass band picking a tune on the back of a flatbed truck for couples square-dancing in front of them. Only white participants appeared in those photographs.[21] Reports of the parade that year included a photo of an unidentified high school band comprising both black and white students. In another photo, black observers stood together as a group among the otherwise white parade crowd. Those photographs contrasted other images of white participants in a variety of activities, including square dancing, a greasy pole climb, a tractor pull, men and kids on motorcycles and minibikes, and Billy Wilson with a raccoon. The paper quoted Jaycee president Don Tarkenton as saying, "It was a fine day, and really worthwhile."[22]

Nothing to do with Race

Residents plainly told me that racial desegregation had nothing to do with parade decline. Alan Resch, editor-publisher of the *Chatham News*, stated that the "desegregation of schools was not what killed the parade. The Jaycees didn't have the manpower to do it. Nobody wanted to do it."[23] Larry Cheek, a member of Corinth AME Zion Church, a town commissioner and a former Jaycee, attended the parades in the 1960s when he was a kid and helped organize parades as a Jaycee. Commenting on the parade decline of the 1970s, he said, "As far as anything racial, it had nothing to do with that."[24] The reason the parades declined, he said, was because the Jaycees declined. Other residents added that without the Jaycees, there was not enough money to keep up the parade. The Jaycees traditionally had paid for big commercial floats, but as funds dried up, they no longer could afford them. He said that local bands wanted to go to other places, such as cities where they would be compensated. Other residents echoed the assessment that people's lifestyles had changed, saying that in the late 1970s residents went away on vacations, rather than staying in Siler City for the parades. In addition, a few residents mentioned that other towns started having their own celebrations. Yet all of the changes they described happened, to my knowledge, after the racial integration of parade participation.

When I asked one of the Jaycees who helped organize the 1976 parade about why the tradition ended so suddenly in the 1970s, he told me what other residents told me: the parades stopped because the Jaycees stopped. A white businessman who still lives in Siler City, he explained that there had not been a Jaycee chapter in Siler City since the early 1980s. In 1976, he said, "There were 30,000 Jaycees in the state of North Carolina and now [in 2011] there were less than 1,000." When I asked why the Jaycees declined, he responded matter-of-factly, as if I had asked him to explain why water ran downhill, that "when the Jaycees took women in, that just killed it all." He said that membership went from eighty business leaders, all of them men, to twenty women, most of them secretaries. According to him, the same thing happened to the Rotary Club: bringing women into the Jaycees nationwide "destroyed" the organization. Back then, he said, the Jaycees did everything in the community. When the Jaycees died, community participation died, and that killed the parade. When I asked if racial desegregation had anything to do with parade decline, he remarked that the Jaycees had a few black members, and there was black participation in the parades. "So no," he answered, "it had nothing to do with the parade." Asked what happened in 1976, he replied that he did not remember anything about that year. And when I specifically asked why the bands canceled and why the Jordan-Matthews band was so disorganized, he offered only that school was out for the summer and they probably weren't excited about having to show up on one of their days off.[25]

Those responses confused me. If the parades died when the Jaycees died, and women killed the Jaycees, as this former member argued, then women, by that logic, also killed the parade. But the parades in question stopped well before women were admitted to the Jaycees in the mid-1980s.[26] That anachronism was telling. It suggested that this Jaycee explained the effects of the institutional changes of racial segregation in the 1970s by using a later memory of what he considered the impact of the inclusion of women in civic organizations. This might help explain, perhaps, why he said race was not a factor: he might have replaced that memory with another.

The argument that local bands were not interested in marching because they did not want to give up a day of vacation also did not fit with what I knew about the parade. Northwood High marched in the 1972 parade, and newspaper coverage documented at least one integrated high school band participating in the 1973 and 1975 parades. Concerns over vacation time did not adequately explain why area bands suddenly canceled in 1976, with Northwood High and Chatham Central canceling at the last minute that year. Based on earlier conversations with longtime residents, it also was my understanding that locals, even if they vacationed elsewhere around the Fourth of July holiday, made sure they were back in town for the parade. Longtime white resident Nelly Cole told me that you "needn't say anything to my kids [to get them to attend the celebration]." Her family, she said, took an annual vacation during the week of the celebration, but they never left town before the parade festivities, "unless we were going to get back home before the Fourth of July." She remembered how downtown was the site of "the biggest Fourth of July celebration around," adding with emphasis, "I mean *all-day-long* July Fourth." She described how the day started with a parade and all kinds of games—"a greasy pig and some kind of watermelon thing"—and culminated with a rodeo or ballgame. Her children, she remembered, loved the Fourth of July in Siler City.[27]

If families like the Coles made sure their kids were in town for the Fourth because they had to see the parade, then why would they suddenly want to leave town on a vacation instead, as suggested by the former Jaycee above? Adding to the incongruity, the paper's description of the Jordan-Matthews marching band's "half-hearted" appearance also seemed odd. Speaking with former Jordan-Matthews band members, I learned that 1976 was the first year that their marching band participated in the Fourth of July parade. The band director that year was Clifton Lloyd, a graduate of North Carolina Agricultural and Technical College, who had previously directed concert and marching bands at Chatham High School, the segregated black high school in Siler City. When I spoke with a former band member of Chatham High School who graduated in 1967, she told me her band marched in the Fourth of July and Christmas parades.[28] She remembered performing the "high-stepping style of A&T," adding that "when they cut street corners their high steps were like goose steps."

The Chatham High band marched in the Fourth of July parade until sometime before 1969, when the school was integrated into Jordan-Matthews High.[29] When Chatham High closed, Lloyd moved to Jordan-Matthews to direct the newly integrated band. A band member who played for Lloyd at both schools, first at Chatham High from fall 1967 to spring 1969 and then at Jordan-Matthews from fall 1969 to spring 1971, did not remember ever playing in the Fourth of July parade during those years, but did remember watching the parade every summer. When we corresponded by e-mail, which was his preference, along with remaining anonymous, he told me that they marched in the Siler City Christmas parade all four of those years. The integrated Jordan-Matthews band, though, did not perform in the high-stepping style, he said, in that parade. He wrote, "We didn't continue the high-stepping the same way that we did at Chatham High, but the drum section kept almost all the beats that Chatham had." He remembered the Jordan-Matthews band as fully integrated, saying that "in concert band, there was no segregation. We were seated based on our instrument. All drummers sat together, trumpets together, saxophones together, etc." He also remembered that they did not have official uniforms at Jordan-Matthews. He stated, "I do remember that either at Chatham or at JM, we had to wear White shirts and Black pants when we performed for a long time, and I think it was at JM because Chatham had uniforms."[30]

After learning more about the situation at Jordan-Matthews—a black band director led them in 1976, they more than likely did not have uniforms, and they kept the same beats performed earlier at Chatham High—I spoke with the Jaycee leader a second time. Asking if he remembered any other details about the 1976 parade, he confirmed, to my surprise, that Northwood High School and Chatham Central had canceled that year. He then added that ten to twelve members of the Jordan-Matthews band showed up, but the Jaycees told them to go home. That was the first time I heard that organizers prohibited Jordan-Matthews band members from marching in the parade. I then mentioned that, according to the news report, at least a few members did march, and I asked him if the band members they sent home were black or white. He said he did not remember, emphasizing that he had no idea, and reminding me that I was asking him about things that happened thirty-five years ago. He recommended that I speak with other Jaycees who also were involved around that time.[31]

Other civic leaders who remembered the 1970s parades offered different versions of a Jaycees declension narrative. A white resident who grew up in Siler City and held a prominent public position for forty years also attributed parade decline in the 1970s to the decline of the Jaycees. He said there used to be sixty members of the Junior Chamber of Commerce, and they organized the parades. That civic group invited the bands and planned the activities, which always included a greasy pole, greasy pig, and a baseball game, among other things. They also gave away a car. The Junior Chamber, he said, died out as people moved away. Membership declined, and it eventually disbanded. Commenting on the present state of civic clubs in 2011, he asserted, there was no Junior Chamber of Commerce in Siler City. He explained that all the civic clubs in town had faded, noting that membership decreased in the Rotary Club and the Lions Club from about sixty to twenty people in each. He further explained that the town lost manufacturing jobs, adding that a young boy might graduate from college but find that there is nothing here for him, unless he teaches school. After recounting the loss of civic participation, he reflected on the days when the parades were a vibrant part of town life. He remembered how the parades used to feature important people like congressmen or state politicians, and they always had a beauty queen—Miss America, Miss USA, or Miss North Carolina—and a dance. Without specifying dates, he added that there were no blacks in the Jaycees at that time. Later on, he said, there were one or two blacks in the Jaycees, but not many. And there were a few blacks in one or two of the bands. He said that some of the blacks did attend, but it was a white parade. Like the Scouts, he said, they had their own groups. When he mentioned the Scouts, I asked if a black Scout troop ever marched in the parade. He said he didn't recall Siler City ever having a black Scout troop. He also didn't recall blacks in the parade. They participated in games, he said, like catching the greasy pig and climbing the greasy pole. But, he repeated, it was primarily a white function. He then interjected, unexpectedly, mixing dates with events, that "things began to decline about 1961, when the Civil Rights Act was passed." He said blacks in Siler City had a strong American Legion. They had a strong affiliation with churches. I told him that I was trying to find out if integration of the public schools had an impact on the parade. He responded by saying that the integration of schools was done without any difficulty in Siler City. He then referenced the sit-ins in Greensboro by saying, "The first thing that happened was a group of A&T College students…" But he did not finish that sentence, stopping short of actually saying "sit-ins." With an implied contrast to Greensboro, he then stated that there always has been a good relationship between blacks and whites in Siler City. "There was no problem with integration," he said. During the conversation, he had told me that he graduated high school in the early 1940s. Knowing this, I asked if he remembered ever seeing blackface in the parades or Halloween celebrations. He said that he didn't recall blackface, stating, "Our relationship—we got along really well and still do." Then, without prompting, he began listing black leaders in town, adding, "We have had a black chief of police, excellent black leaders, black county commissioner, excellent black high school teachers, excellent principals that were black." He said it was a "matter of cooperation." There were blacks on the city council and the county commissioners board.[32]

In his unprompted response, that white resident constructed a narrative of civic cooperation that acknowledged a historical period of racial segregation but glossed over the harsher realities of that period. He cited evidence of black leadership after desegregation to bolster the claim that perpetual racial harmony was present even in the midst of segregation in the 1950s and 1960s. That was, to him, as it always had been. Since he attended local schools in the 1940s and was a prominent public figure in Siler, this resident, I am fairly confident, encountered public performances of blackface in streets or in shows. He was from the same generation that included the two white residents who told me about the performance of blackface in Siler City, when I had asked them about it. I would be surprised if he had completely different experiences than his peers. Yet, like the many other white residents I spoke with from that generation, except those two, he did not acknowledge those performances as part of the town's history.

Personal experiences of black students at Jordan-Matthews High School during the initial years of desegregation challenged white memories of racial harmony. The band member who told me about his time at Jordan-Matthews during the first two years after it was integrated remembered seeing the school mascot, "the Phantom," painted on the outside of the gym and recalled how it resembled, in his words, "a person in a sheet (aka KKK)."[33] Confirming that account, Reverend Barry Gray, pastor of First Missionary Baptist Church in Siler City, told journalist Paul Cuadros that "the African American people felt like [the Jordan-Matthews mascot, the Blue Phantoms,] represented the emblem of the Ku Klux Klan." According to Cuadros, Gray "remembered times during the football games when the mascot would come out onto the field in a sheet to the cheering crowds."[34] Another resident told me about a riot at Jordan-Matthews over the mascot, sometime in the second year after integration. She said that from what she heard from older residents, the riot began when they got ready to take sports photos for the yearbook. They tried to make the black football players sit on the floor, while the white football players stood behind them. As she put it, that is when the black students said they had had enough. The police were called, school was dismissed, and students were sent home on buses. By 1971, Jordan-Matthews High School had changed its mascot from the Phantoms to the Jets.

As part of our e-mail exchange, I also asked the former band member at Jordan-Matthews who graduated in 1971 if he remembered any other racial incidents during his time there. He wrote:

> The band, track team, and basketball team worked hard together, and seemed to get along well. That is until one morning, there was a message written on a poster board in a hallway saying, NIG_ _ _ _S go home. I lived in a suburban/rural area, and always arrived at school earlier than the buses that picked up persons from Lincoln Heights. When those buses arrived there was MUCH unrest. There was definitely a division THAT DAY. Two huge groups gathered, one black and one white. The guys on the basketball team that I thought were friends were shouting with the rest of them, Nig _ _ _, Nig _ _ _, Nig _ _ _ towards the group of Blacks.

This former resident's description suggests that racial cooperation was an illusory and temporary state between polarizing moments. Everyone, he said, "seemed to get along well." But once sparked by the racist actions of others, even those he considered friends were charged with animus.[35]

Ignoring those incidents, southern whites glossed their memories with a shiny veneer. Longtime residents remembered the fun times and the trivial facts of earlier parades, but always detached those good feelings from the physical and psychological pain inflicted by racial segregation. Another white resident who had grown up in Siler in the 1940s and 1950s told me that when he was younger he attended all the parades. He rode on floats, and he said it used to be an all-day affair. The parades, he said, were a big deal. You just went downtown, found a spot on the sidewalk, and watched the parade. Kids rode on the fire truck. After the parade, there was the greasy pole, the greasy pig contest, and watermelon fights. He also remembered that in the 1950s students at Siler City High School put a float together in which girls dressed in bathing suits and held signs saying they wanted a municipal pool. Laughing, he said the pool was built a year later.[36]

After we spoke, I found a photo in the *Chatham News* from the 1952 parade of a float with white girls in swimsuits that confirmed his account. Attached to the float was the sign, "We Want Pool." Two year later, Siler City opened a public pool. A photo of the municipal opening in 1954 showed white girls in swimsuits at the edge of the water. The caption read, "Opening day at Siler City's new $90,000 municipal swimming pool saw these five young beauties giving the pool their unanimous approval."[37]

In its coverage, the newspaper associated the public pool with the presence of "beauties." Yet, like the local resident who remembered the parade float that led to the pool opening, the reporter never acknowledged the racial status of those "beauties" or the racial segregation of pool space. The display of town "beauties" and the maintenance of the public pool continued the historical tradition of a religiously sanctioned racial order, one that entailed the presentation and protection of white femininity. But unlike in the early twentieth century, when Lillian White spoke of Colonel Lane, there was no need to say anything that might imply that was the case. By mid-century, just as they referred to that Methodist neighborhood as the Hill instead of Palestine, white residents no longer publicly professed their religious understanding of gendered protection. They did not need to say so explicitly, because it was, as described in the previous chapter, common sense.

Institutional desegregation disrupted that secular display of sacred order. The former Jordan-Matthews band member, who told me about the incidents in the first two years of desegregation, also remembered his experiences at the public pool. He said that the first time he and two black friends got into the pool, all the whites got out of the water. He wrote, "Me and two friends went to the Bray Park swimming pool. I remember everyone else getting out of the water and watching us swim, however nothing else happened." The next time he went to the pool with a friend, he remembered, "People stayed away from us but stayed in the pool."[38] As that resident's experiences suggest, some white residents developed spatial strategies to stay in the public pool following racial desegregation. Others, though, decided to go elsewhere.

Everyone Is Elsewhere

Rodney Kimery, a white resident, drove his "antique fire truck...decked out with American flags and bunting" in the Fourth of July parade for "many years." When the parade was canceled in 1977, the *Chatham News* ran a photo of Kimery driving his fire truck on the "deserted" street of Chatham Avenue. The reporter wondered if he was there out of a "force of habit or maybe mild protest." Below the image of him in the truck with a phone to his ear, the caption read, "Hello! Where Is Everyone?"[39]

In 1978, the second consecutive year without a parade, the *Chatham News* remembered the Fourth of July in Siler City as "one of the best and better known celebrations in the state," listing what used to be the "usual bands and parades, greased pig and pole contests, ball games, rodeos, and other activities associated with old-fashioned Fourth of July celebrations." The parade festivities, according to the article, had become "such a custom that several cars loaded with children were seen [in] downtown Siler City on Tuesday morning expecting to see a parade and to participate in the customary Fourth of July activities." In the absence of the usual festivities, the Siler City Moose Lodge "held a street dance," Jordan-Matthews High School hosted professional wrestling, and the Siler City American Legion baseball team defeated Burlington at Paul Braxton field, all on Monday night. But that Tuesday, the Fourth of July, was "very quiet." Residents were "doing their own things, such as puttering around the house and yard gardening, family picnics, swimming, fishing, tennis and golf."[40]

Without a celebration in 1978, a group of white children planned and performed their own Fourth of July parade in the Pine Forest neighborhood surrounding the Siler City Country Club. Lee Moody, one of the participants in that private celebration, told me that the parade was his older brother's idea. Lee, who was eight at the time, dressed as a clown. His brother was eleven and dressed as a Revolutionary soldier. The parade included homemade floats, which boys pulled with lawnmowers, a baton girl, a girl holding an American flag, and a boy on what Lee remembered as an "Evel Knievel" bike. He said the parade route began in his backyard and moved through the neighborhood streets. Other kids, he remembered, came from the Country Club pool to join them. Club members and golfers waved at the participants as they paraded past the clubhouse and near the course.[41]

In 1979, for a third straight year, there was no downtown parade in Siler City. In its absence, attendance increased at Fourth of July celebrations in surrounding rural towns. The paper reported, "Activities were held all around the area, with two of the best at Antioch and Snow Camp." Photographs of Fourth of July celebrations at Snow Camp and Carbonton, small towns within twenty miles of Siler City, showed only white children and adults participating in "watermelon eating, greasy pig, sack race, tug of war, horse shoes, (and) greasy pole." According to the paper, "most of the activities were attended by unusually large crowds, no doubt in part because of people staying close to home because of questions of gas availability."[42]

After another year without a Siler City parade in 1980, a "reorganized" Jaycees renewed the downtown Fourth of July celebration in 1981. Photographs of the event suggest black participation in the parade and showed old cars, horses and buggies, old tractors, go-carts, a watermelon-eating contest, and cars from the Chatham Street Rod Association, Inc. Roy Key, the *Chatham News* editor, wrote that the "Jaycees should be commended." He praised them for bringing back the celebration "which has been sorely missed in the past couple of years." He said it was a "good feeling" to see the "large crowds" in downtown. The Jaycees, he said, "did a good job in spite of the odds against them." Key noted that for "most of the Jaycees," organizing the parade and festivities was "new for them." He hoped that with a "year's experience under their belts" they could sponsor even "better celebrations" that would "once again attract thousands to Siler City for the annual parade."[43]

The reorganized Jaycees tried again in 1982. Photographs suggest continued black and white participation. Included in the images were the watermelon contest, a clown, fireworks, old cars, and a rodeo.[44] The parade organizers were unable, though, to continue their efforts for long. I could not find issues of the *Chatham News* from 1983 to 1987 in the paper's collection to verify exactly when that renewal attempt stopped. But based on conversations with residents, the Jaycees canceled the parade sometime during that period over an incident at Bray Park in which a tractor pull contestant knocked down a light pole on the baseball field. I was told the Jaycees could not overcome the cost and controversy of that accident. By 1988, at the latest, the Jaycees abandoned all attempts to keep the parade afloat. That year, the front page of the *Chatham News* ran a photo of a ten-year-old white girl carrying an American flag and walking along an empty Chatham Avenue. The caption read, "Where's the parade?"[45]

Between 1988 and 1996, other civic organizations offered Fourth of July celebrations, some with a small parade. But none were as successful as, nor garnered attention like, the earlier Jaycee-sponsored festivities.[46] The most recent approximation was a third renewal effort in 1997, which I discuss in the postscript. Despite renewal attempts by a younger generation, the downtown parade never was the same after 1976. Longtime white residents were still interested in celebrating the Fourth of July and observing the old-time parades. But after public participation was racially integrated, that interest was elsewhere, in surrounding rural towns and the private space of a resident's backyard.

The Emerson-Marsh Celebration

In 1977, Tommy Emerson and his brother-in-law Dalton Marsh hosted the first annual Emerson-Marsh Fourth of July celebration at the Emerson home. Tommy told me that they started the private party soon after their parents died. While his parents were living, he explained, his extended family always came to town. But once they passed, and the parade stopped, there was no reason for a reunion. Anna Emerson, his wife, remembered hosting the Fourth of July party at their house in 1977 because, she said, it was the year after her mother passed away.

Dalton told me that Tommy got the idea for the private celebration after reading Raleigh and Greensboro newspaper reports about politicians and legislators having a "pig pickin'." Dalton remembered Tommy saying, "If they can have one in Raleigh, we could have one in Siler City."[47] Tommy told me that he didn't remember that part of the story. He said that Dr. Dicroce, whose son married Anna's sister, was at Mrs. Marsh's funeral and that he was the one who suggested that they organize a pig pickin'.

Dalton learned to cook from a man who ran a barbecue place in Lexington, North Carolina, where he had lived until his father died in 1969. The first year of the party, Dalton borrowed a cooker from a man in Hillsboro. They started cooking whole hogs, he said, then later they cooked just shoulders.

When I asked Tommy why the downtown parades ended so abruptly, he told me that he really did not know the reason. He said, "They just stopped it," adding that the parades of the last few years were different than the earlier ones. Tradtionally, the parade organizers used to block off the whole town, all the downtown streets. But the parade started dwindling in the late 1960s and

1970s. The renewed parades of the early 1980s, he said, were "not old-time." Tommy fondly remembered the 1950s Fourth of July celebrations as some of the best moments of his childhood. As a kid, he rode his pony in the parade and anticipated the festivities with as much excitement as he did Christmas morning. He competed in the sack race and the watermelon-eating contest. He tried to catch the greasy pig on the ball field. He tried to climb the greasy pole, which always had a watch or bag of money at the top. He also joined in another type of watermelon game that differed from the watermelon-eating contest. In this other game, the local fire department put a watermelon in the middle of the street and used a fire hose to blast anyone who tried to retrieve it. Tommy remembered running into the street to get the watermelon and getting soaked with water.[48] He also remembered watching the semipro baseball games between the Siler City Millers and a visiting opponent. He remembered that the veterans marched in the parades, as did marching bands and beauty queens, which included on occasion the Fort Bragg military band and Miss North Carolina. He recalled how churches entered floats in the parade. He ate barbecue dinners in the Paul Braxton gym. Some years, he attended the evening rodeo. And the opening events, he said, always included a prayer given by a local pastor, a patriotic message from a featured speaker, and a time to honor any veterans who were present.

The Emerson-Marsh celebration collectively performed Tommy's memories of that old-time tradition in a private space, though it did so without an actual parade. In the absence of a parade, it substituted the pig pickin', with its prep, presentation, and consumption, as the central communal rite. It infused in that event the ritual order of the former downtown festivities, keeping the prayer from a local pastor, a patriotic message, and a time to honor veterans. It also replicated the old-time games and contests. Tommy mentioned in particular that he and the other party organizers retained the greasy pole contest, placing dollar bills in bags at the top of a greased pole on the Emerson lawn. In the private party, he said, "We are like we used to be."[49]

At the invitation of FBC members Barbara and Murray Andrew, I attended the 2006 Emerson-Marsh celebration with my spouse, Emily. That year, it was held at the Marsh home. We arrived around 12:30 p.m. and parked in a grassy field. Emily brought an apple crisp. As we approached the side of the house, a high-school-aged girl with braces greeted us and took the dish. Emily asked her how the celebration worked, since it was our first time. She smiled and told us to register at the tent with the line of people.

The woman just ahead of us in line wore blue flip-flops. I heard another woman near us say in conversation, "He goes to our church," and, "They still

go to our church." On a table was a photo album with pictures of the celebration from earlier years. Most of the photographs were from the 1980s with
kids in tube socks. We signed the guest list. A woman seated behind the table
handed us each a homemade fan with the schedule of events printed on one
side and a photo of the Emerson and Marsh families on the other. She told
us to guess how many gumballs there were in the container on the table. At
intermission, she said, they would hand out door prizes and reveal the number of gumballs. The person who guessed closest to the actual number would
get to keep the full container.

Everyone was gathered in the backyard. I estimated that there were about
four hundred people present, most of them older adults. They brought their
own lawn chairs and arranged them in rows around a stage with red, white,
and blue bunting. Two large tents, one for barbecue and the other for desserts,
bordered two sides of the crowd. It was a hot July day, so the prime seats were
under the large trees. Barbara had told me they liked to arrive early in order
to make sure they got a spot in the shade. We sat near them. Kids ran around
the edges of the crowd and several kids swam in the pool behind the house.
I noticed a black girl swimming with the white kids in the pool. I saw only one
black family that day; the rest of the attendees were white.

The celebration followed the schedule printed on the program. The hosts,
Dalton and Marie Marsh and Tommy and Anna Emerson, stood together
onstage to welcome their guests. Dalton used a microphone, saying that he
didn't have any other words, other than "Welcome." Stepping forward, Tommy
led rounds of honor for "the vets in the audience." He began with World War

FIGURE 4.1 Emerson-Marsh Fourth of July Celebration Program, 2006.

II veterans and moved through Korea, Vietnam, Grenada, Panama, the first Gulf War, Afghanistan, and Iraq. Each time he called out a war or conflict, he asked, "Would the men from..." or "the guys from..." or "the boys from..." please stand up. Some of the men wore baseball hats with insignia that designated their service. As they stood, the crowd applauded. After the recognition of veterans (all of them men), Bryce Marsh, a young boy, led the crowd in the Pledge of Allegiance. The entertainment, Dave and Ellen Holder, directed those gathered to join them in the National Anthem, though the program listed "God Bless America." As the crowd finished the last verse, a man yelled out from the back, "Play ball!"

The Reverend Jim Wall, pastor of First Baptist Church, followed, offering from the stage his "Patriotic Words and Blessing." He thanked Dalton and Tommy for inviting him to speak for thirty minutes, which drew a few laughs from the crowd. But he promised to keep his comments to five, pausing to say he meant the five points of his talk, not five minutes. After the opening round of jokes, Pastor Wall delivered a mini-sermon on the meaning of the Fourth of July. He spoke about "a short list of what to do on the Fourth," on a day, he said, "to celebrate freedom and liberty." First, pray for the country and her leaders. Second, visit the library and read about the history of the wars that American veterans have fought. Third, go vote. He said that he knew there was not any voting today, but asked what would happen if we did vote on July Fourth. "Just something to think about," he said. Fourth, read the Declaration of Independence, "still one of the most interesting documents ever written." And fifth, thank the servicemen for making a sacrifice for freedom.

Reverend Wall elaborated each point and closed by saying that he loved to eat homemade ice cream on the Fourth of July. He said, "Freedom, like homemade ice cream, is rich and sweet." He asked those gathered to bow their heads for prayer as he blessed the food. Invoking "our heavenly Father and his son," Reverend Wall claimed the "resurrection" of Jesus as a visible sign of victory over sin and death. He said that Jesus made a sacrifice on the cross for salvation and freedom from sin. In the prayer, he related the sacrifice Jesus made to the sacrifice soldiers make for freedom, a sacrifice celebrated in the Fourth of July and symbolized, for him, in homemade ice cream.

After the prayer, Emily and I followed Barbara and Murray to the barbecue tent. The tent was surrounded by heavy-duty smokers, which the men used to prepare the pork. We stood in the back of one of four lines. In each line, men served barbecue onto Styrofoam trays. As we waited, Emily and I talked about how we would accept the plates, since she is a vegetarian and does not eat barbecue. She stood ahead of me and decided that when they

FIGURE 4.2 BBQ Tent at Emerson-Marsh Fourth of July Celebration, 2006. Photo by Author.

handed her a plate, she would just hand it to me. That was our plan. But when she did that, the man serving her looked confused. He turned to me, as I was holding her plate, and said, "That's a lady's plate." He then handed me another plate with a larger serving. Now holding two plates, I gave the second, the larger of the two, to the woman behind me. Again, he looked confused. This time he said to me, "No. That's a man's plate. You have a lady's plate." I said thanks and moved on to the beans, chips, and coleslaw. I couldn't handle the larger portion, and the woman behind me did not complain.

At the end of the line, we filled our plastic cups with iced tea from the jug labeled with "Sugar," not the one labeled with "Sweet 'N Low." A woman noticed that Emily did not have any barbecue and commented, "Oh, you must want a hot dog." She helpfully pointed to another tent for kids. Emily said, "Thanks, but I don't eat meat." To that, the woman responded, "Oh, you must be on a diet."

In the barbecue tent, men prepared and served pork. In the dessert tent, women presented and organized the cakes and pies on several long tables. By the time we made our way to the dessert tent, the homemade ice cream was all gone. There were still plenty of cakes, pies, and cookies, although some were almost gone. Nobody, however, had touched the apple crisp, probably because they didn't know who had made it.

As we ate in our lawn chairs with the folks we knew, the Holders played keyboard and sang for the crowd. I recognized at least one Jimmy Buffet song.

FIGURE 4.3 Dessert Tent at Emerson-Marsh Fourth of July Celebration, 2006. Photo by Author.

Later, after we had finished eating, Tommy walked over to the sheriff, who happened to be sitting near us, and challenged him to a race to the top of the climbing wall. With his hat turned backwards, Tommy reached the top first. When he came back, he joked that his victory had nothing to do with politics.

Maintaining Gendered Order

In the separate space of a private lawn, the organizers of the Emerson-Marsh Fourth of July celebration performed a sacred order previously displayed in the "old-time" parades in downtown Siler City. They expressed their secular sacrality in explicitly gendered spatial divisions without directly referencing racial differences. The celebration continued a tradition of a city official recognizing the masculine sacrifice of southern soldiers and then a Protestant minister consecrating that sacrifice with a public prayer. In 1911, the Honorable E. J. Justice recognized veterans and the Reverend A. H. Perry prayed on their behalf. In 2006, County Commissioner Emerson and Baptist Minister Wall performed those duties.

The celebration also included the types of athletic games and entertainment that Tommy associated with old-time parades. That year, a climbing wall substituted for the greasy pole and the festivities included a hula-hoop contest and a mens' pantyhose contest.[50] By challenging the sheriff to climb the wall, Tommy performed a type of masculine fitness that characterized muscular Christians. And in the pantyhose contest, in which men were judged on the attractiveness of their legs, the celebration performed the type of inverted gender control evident in earlier parades.

But not everything was exactly as it had been. I did not see any white men dressed as mammies in blackface. Nor were there any minstrel shows. Those displays, even in the private celebration, were unacceptable. The celebration served as a ritual device to reconfigure the historical memory of southern whites. Just as they disremembered blackface after those performances were publicly declared racist, they purified the private celebration of the blatant racial elements displayed in the old-time parades. These changes evidenced the continued secularization of the secular display. The parade tradition had moved from public to private space. The parade had stopped, but the tradition continued. To maintain the universality of their particularity, to perpetuate racial difference without mentioning race, they kept some but not all of their "old-time" practices. They no longer enforced strict racial divisions, as evidenced by the presence of an African American family in the crowd and African American kids in the swimming pool. In this sense, the celebration was not a segregated event. And it seemed to me that all the kids in the pool were having fun. Citing that evidence, race was "not a factor," as residents had earlier ruled regarding the parade's decline.

Race, of course, still was ever present that day. The celebration obviously was an event organized for whites. The invitation list began with First Baptist Church, not Corinth AME Zion Church or First Missionary Baptist Church. The greeters, the hosts, the pastor, the entertainment, the soldiers—all of them were white. Those who oversaw the desserts were white. Even those who prepared the pork were white. That differed from earlier patterns, when, for example, Milton Foushee, "the good colored citizen who [knew] well his business," prepared barbecued pork and mutton in 1918. Yet, it would be misleading to say that the event organizers or the attendees that day were strictly concerned with regulating racial divisions. This was, after all, a civil crowd, and on other occasions they had celebrated the legacy of Tod Edwards and his presence in the white business district. A black family was, I am sure, welcome anytime. But that was different from offering a formal invitation to members of black congregations in town. As sociologist Korie Edwards has argued, white Protestants who celebrate racial inclusion often do so as long as they remain in charge and maintain leadership roles.[51] After the delayed impact of the Civil Rights Act, public spaces like the municipal pool were no longer theirs alone, and the downtown parade in the 1970s demonstrated that loss of control. But in the private party, it was their pool and their yard.

I would be surprised, though, if all the white residents that day were comfortable with the presence of African Americans. As I observed the event and talked to some of the residents over the course of the day, I overheard snatches of conversations around me that included phrases that were never offered directly to me. I distinctly remember two exchanges, which I wrote down with my notes after leaving at the end of the day. I heard a white woman say to another white woman, "I haven't seen you in a coon's age." And I heard a white woman ask another white woman, "Who's that colored boy?" The first exchange contained a racial slur, which likely was unrecognized as one. The second exchange was racially charged and suggested much. But despite those personal exchanges, I did not see a white organizer or attendee leave the party when the black family arrived. Nor did I see the white kids move to the other end of the pool when a black girl jumped off the diving board. This was not the 1970s.

Racial differentiation, then, was a second-order function of the celebration, limited to private conversations and reconciled in public encounters. The first-order function of the private celebration was to protect gendered order. As long as gender was emplaced, as it had been for a century, then racial boundaries could be reconfigured within white-controlled spaces. The ritual order of the celebration hinged on the gendered divisions of men and ladies; it was what made that performance "old-time." As the downtown Fourth of July parade in Siler City had done since 1901, this private celebration marked white men as masculine protectors of white ladies. Colonel Lane had, after all, fought to protect Christian homes, not to defend slavery. The soldiers present that day were descendants of his stock. Like him, they were Bible-believing Baptists with a patriotic spirit. And like him, many had gone to war to protect freedom.

At the private celebration, the gender-segregated tents were the spatial placeholders of parade order. The barbecue tent contained the ritual sacrifice carved with masculine muscle. The dessert tent contained the sweet reward tended by fairer hands. The sacrifice preceded the reward, as the line moved first through the barbecue tent before culminating in the dessert tent. In his sermon, Wall explained that unspoken secular differentiation in explicitly religious terms. He referenced both spiritual and political freedom, moving from the sacrifice of Christ for personal salvation to the sacrifice of soldiers for personal liberty. He then, intentionally or not, gendered political freedom by comparing it to homemade ice cream, which was located within the feminine space of the dessert tent. The pastor did not compare freedom to a pork shoulder. Freedom was not spice and vinegar; it was rich and sweet.[52]

When Emily handed me a "lady's plate" and I handed the woman behind me a "man's plate," we unwittingly broke barbecue protocol and violated a core principle of the patriotic celebration. We mixed up symbolic markers of masculine difference. At that moment, the line stalled. If I had asked for another man's plate and handed it to another woman in line, or if Emily had asked for another lady's plate and handed it to another man in line, would the barbecue procession have stopped like the downtown parade? How much confusion could the servers tolerate? I dared not find out because despite my own perceived differences, my vegetarian sympathies, and my support for equal portions, I was not all that different from everyone else in line. I just wanted to keep moving forward.

Conclusion

In the earlier movements from the Hill to the Club, white Methodists bypassed the public streets. They stopped processing where the rest of the town could see them, right around the time residents whom they considered lower class moved into their neighborhood, which was right around the time they moved their prestige show to the exclusive space of the country club. In the Emerson-Marsh celebration, white Baptists, few of whom ever lived in Palestine, demonstrated a similar secularizing pattern at a later historical moment. The downtown Fourth of July celebration stopped soon after the "de facto desegregation" of parade participation. That change disrupted the public display of a divinely sanctioned racial order predicated on the spatial differentiation and masculine protection of white feminine beauty. The issue was not race in itself, the point residents made when they balked at my inquiries. Rather, it was race *and* gender. In the first half of the twentieth century, white residents conflated those two identities. But after the Civil Rights Act, they could only remember one but not the other. Racial integration threatened their divinely sanctioned moral order not because blacks and whites came into contact with one another. They had encountered one another in close spaces for over two centuries. But whites always had controlled those spaces, and they always had been able to separate difference as they saw fit. To allow blacks to march with whites in the same bands or to ride the same floats was akin to putting the barbecue and the ice cream under the same tent. It disrupted a sacred ritual based on the spiritual purity of white women. For southern whites, racial difference was inseparable from gendered difference. This was, by their account, the disruption that precipitated parade decline. White women no longer were in a place where white men could protect them. After the civic death of the "old-time parades," a group of white Baptists retreated to the private space of their religious congregation and then carried their gendered order outside again, this time to the backyard and not the streets. When a younger generation of residents reorganized the Jaycees in the 1980s and tried to bring the parades back to downtown, those older white residents did not rejoin the group, because, much like the arrival of the lower classes on the Hill, its integrated participation signaled an end to spatial exclusivity. They no longer controlled the collective presentation of that sacred order. Privatization offered a means to retain the social power of public religion for a select public. After the local arrival of external forces of competing secularism in the 1970s, it was no longer feasible to maintain that order. Up to that point, paternalistic whites successfully resisted those social changes using strategies of civility, conceding as little as required to maintain control. They could not, however, indefinitely fend off institutional integration. By privatizing the Fourth of July, they avoided the type of public commerce that placed them at risk of federal regulation.

5

Migration

WHEN PARISHIONERS OF Saint Julia Catholic Church in Siler City first performed a Good Friday procession in 1996, they stopped at one point, according to Joyce Clark, a reporter for Raleigh's *News and Observer*, to "bandage a cut that Gerardo Zigala, who portrayed Jesus, received from the crown of thorns on his head." Prior to the stoppage, close to one hundred observers accompanied the processants through a neighborhood just west of downtown, along a city street, en route to the church lot. As neighborhood residents and passing drivers caught a glimpse of the Good Friday scene, with everyone gathered around a bleeding Jesus, they moved closer. "After the interruption," Clark reported, "the crowd grew steadily, swelled by dozens of curious onlookers who had stopped their cars and come out of their homes to watch a barefoot Zigala tread through the streets and fall repeatedly under the weight of the giant wooden cross."[1]

FIGURE 5.1 Good Friday Procession 1996. Credit: Joyce Clark, "Newcomers Re-create Christ's Passion in Siler City: Holy Drama the Latino Way," *News and Observer*, April 6, 1996, B1.

Seven years later, Reverend Sam McGregor, Jr., former pastor of Siler City Presbyterian Church, remembered the procession. In an Easter homily to a Protestant congregation in Lake Wylie, South Carolina, he said, "I am reminded of the Stations of the Cross in Siler City where the Hispanic man had to be hospitalized because he put the crown of thorns on his head to dramatize Jesus and he lost so much blood he passed out. Now that is a culture that understands Good Friday. I almost want to get in my car and drive there in order to experience the pain of Good Friday."[2]

New migrants—many, but not all of them, Roman Catholic—brought diverse sets of cultural and religious practices to a town historically dominated by southern Protestants. In the midst of that diversity, which prompted a second stage of local restructuring in the town, white observers focused on the public display of the Good Friday processions as symbolically representing a homogenous Hispanic identity. As Pastor McGregor's comments indicate, they associated Spanish-speaking Catholics with an imagined "culture of suffering" and viewed the pain visually displayed in the processions as a sign of proximity to the sacred. Sighting that religious performance, white observers used it to mark a secular difference between Latino migrants and other Americans. Catholics were present in Siler City before migrant arrival, but white Protestants, in particular, seldom recognized their bodies as religiously different from their own. From the 1960s through the 1980s, almost all of the parishioners at Saint Julia Church were white, and they never carried religious iconography through the city streets. Because of their skin color, and their less visible devotional practices, Catholics flew under the radar in Siler City during that period, as one white parishioner put it. But the arrival of Latinos put them on the local religious map.

Migrant Arrivals

The earliest Latino residents in Siler City arrived in the late 1970s and early 1980s. Most, though, came in the 1990s. Locals claim Roberto Vásquez, a Salvadoran migrant worker, as their first Latino resident. According to a story published in the *News and Observer,* a fellow farmhand kidnapped Roberto in the eastern part of the state in 1977 and forced him to drive west. When they stopped at a gas station and the kidnapper left the car with the keys still inside, Roberto sped off and continued to travel west. After asking several strangers for help, a convenience store clerk and at least one other intermediary directed him to Hank Wilson, a white resident in Siler City. Hank provided room and board, while Roberto learned English and sought employment.

Within a year, Roberto was living on his own and working at the Food Lion grocery store. Around 1980, Roberto encountered four Mexican men walking in downtown Siler City. Using his bilingual skills, he helped the men apply for jobs at the Townsend poultry plant. Roberto later helped two of his brothers and a Salvadoran friend get a job there.[3] According to a longtime member of First Baptist Church, Roberto married a "local girl" and they attended Loves Creek Baptist Church, where he helped organize a mission program for newly arriving Latino workers.

Roberto was among those Latinos that moved out of seasonal farm-labor circuits to year-round employment in the American South, albeit under dramatic circumstances. The majority of later arriving Latino migrants to Siler, however, were recruited directly from Mexico by industrial corporations, particularly those that operated poultry processing plants. It is widely known among Siler residents that corporations posted signs on the US-Mexico border inviting workers to "Come to Siler City." Journalist Barry Yeoman described how plant operators targeted new migrants disconnected from institutional support structures because they were "less likely to seek medical care or protest dangerous working conditions." A supervisor of a North Carolina meatpacking company admitted, "I don't want them after they've been here a year and know how to get around. I want them right off the bus."[4] Short of kidnapping, those corporations strategically kept migrant workers in a bewildered state, in an effort to prevent them from seeking out help or too quickly escaping their industrial machine.

In some cases, poultry plants directly called Mexican towns to request migrant labor. When Chatham County Commissioner Rick Givens went with a group from Siler on a "fact-finding mission" to a sending community in Mexico, he found a person operating a phone specifically for the purpose of receiving calls from poultry plants in the United States.[5] He recounts the experience:

> We visited a village. They had a telephone line and a person manned the phone twenty-four hours a day in this little village. That was their job. I said, "Have you heard of Siler City?" "Oh, yeah, many people call from Siler City." I said, "What do they say?" And then she said, "Well, if Townsend has a job opening for four people, they call us on Wednesday. We'll have them there by Monday morning." And the whole group worked together to get the people to where they need to go.

As with other new Latino destinations, US companies were the driving force of migrant arrival in Siler. City officials ultimately were responsible for inviting those companies to their town, believing that their presence would benefit the local economy. Yet, as Givens's comments indicate, they were not fully aware that companies like Townsend would recruit migrant workers directly from Mexico. Nor did they foresee that business leaders' attempts to revitalize the local economy through the recruitment and retention of major corporations ultimately would lead to the restructuring of Siler as a new migrant destination.

Poultry plants and other industries in Siler City let the cost burdens and moral obligations of migrant labor fall to the broader community; for example, they seldom provided their newly relocated employees housing and health care. Even when willing, the town of Siler City lacked the necessary resources and infrastructure to accommodate the massive influx of Spanish-speaking migrants in the mid-1990s. Adequate housing was scarce, proper health care was limited, and public schools were overwhelmed. Local and area agencies worked to provide housing. But price gouging was common, as demand far exceeded supply. The health-care system, which already was challenged before migrant arrival, did not have the institutional mechanisms in place that were needed to deal with the rapid changes. Added to that, many migrants stayed away from the hospital or doctor's office because they feared deportation, their employer did not provide health-care coverage, or they were unfamiliar with the local resources. As more Latino students enrolled in public schools, a number of middle-class white parents, including a former school official, withdrew their children and enrolled them in private schools. Hindered by inadequate resources and a lack of bilingual teachers, the public school system struggled to keep up with demographic changes.[6]

Local nonprofit organizations, churches, and activists provided advocacy and support for migrants, as they adjusted to life in Siler City. El Vínculo Hispano, or the Hispanic Liaison, founded in 1995, was at the forefront of social service and public advocacy for Latinos in Siler City. When I spoke with director Ilana Dubester in 2004, the Liaison sponsored two radio programs in Spanish, *La Charla* (The Chat) and *Grito Juvenil* (Teen Shout). For *Grito Juvenil*, Hispanic students would organize their own material for a thirty-minute music and talk show that addressed topics ranging from immigration laws to drug awareness.[7] The Hispanic Liaison also sponsored the annual Latino Festival. Those efforts helped connect diverse Latino groups and provided grassroots networks for public displays of solidarity, such as the local Pilgrimage for Peace and Justice, part of the National Day of Action in 2006, which culminated in a rally in front of Siler City Town Hall.[8]

In the 1990s, a typical poultry worker made around $250 a week in Siler City.[9] Unable to pay for a place of their own, Latino men, who were the first wave of workers to arrive in Siler, pooled their resources and shared rental properties. They initially moved into the historically African American neighborhood of Lincoln Heights in the northernmost section of the city, and then later into lower-income, predominately white neighborhoods near downtown. Tensions arose as Latino arrival disrupted segregated residential patterns. Some black residents expressed a sense of displacement. Paul Farrish, a black resident of Snipes Trailer Park, one of the areas of town where new migrants first took residence, told a reporter in 1997 that Mexicans "really ruined" Siler City and that he has "seen black folks trying to get a house, but they can't get one because the Mexicans have them." He also complained that they "play some of the weirdest music" and that he has "called the law a lot of times to make them turn it down."[10]

Living conditions in Snipes Trailer Park, as well as around the North Chatham Avenue corridor that runs through Lincoln Heights, were substandard compared to the rest of the town. When journalist Paul Cuadros visited that part of town in 2001, he found groups of Latino men living together in trailers and small run-down houses, some without heat or hot water. Drugs and prostitution were prevalent. Young white women addicted to crack cocaine solicited Latino men in the trailers and nearby homes, typically on Friday nights after the men had received their pay from the poultry plant. The number of syphilis cases in Chatham County increased from four in 1996 to fifty-four in 1999. In response to that outbreak, the health department developed an intervention program for those areas of town. They eventually closed Snipes Trailer Park due to exposed sewage.[11]

Many long-term residents cited North Chatham as a sign of cultural and economic decline in Siler City following migrant arrival. On separate occasions, three different white male residents drove me around town. All three were Methodists. Two of them had grown up in Siler and were old enough to remember the town as it was in the 1950s, while the third had moved to Siler with his wife and young children at the end of the 1990s. Each one took me past the ramshackle trailers of Snipes and pointed to that area as the blight of Siler City. One of the men identified a woman walking on the side of the road as a prostitute. Later on that same driving tour, he showed me a city park in another part of town. When I mentioned that I had recently attended the Latino festival in that park, he mockingly referred to the event as the "festival de la resistance," an offhand comment aimed at the outsider support for Latino residents in Siler City. Based on my observations at the festival, it affirmed more so than it denied the market commerce and consumptive habits that were familiar to longtime residents. The event demonstrated in a bilingual transcultural setting the economic impact of new migration as well as the rise of a Latino consumer class in Siler. When I was there, I saw children playing games, vendors serving ethnic foods, a mariachi band, and an array of business representatives, from car dealers to cell phone companies to money services. In its promotion of corporate products and services, I did not find it revolutionary. But for that resident, because it was organized by outsiders in support of Latinos as equal economic members of the community, it carried a spirit of "resistance."

Despite a general public perception that migrants drained the town of its resources and that they needed significant assistance from nonprofit and social service agencies, new Latino residents measurably benefited the local economy, particularly the real estate market.[12] Holly Kozelsky, a bilingual real estate agent, told Cuadros that a typical two-bedroom, one-bathroom house increased roughly 30 percent in price, from $39,0000 to $59,000, while interest rates rose from 6.7 to 8.5 percent from 1999 to 2001. Families dependent on the annual income of a single poultry worker, which was around $14,000, were priced out of that market.[13]

Latino residents who could afford homes were discouraged from buying in white neighborhoods. Adolfo Aguilar migrated from Mexico to Los Angeles in 1981 and later relocated to Siler City after visiting a friend there. He planned to stay only a few months, make some money, and move on. But he grew to like the quiet feel of the small town and decided to stay. When he was ready to buy a house, the real estate agent refused to show him homes in white sections of town.[14] He remembered:

> I'm trying to buy my house, my first house I'm trying to buy in this country. And I say, "I want to see a house on the other side of Siler City." They told me, "No, we have a house back in this area." They used to divide the community. They want to sell the Hispanic people on the west side of Siler City and the black on the east, and the rest was for the white people. And I mean that thing happens to me, because I can't believe it. I mean, how many houses was for sale in that time and he didn't show me but one house? But I was excited because he said, "You can be approved for this house with no problem." So I buy the house, but not the house I really want. It is the house that they want to sell to me.

In the early years of migration, few Latino residents could afford to move into white neighborhoods. But as Adolfo's experience indicates, those who could were constrained by organizational structures that worked to maintain the town's historical patterns of spatial segregation.

Despite those constraints, members of an upwardly mobile Latino working class did make their way into white middle-class neighborhoods. They were aided by the emergence of Spanish-speaking real estate agents in the area. Latino residents with combined incomes, which sometimes included multiple families, bought homes in the historically white neighborhoods closest to downtown, including homes near the Hill. Most Latino residents, though, lived in old mill houses on the west side of town, or in one of the numerous trailer parks constructed on the outskirts of town, where rows of prefab homes filled open fields. Latinos worked in wealthier white neighborhoods, particularly the area around the Siler City Country Club southwest of downtown, but they did not live there.[15] As I recounted in the Introduction, when I visited the country club in 2006 for lunch with a white Methodist resident, Latinos bussed tables and worked in the kitchen. But based on census records and personal observations, no Hispanics or Latinos lived in the surrounding neighborhood at that time.[16]

Contested Arrivals

In February 2000, after a decade of rapid change, a small group of white residents held an anti-immigration rally in downtown Siler City.[17] Their featured speaker, David Duke, former Klansman and Louisiana state legislator, verbally assaulted the town's new migrants from the steps of City Hall. Representing the National Organization for European-American Rights, Duke blamed Spanish-speaking minorities, particularly Mexicans, for destroying the moral and social foundations of white America.[18] The former KKK Grand Wizard later wrote that what was happening in Siler City was a "process...going on all over America."[19] More than one hundred people assembled in support of Duke, many carrying signs with epithets such as "To Hell with the Wretched Refuse," with a larger number of counterprotesters gathered across the street in front of First Baptist Church. At one point, someone from that crowd yelled back, referencing the tobacco road rivalry, "Duke who? Go Heels!"[20]

Responding to the anti-immigration rally, the Carolina Interfaith Task Force on Central America (CITCA) added Siler City to its annual Pilgrimage

FIGURE 5.2 David Duke in Downtown Siler City, February 19, 2000. Credit: Paul Cuadros Photographic Collection, 1993-2001. Credit: North Carolina Collection, University of North Carolina Library at Chapel Hill.

for Peace and Justice during Holy Week of that year. Drawing on the ritual resources of processional traditions, those North Carolina Catholics organized an ecumenical display of support for Latinos. Pilgrims began their journey in Greensboro on Palm Sunday and ended in Raleigh on Good Friday. Each day, they stopped in select towns to protest social and economic injustice. On Tuesday, April 18, the pilgrims joined other Catholics from St. Julia Church, along with representatives of Siler City's Protestant congregations, including historically black churches, and marched to the steps of city hall, where Duke had stood two months earlier. According to the event's organizer, "People felt like it was very important to reclaim that space and give it a positive image again."[21]

Six years later, on April 10, 2006, CITCA pilgrims returned to Siler City, met other demonstrators at a nearby parking lot, and marched into downtown for the Latino immigration rally, a public display of support for immigrant rights in more than one hundred U.S. cities.[22] Protestors carried white crosses with phrases written across the horizontal beams such as, "*No más MUERTES en la FRONTERA!*" (No more Deaths on the Border). Other crosses contained messages not directly related to migrant rights, such as "Bread Not Bombs" and "*Paz in Palestinia.*" An estimated three thousand people filled Chatham Avenue, their faces to City Hall, their backs to First Baptist Church. Demonstrators waved American flags and chanted "*Sí, se puede!*" They displayed signs in Spanish and English with statements like,

"Reward Hard Work," "*Trabajador: No Criminal*," "We Love America," "We Love Siler City," "We Pay Taxes," "Abuse by Police—No More," "*Ningún Ser Humano Es Ilegal*," "*Somos Inmigrantes, Somos America*," "Immigrants Contribute 9.2 Billion to NC Economy," "My Parents are not Criminals," "DMV: License for All," and "We're Not Alone, Our Lawyer is Jesus Christ."[23]

Standing in the middle of the crowded street, I saw activists address those gathered from atop the City Hall steps. One by one supporters took the podium, used the microphone plugged into the portable speakers, and protested the daily discrimination against Latino workers in Siler City. I recognized Ilana Dubester, director of the Hispanic Liason, the nonprofit that organized the local event, who spoke against the city's use of random driver's license checkpoints to intimidate new residents, shouting to officials, "Shame on you!" A representative from the AFL-CIO labor union used a translator to tell Latino workers in Spanish that now was their time to assert themselves. A black Protestant minister, who worked with an organization to improve African American and Latino relationships, spoke bilingually on the topic of Christian reconciliation. A white male speaker invoked the legacy of Martin Luther King, Jr., and the "power of love." And a white woman delivered a short speech that referenced Pete Seeger and Woody Guthrie and then sang "This Land Is Your Land."

Positioned behind the speakers' podium on a balcony directly underneath the large block letters of "CITY HALL," officials kept a watchful eye on the event, as can be seen in Figure 5.3. A white man in blue jeans and a khaki vest

FIGURE 5.3 Government Officials on City Hall Balcony, Immigration Rally in Downtown Siler City, April 10, 2006. Credit: Stephanie Gagnon.

peered through binoculars. A white officer in sunglasses leaned on the railing. To his left, a black officer gazed across the distance. Next to one of the tall columns, a white-haired man held a walkie-talkie to his face. He wore a gold wristwatch, and a roll of papers jutted halfway out of his pants pocket. Additional officers and personnel filled the balcony and more on the ground patrolled the boundary.[24] From their position, those officials clearly saw the visual displays of protesters below.

Among the flags and signs were several paintings with images of Our Lady of Guadalupe. The largest of the artworks, carried by two men, depicted the struggle of Mexican farmworkers in the United States. At its center, a split image of Our Lady of Guadalupe and the Statue of Liberty hovered within a border of barbed wire. Mexican and American flags distinguished one side from the other. On the Mexican side, a farmer stood in a field of tall corn. A shoulder bag hung at his waist, and he wore a wide-brimmed yellow hat. On the American side, two farmworkers hunched over to pick tobacco leaves. One was dressed in white, the other in yellow, and both wore white baseball caps. The Mexican flag blended into brown earth, contrasting the American flag, which faded into a blood stained landscape marked with white crosses, signifying migrant worker deaths on U.S. soil. Conveying a social message of immigrant struggle and sacrifice, the painting starkly divided the Mexican and American experience while connecting both to the same body through the steadfast gaze of Our Lady of Guadalupe/Lady Liberty.

FIGURE 5.4 Mural Displayed at Immigration Rally in Downtown Siler City, April 10, 2006. Credit: Stephanie Gagnon.

After two hours of speeches and songs, the rally ended without notice-able conflict. As the crowd dispersed, I headed to my car. While walking by, a young Latino to my right struck the bell that stood in the center of a small green gazebo in Collins Park, adjacent to City Hall. Those nearby turned their heads to the sound. A police officer eyed the scene but did not move. The young man walked on, with what looked like a wry smile on his face.

At that moment, I did not know the historical significance of the bell. Later, when I revisited the park, I noticed it sat atop a waist-high block monu-ment. Engraved on one side of the block in all capital letters was a description that read in part:

> Siler City, N.C. Incorporated March 7, 1887. Place first known as Matthews Crossroads. A rural post office named Energy opened here in 1880. The coming of the railroad in 1885 stimulated the develop-ment of a town first known as Siler Station. Population in 1890 was 254. Above is the school bell used by Siler City from 1887 to 1972.

That description designated the Siler City bell as a historical artifact of the southern town. The engraving on the monument connected the bell to the historical period from incorporation to racial integration. Ringing the bell, the Latino demonstrator touched the artifact and used it to announce his presence in that public space.

Like the ringing of the Siler City bell, the April tenth rally demonstrated how Siler City had become a contact zone for the spatial encounter between new migrants, who carried with them religious and cultural histories that spanned the Americas, and southern Protestants, who had for the last cen-tury controlled the construction and presentation of religious and cultural markers in that town.[25] Chatham Avenue between City Hall and First Baptist Church historically had been considered southern Protestant space. It was where residents performed their annual Fourth of July parade, where promi-nent white citizens strolled in blackface during holiday celebrations through the 1950s, where locals shopped, where Tod Edwards operated his jewelry store, and where the Farmers' Alliance has been open for business for more than a century. Joined by outsider activists, Latino residents stood together on that street and on the steps of City Hall and symbolically claimed their place in Siler City's local history within full view of the town establishment. The public performance of religion was entangled with secular claims to American nationalism.[26] Rally leaders evoked legacies of African American Protestantism, the civil rights movement, and protest traditions of the

1960s, referencing Martin Luther King, Jr., in speeches and invoking Woody Guthrie in their songs, while those in the crowd utilized popular Catholic traditions developed in the contexts of Mexico, Central America, and the American Southwest to display their transnational presence.[27] Not all of the visual displays in the crowd were distinctly Christian. Organizers encouraged protestors to wave American flags—secular displays of nationalism that outnumbered visible religious symbols. But the sight of religious displays was unavoidable, including the images of Our Lady of Guadalupe, handmade crosses with moral protests written in Spanish, and declarations of Jesus on the side of the oppressed, such as the sign that claimed him as their lawyer. Those religious displays connected Siler City to a Latino Catholic trajectory in American religious history that starkly contrasted with the town's southern Protestant past. Observers of Latino presence, more often than not, focused on the public performance of that religious contrast, more so than any visible signs of secular convergence.

Catholic Presence

In the New South, public Protestantism was the dominant mode of religious performance for secular differentiation. In an emergent "Nuevo South," popular Catholicism took on that role.[28] Latino Protestantism has played a significant role in the development of a Nuevo South, as parallel congregations emerged within existing white Baptist, Methodist, and Presbyterian churches. Latino Pentecostal churches also filled former storefront businesses on Chatham Avenue, and their members held revivals in old mill parking lots.[29] Those developments provided a different type of Latino presence in Siler than that marked with Catholic iconography and accompanying ritual performances. In contrast to the spatial disruption of Good Friday processions, for example, Latino Protestant congregations signified an ethnic reconfiguration of town space within long-standing Protestant spatial boundaries.

To illustrate this point, in the mid-1990s, a small group of Latino Protestants visited the only Presbyterian congregation in Siler City. They had been attending the Spanish-speaking mission at Loves Creek Baptist Church, the largest Latino Protestant gathering in the area at that time.[30] But they considered themselves Presbyterians, as they had defined themselves as such before migrating from Central America. Reverend McGregor told me that when he was pastor the Latino worshipers knocked on the church door and asked if they could use the building for services. McGregor consulted his English-speaking congregants and they agreed to offer their meeting site.

Tensions developed, though, as the small number of Latino Presbyterians grew from about fifteen to over one hundred. In a short amount of time, they outnumbered white congregants two to one, and long-standing members objected to what they considered a "takeover" of their facilities.[31] To help ease the tension, McGregor initiated a bilingual service, but this attempt proved ineffective. White members complained that the services were too long and worried they were losing their congregational identity. After deliberation, English-speaking congregants asked the Latino worshipers to no longer use their church facility. With denominational support, they helped construct a separate church building for Latino Presbyterians to meet as an independent congregation.[32]

Like the new members of the Presbyterian Church, Latino Protestants were dispersed to their own congregations. Their arrival altered the local religious landscape, but in a way that differed from the impact made by Latino Catholics. White residents often mentioned to me that Loves Creek Baptist Church and First United Methodist sponsored Hispanic missions. Because long-standing historically white congregations supported those outreach efforts, they perpetuated familiar paternalistic patterns. Latino Protestant presence, even when unwelcome, ultimately did not challenge a narrative of white control and supervision. As white members demonstrated at Siler City Presbyterian Church, when they felt threatened, they simply removed Latinos from their spaces and relegated them to their own sites.

Latino Catholicism, however, did challenge that narrative of white paternalism, though it did not completely displace it. During the early years of migrant arrival, white and Hispanic members met together for bilingual Mass. Services lasted two hours or longer. Frustrated by the liturgical changes, some long-standing white members requested a separate church for Hispanic Catholics, much like the laity at their neighboring Presbyterian church had done. But as David Kalbacker, a relocated white Catholic from the northeast who joined St. Julia in 1984 told me, the Bishop of the Diocese of Raleigh refused those requests, stating that, "We don't build separate churches for Hispanics."[33] With its institutional authority, the diocese held the racially and ethnically diverse laity of St. Julia Church together under the same roof.

In contrast to the denominational varieties of Latino Protestants in Siler City, Latino Catholics had only one church, the St. Julia parish. Because of that, it was the single most recognizable religious marker of Latino presence, ethnic difference, and cultural transformation in Siler City. The church and its new members drew attention from a range of residents and outsiders, including newspaper and television reporters, government agencies, white supremacists, and community advocates. The PBS documentary, *The Divide*, which I discuss in more detail in the postscript, included a clip of services in the old church as evidence of cultural change.[34] Siler City police set up driver's license checkpoints near the church, stopping migrants on their way to Mass.[35] During David Duke's visit, white supremacists targeted the newly constructed St. Julia church building, rearranging the letters on the church marquee to spell "White Power."[36] Researchers from the School of Public Health at the University of North Carolina held information sessions at St. Julia Church and enlisted *promotoros*, or bridge persons, for the congregation to help connect health services to Latino communities.[37] For different persons and groups— those wanting to document and observe, those wanting to enforce immigration law, those wanting to intimidate or harm, or those wanting to help—St. Julia Church was a key site for locating new Latino residents.

Prior to migrant arrival, Catholics and their church building were inconspicuous in the surrounding Protestant landscape. In the 1980s, St. Julia Church was a middle-class white congregation with a few African American members. They met in a small building that looked more like a house than a church in a white residential area about a mile west of Chatham Avenue. Most of those parishioners had relocated from outside the area, several from the northeast.

According to Hadley, a small group of Catholics held their first service in Siler in a downtown furniture store in 1951. That same year, the furniture store burned and, without a meeting place, Catholics attended services in nearby Asheboro, North Carolina. Two years later, a visiting priest officiated the first Mass in Siler in a private domestic space. Official church records note that "Fr. Paul Byron presided at the celebration of the first Catholic Mass in Siler City in 1953 at the home of Mrs. Charlie Ellis, a devoted Baptist woman." Kalbacker remembered that Mrs. Ellis's sister Katherine married Rudy Dudek, a Polish American Catholic who served in the US military. Katherine's conversion to Catholicism through marriage and her family ties brought the first Catholic Mass in Siler into her sister's Protestant home.

In 1960, Catholics in Siler discussed plans to construct a church building over a "covered dish dinner at the home of Mrs. T. A. Brown." After dinner, local industrialist John J. White offered to sponsor a fund drive for its construction. The congregation broke ground in April and opened its doors as a "mission of neighboring parishes" with eight families in November of 1961. By 1980, the mission included thirty-five families.[38]

As a mission, St. Julia Church did not have a full-time priest, administrator, or sacramental minister. Kalbacker, who was a member of the parish council, said that because they were such a small church, they had to do everything themselves, and that gave them a taste for "Protestant democracy." A committee of lay members made rulings on major issues within the congregation, which was atypical of larger Catholic churches. Proximity to hierarchical authority came periodically, when a priest or church official from the diocese visited Siler to consecrate the sacraments. The rest of the time, he said, they were "left to their own devices."[39]

During those years, Kalbacker noted that it was assumed in Siler that if you were Christian you were a Protestant. Reframing language of racial difference as religious difference, he explained, "We can pass, because we don't have a sign on us that says we're Catholic." When he first arrived in Siler, a white resident gave him a tour around town; when they drove by the Catholic Church, the man said to David, "You won't need that." When he later learned David was Catholic, his response was, "At least you go to church." In his experience living in Siler, Kalbacker felt as though "Catholics don't show up on the radar." To illustrate his point, he recalled how around 2001, when he moderated a quiz bowl for three area high schools, he asked the students, "What is the largest organized religion?" He said that the first student answered "Baptist," the second student answered, "Methodist," and the third student did not respond. After a brief silence, David then answered, "Roman Catholicism."

In 1989, when the church held its first Spanish Mass, the parish included forty-five families. With the arrival of Spanish-speaking Catholics, the diocese promptly assigned a church official to serve the mission. In 1990, "the diocese hired Sister Anita Gutierrez, a Mexican American bilingual woman as pastoral administrator with a friar-priest coming weekly from the parish in Burlington for Sunday Mass." In 1993, a friar-priest, Father Daniel Quakenbush, replaced Sister Anita as part-time administrator and continued as sacramental minister while still "serving as an associate pastor of Blessed Sacrament in Burlington." In 1997, Father Daniel left his duties in Burlington to serve full-time as pastoral administrator at St. Julia.[40]

The congregation quickly outgrew its building space and in 1996 initiated talks to either expand its 125-seat capacity or build a larger space. As it planned for expansion, it added multiple services, but still could not accommodate the growing number of newly arriving Spanish-speaking Catholics. According to church records, in 2000, the year before a new church building was completed, "the 8:00 a.m. Spanish Mass had over 150 people, the 12:00 [p.m.] Spanish Mass had over 300 people, while the Feast of Our Lady of Guadalupe, Palm Sunday, and First Communion Day would see almost 700 people in Mass. People would sit in the aisles and children would sit in the sanctuary." In 1999, the church was granted parish status, and on December 9, 2001, F. Joseph Gossman, the bishop of the diocese of Raleigh, "consecrated the parish church" at a new church building approximately six miles east of the city. By 2011, the church counted five hundred families in its parish, approximately 80 percent of them Spanish speaking.[41]

Ritual Innovation

Mexican American Catholics were the driving force of ritual innovation at St. Julia Church. Changes to church liturgy or tradition, though, required the tacit approval of the church committee, comprising mostly longtime white members who advised church leaders—Sister Anita initially and later Father Daniel (who I was told was more open to including popular Catholic practices in church life). Some changes, like the addition of *quinceañeras*, or celebrations of a girl's fifteenth birthday, required approval to use church space but were lay-led, though always supervised. Other changes required more negotiation. When new members wanted to introduce Las Posadas (a traditional Christmas procession) to the congregation, church leadership, under the advisement of a longtime white member, adapted the tradition by singing Christmas carols in Snipes Trailer Park, where members previously did volunteer work. In the early 1990s, when Mexican Catholics requested permission to celebrate the Day of the Dead, wanting to process with a coffin through city streets, white church members advised Father Daniel that the procession would not go over well in town and suggested he redirect their energy to having a float in the Christmas parade. As a result, the church entered its first holiday float, instead of processing with a coffin in city streets. The float included lots of kids, a Christmas tree, lights, and fake snow, and everyone sang "Feliz Navidad" as they moved through the downtown crowd.

Through their influence, the parish committee rejected the public performance of the traditional Mexican Day of the Dead procession, concerned that it would cause backlash against Latino Catholics and St. Julia Church in Siler City, and replaced it with a local tradition, a parade. They intended their redirection to offer a more effective way of integrating Hispanic Catholics into the public life of the church.[42] However, in contrast to the earlier dismissals and redirections, the church leadership and parish committee heartily approved a request by Mexican American Catholics to perform Good Friday processions, offering support and promoting the performance in the broader community.[43]

In the Good Friday processions, Latinos publicly performed Catholic presence. Prior to the arrival of Latino members, Catholicism in Siler City had been relegated to a more private sphere. As Kalbacker's comments about the quiz bowl and his own personal experiences as a newly arrived Catholic to the southern town attest, Catholicism was excluded from the recognizable sites of public religion. To be religious in Siler City was to be a Protestant of one brand or another. By the end of the twentieth century, as I noted in the previous chapter, public Protestantism had become increasingly privatized. The movements of the Emerson-Marsh private Fourth of July celebrations tracked from church to home, intentionally bypassing the streets. The Good Friday processions followed a different track to privatization, moving from the streets to the church. That was not necessarily intentional, but perhaps more a matter of civic logistics. The first public performance in 1996, according to St. Julia member Louis Rodriguez, crossed major interesections as it moved through the town. But, he said, because it disrupted traffic, the Siler City police required that they have an officer at each intersection to direct the cars. The congregation, however, did not have the money to pay the fees, he said, so in following years they processed through the neighborhood near the church.[44] According to Father Quakenbush, those later processions began in the private driveway of the Dudek family home on North Glenn Avenue and followed that street, "station by station," until they arrived "at the back of St. Julia's old church—presently Siler City Pediatrics, owned by Dr. Jim Schwankl." Yet, because of the public visibility of the first procession, because of the spectacle of Catholic blood in the streets, observers came to see the later processions. Father Daniel described those performances:

> We did not go on any of the main streets in Siler City. Although the word got out, as the yearly Via Crucis continued, and a number of non-Catholic people from the community came each year. It was great to see our Baptist brothers and sisters show up for these Good Friday services, which we made prayerful; it cultivated an ecumenical spirit, but also helped to promote a respect for the Hispanic immigrants among us, and their faith.[45]

Despite the semiprivate quality of those performances, the processions offered the broader public a chance to see Catholics outside the church. Unlike the Emerson-Marsh celebration, this was not an invitation-only event. And unlike the more exclusive streets of Pine Forest, the processions moved through an easily sighted neighborhood between downtown and Chatham Hospital.

As the word got out, procession observers came to see Latinos, not white Catholics like Kalbacker. Protestants had encountered white Catholics outside the church, around town. But they never carried a cross, wore a crown of thorns, or bled so much that they lost consciousness. [46] For Protestant Christians familiar with the story of Jesus, the visual displays of the Good Friday processions did not need translation, even if the priest offered bilingual descriptions at each station. Protestant observers readily recognized the bleeding Latino man carrying the cross. They may not have known him personally, but they knew the man he portrayed. Without that religious display, white Protestants, unless they were close friends or family, seldom suspected that white Catholics in Siler City were anything other than Protestant. In that context, white Catholics had reason to celebrate the processions. For Kalbacker and others, Protestants finally took notice of Catholicism in Siler City.

Processional participants described the performance as a way to maintain their faith traditions and as an expression of their spiritual sincerity, diligently preparing to respectfully display both. Jorge Ocampo, who performed as Jesus in the 1999 procession, prepared for his role by growing his "wavy black hair down to his shoulders," using Grecian Formula to take the gray out of his beard, and watching Franco Zeffirelli's movie *Jesus of Nazareth*. Ocampo worried about accurately portraying Jesus, telling reporter Carol Hall, "I came to Mass every Sunday, and I asked God to forgive me if I do it wrong." He also responded to objections to the performance by saying, "A lot of people tell you we're not supposed to do it because the Bible says only Jesus does it. But we're just trying to do something for him and show how he died on the cross for us." Marlene Rodriguez, who worked at the Hispanic Task Force in Sanford and attended North Carolina State University at the time, directed the performance. She told Hall, "Today, as we act it out, it becomes a spiritual experience. Before today, it's really nerve-wracking." Hall estimated that thirty people participated in the dramatic performance, with a crowd of about four hundred watching.

Prior to the arrival of Mexican American Catholics, St. Julia Church did not have any type of Holy Week performance. Much like neighboring Protestant congregations, members met for a covered dish meal, played piano, and sang songs on Easter. The processional tradition had not been a part of their church life. Father Daniel had never witnessed that type of performance.[47] He told Hall, "I'd been a priest for 10 years and I'd never seen it done before. The first gentleman who did it here was from Mexico, and he had done it at home. It has pulled our congregation together and allowed our (non-Hispanic) population to see what devout Christians our Hispanic members are."[48]

When I corresponded with Father Daniel, he said that he was "always very impressed by the sincerity of the participants." He wrote that:

> The first year the young Hispanic man, who played the role of Jesus, fasted for an entire day and went to confession before we began. He was a little overzealous, in that he put slits with a razor blade in his forehead before the performance. This caused considerable bleeding at the scourging post up at the Dudeks'. One little girl began to cry and I thought we would have to suspend the performance.
> Thanks to the presence of Dr. Jim Schwankl, as well as the crown of thorns [the performer] wore—we were able to stop the bleeding and continue. His long hair and vital appearance, along with the presence of real blood, made the production all the more realistic.

Reflecting on the sincerity and realism of the performance, Father Daniel described the man who played the role of Jesus that year as a "wonderful young Hispanic man, a husband and father of three young children, whose family remained back in Mexico (as he worked in North Carolina, blue-collar labor, which most, if not all, North Americans would not want to have)." He remembered him as a "fine guitarist and the head of the Spanish choir at Blessed Sacrament Church in Burlington" who also organized the processions every year until he returned home to Guadalajara. He said that, "it was [his] idea to bring this Mexican custom to our faith communities in central North Carolina. He knew that we had a higher concentration of young Hispanic men and women at St. Julia's, so we began the project of the Via Crucis there."[49]

Good Friday at the New Church

In 2002, St. Julia members moved the Good Friday processions from the neighborhood streets near downtown to their new church building outside of town. The design for the new church building was to be chosen by a parish committee comprising longtime white members and two Latino members, in consultation with Father Daniel. With generous but limited financial resources from church members, family of clergy, and the diocese, the parish committee considered several architectural designs, looking for something that would reflect the congregation's changing population while remaining cost effective.[50]

The committee chose the submission of Jim Spencer, an architect in Raleigh, whose vision for St. Julia Church was modeled on the Spanish Mission style of the southwest United States. Spencer, a white Episcopalian, previously worked on two projects for the Diocese of Raleigh. He told me that before developing the design for St. Julia Church, he learned about Catholic liturgy by working with Father Philip Leach on a renovation of the Newman Catholic Center at the University of North Carolina at Chapel Hill.[51] The building committee, he said, told him they wanted something that looked like a church, not a warehouse or office building.[52] The construction had to be affordable, they needed indoor seating for around 350 people, and they needed quality outdoor space. The committee emphasized that the design should reflect the congregation's Latino parishioners; Spencer remembered that this was a universal message delivered by everyone he encountered.

Spencer's design included an adobe chapel with a high bell tower above the pitched sanctuary contrasted by an attached low-lying office and activities building with a covered walkway that framed three sides of a courtyard.[53] To save money on construction materials, a concrete company in Raleigh poured the walls and then installed them on-site. The building cost an estimated $1.3 million and seated 450 people.[54] As described by Pastor Joseph Madden, the courtyard featured a "plaza where people sit in the sun," which he noted as one design component of a facility that was "welcoming to [the city's] Spanish [-speaking] population."[55]

When I asked Spencer about the inspiration for his design, he specifically cited sacred sites in New Mexico, such as El Sanctuario de Chimayó, noting

FIGURE 5.5 Good Friday Procession, St. Julia Catholic Church, Siler City, NC, 2006. Photo by Author.

its "spiritual quality and beauty"; Ranchos de Taos church, as portrayed in the O'Keeffe painting; and the church at Acoma Pueblo. I later asked if he considered the contested role that white Protestants played in their efforts to preserve the Mission style of the southwest United States in the early twentieth century.[56] He said that he was aware of that history and noted that the southwest Mission style was a European adaptation to the local context and was formed through that colonizing process. To illustrate this point, Spencer recounted that when he toured the pueblo in Acoma, the guide explained that the church was built with slave labor. One of the white tourists asked who the slaves had been. He said the Hispanic guide then responded, "We were the slaves." Acknowledging the colonial context in which the Mission style was developed, Spencer described his intent to take a recognizable American form associated with the Spanish Catholic history of the southwest United States and adapt it to the rural South.[57] For the attached building, he incorporated the low-pitched roof design used in chicken coops around the Siler City area. Using this utilitarian architectural form, he appropriated the Mission-style chapel and localized it within the surrounding southern landscape.

Along with the celebration for Our Lady of Guadalupe and other ritual traditions, Latino Catholics carried Good Friday processions to the new St. Julia church and used them to publicly sanctify the building space as their sacred place. When I attended the performance in 2004, cars rolled off Highway 64 onto the access road, moved along the right side of the circle drive next to the church, and parked in the adjacent soccer field. When the procession began shortly after noon, cars filled half the field. Latino families and groups of men arrived in new SUVs, trucks, and older compact cars. By the end of the performance, when they lowered Jesus from the cross and prepared him for burial, about an hour and a half later, cars overflowed the field onto the grassy space below the church.

As I walked up the hill to the church, I noticed that the processants had gathered at the far end of the annex building to prepare. Those who played the roles of the Roman soldiers, crying mothers, the Messiah, and the two thieves to be crucified had their heads down and their backs to the four walls of the room. They held hands in a circle for a pre-performance prayer. When I walked back down to the front of the church, I saw the crowd gathering beneath the front steps. Most of the men wore jeans, some with belts with large buckles. A few of the men wore baseball caps; others wore cowboy hats. One man wore a "New York" cap turned around backwards. An older woman wore all black and walked underneath a black parasol. A woman carried a pink Mary Kay umbrella. A man wore a T-shirt with "Jesus to the Rescue" printed in block letters on the back. Women pushed babies in strollers. The priest urged them, in Spanish, to move closer. They surrounded three wooden crosses laid bare on the asphalt drive. As I approached the gathering, a Latina parishioner handed me a pink piece of paper describing the Stations of the Cross in Spanish and English. Two Latino narrators used a microphone attached to a portable boom box to offer descriptions of each station, the man in Spanish, the woman in English.

After some time passed, Jesus emerged from the church, wearing white from shoulders to knee, a red cloth draped across his back. He was condemned at the top of the stairs in front of the church and then walked down the stairs to take his cross. The thieves followed him, their legs and arms more exposed. The soldiers surrounded them, red capes from their shoulders, red crest on their heads, spears in their hands, and sandals on their feet. Jesus and the thieves stood in a line behind the crosses, the older soldiers in red behind them. Younger soldiers dressed in similar uniforms but with yellow capes stood in another line facing them a few yards ahead.

The processional route followed fourteen stations, from sentencing to crucifixion to burial, clockwise along the circle drive from the front to the back of the church. Every movement was well documented. At one point, I counted twelve Latinos and Latinas filming the performance, including a child with a handheld video camera. I watched the WRAL Channel Five News cameraman film a Latina observer as she filmed the procession. They had parked their large broadcast truck on one side of the circle drive. Two white reporters took photographs. They wielded more professional equipment than my own, big bags and expensive cameras. That year, I only had a small digital camera. Toward the end of the procession, the priest walked away from the crowd, up the hill to the church. He looked back down at the performance and snapped a photo.

At the fourth station, Jesus met his mother, a woman dressed in black, wearing a wimple. She wept upon seeing him. When everyone moved to the next station, she and two other women walked closest to the cross.

As the procession turned the first curve, Simon, in striped cloth, took the cross from Jesus. While walking the processional route along the circle drive, I noticed two T-shirts covering the front seats of one of the cars in the center grassy space. "Guadalajara, Mexico" was printed on the driver's side shirt, and "Lead Mine Leopards Are #1, Class of 2001" (a reference to Lead Mine Elementary School in nearby Raleigh) was printed on the shirt on the passenger's seat. At the second curve, I noticed a man in an Adidas shirt on the edge of the circle standing beside a cart with images of pineapples, strawberries, and other fruit below the words "La Princesa," written in cursive. As the procession

FIGURE 5.6 Good Friday Procession, Station Four: Jesus Meets his Mother, St. Julia Catholic Church, Good Friday 2004. Photo by Author.

passed the cart and then the WRAL news truck, a group of women dressed in white, came into view. They were the daughters of Jerusalem, as listed in the Stations of the Cross description, and they stood at the end of the long wall on the left side of the church and wailed audibly as Jesus approached them.

The procession rounded the third curve and stopped behind the church in front of a nineteenth-century cemetery filled with leaning obelisk markers. Soldiers stripped Jesus of his outer clothing, nailed him to his cross, and used ropes to lift him and the two thieves upright. Jesus looked down at the crowd standing between him and the church, his back to an empty field with grain silos in the distance. During this time, most of the crowd came even closer and knelt in prayer. I noticed that some observers, though, lingered back at the third curve. A Latino family—a man, woman, and two boys—held the frozen fruit they had purchased from the "La Princesa" street vendor as they watched the crucifixion scene from a distance. Lay parishioners carried offering baskets through the crowd. The WRAL reporter stood just off to the side as the cameraman angled for a shot of the crucifix in the background. Young kids sat on a cattle fence bordering one side of the graveyard. Jesus and the two thieves remained on the crosses half an hour or more, then soldiers lowered them to the ground. The procession concluded with the body of Christ carried around a fourth curve to the front of the church, completing the full circle. As Jesus was removed from view, the gathering slowly broke into smaller groups, and observers headed in the direction of their cars.

In the 2004 Good Friday procession, Latino parishioners encircled St. Julia Church and sanctified it, ritually transforming a southern space into a Latino

FIGURE 5.7 Good Friday Procession Crowd, St. Julia Catholic Church, 2004. Photo by Author.

Catholic place.[58] The cemetery directly behind the church, which provided the backdrop for the crucifixion scene, was for the John Joseph "Chatham Jack" Alston, Jr., family. Its graves were marked with large stone monuments with "lengthy and unusual epitaphs," as described by the Chatham County Historical Association. The first burial was in 1841, and the last was in 1891.[59] Chatham Jack, also known as "40-mile Jack" for the amount of land he owned, was one of the largest slave owners in Chatham County.[60] The family's grave markers connected that plot of land to historical artifacts of the American South. The rest of the surrounding land, once part of Chatham Jack's plantation, was now open fields meted by farm fences, silos, and tree lines, with the exception of the Hart furniture store a few hundred yards east of the church on the access road. The new St. Julia church building stood out within these surroundings. Its intentional Mission-style design marked a self-projecting religious ethnicity onto the land and symbolized the presence of Latino Catholics in rural North Carolina.[61] Raising a Latino Christ outdoors in front of the grave markers of an antebellum past and against the grain silos of Carolina countryside, lay parishioners at St. Julia Church sanctified that land east of Siler as their own Nuevo South.[62]

In other years, Latinos performed the crucifixion scene in front of the church. When I attended the 2006 performance on a sunny and warm Good Friday, the final stations were observed within the Plaza of the Sun. The procession began in the same place as before, at the top of the stairs in front of the church, and followed the circle drive in the same clockwise manner, but then continued around the church to raise Jesus, the two thieves, and the three

FIGURE 5.8 View of Crucifixion Scene from Alston Cemetery, St. Julia Catholic Church, 2004. Photo by Author.

crosses in front of the church and in full view of the highway. As the thieves were raised up to be crucified, one of the cross beams broke. The performance stopped as a few men walked to their trucks, brought back tools, and repaired the broken cross. Once lifted in view, it was difficult for passing motorists to miss the three Latino men hanging from crosses against a nuevo horizon. That year, I heard several drivers honk their car horns as they drove past the church. Whether that gesture was offered in protest or support, I am not entirely sure, but certainly none of the observers that day offered any similar kind of interruption, so I assumed the drivers were indicating their opposition to what

FIGURE 5.9 Crucifixion Scene in the Plaza of the Sun, St. Julia Church, 2006. Photo by Author.

they saw. In either case, the honking confirmed that the processions could be seen from the highway.[63]

Southern Protestantism and Catholic Presence

Two related impulses within southern Protestantism contributed to the public perception of St. Julia Church and its Latino members. The first was a strict fundamentalist sentiment that Catholics were not "real" Christians and needed to be de-converted and return to the teachings of the "true New Testament church." The second was a more moderate view that Catholics were fellow Christians who differed theologically and liturgically from Protestants, but nevertheless shared a common belief in the saving power of Christ's blood. In my conversations with white Protestants in Siler, I encountered the second view more often than the first, though both endured.

In January 2006, I heard a student from Southeastern Theological Seminary deliver an angry sermon ("What Does a Real Christian Look Like?") at the 11 a.m. service at Loves Creek Baptist Church. The guest pastor, a younger white man dressed in a dark suit with contrasting tie and yellow shirt, excluded Catholics from the category of "real Christians." In his schema, real Christians included "Bible-believing conservatives" and "evangelicals," while "so-called Christians" ranged from "Roman Catholics" to "Jehovah's Witnesses."[64] Most of the Baptists I spoke with at Loves Creek and FBC Siler, though, did not share that view. They remembered a more moderate church, well before the fundamentalist takeover of Southern Baptist seminaries in the 1980s and the resulting changes to pastoral education that produced ministers like the guest speaker—ministers more willing to draw a hard line.[65]

Most of the Protestants I talked with and read about shared that second, more moderate position I described above. They believed that Catholics were indeed Christians, although they still considered Catholics to be religiously different, beyond just mere theological disagreement. When I sat with a table of men at a pizza dinner at Rocky River Baptist, prior to the performance of their drive-through Easter pageant, I asked them about the differences between Catholics and Baptists. The first to speak said that the two are not different at all, they just have different worship services. In the end, he said, the beliefs are the same. The next person, however, said, "They go through Mary." Then another added, "They pray to Mary." And another said, "They don't believe you can talk directly to God." The first person then interjected, qualifying those statements, saying that it "don't matter how you get there, as long as you do." After a long pause, one of the men told me that the fire alarm system at St. Julia goes off from the burning of too many candles. He knows this because a fellow Baptist is a fireman in Siler City. Another man then told me he had been to a Catholic funeral in Wilmington. He said, "I was going up, down. I couldn't understand what they were saying."[66]

The types of perceived differences expressed by these laymen also were evident in varied pastoral attempts at ecumenical dialogue with Catholics in Siler. At one meeting, conservative members of a Baptist ministerial organization expressed interest in learning more about Catholicism for the purpose of evangelizing new Latino residents. A more moderate Baptist minister responded to this request by offering to invite a Franciscan priest, a personal friend of his, to come from St. Julia to speak to the group. But the other members objected. One pastor complained that the priest "actually believes in it." Another remarked, "I have studied Catholicism, and Catholicism is a cult." As a result of these complaints, the organization opted to invite a representative from the Southern Baptist State Convention who was trained in Catholicism solely for the purpose of evangelizing Catholics.[67]

Other evidence suggests that in contrast to blatantly anti-Catholic views, Baptists in Siler expressed a more moderate impulse within southern Protestantism, which often romanticized Catholicism and Catholic ritual as more accurately approximating the "real" suffering of Christ in its bodily displays. Since the arrival of new migrants, white Protestants espousing this view were more likely to associate visual displays of suffering with Latinos in Siler. In 2003, for example, First Baptist Church borrowed costumes from St. Julia Church for its Christmas cantata. According to one FBC member, "We knew that our Catholic Church had the soldiers' uniforms." This member was referring to the uniforms of Roman soldiers used by Latino Catholics at St. Julia in their Good Friday processions. Having seen or heard that those costumes were "very realistic," First Baptist members approached their Catholic neighbors in a spirit of ecumenical cooperation.[68] They too wanted to look realistic in their church performance.

Other white observers associated St. Julia Church and the Good Friday processions with what they considered the more realistic culture of suffering among Mexican and other Spanish-speaking Catholics, whom they often conflated as one and the same, and whose experience they considered essentially different from their own. Elizabeth Hains, who traveled from the neighboring town of Pittsboro to see the Good Friday processions remarked, "It's not very Anglo-Saxon, is it? But it's wonderful. It's what this day is all about."[69] Sylvia Navarette, who traveled to Siler with a group from Blessed Sacrament Catholic Church in nearby Burlington, felt that the Good Friday procession "seems pretty realistic" and added, "I never could picture it until now. I'll never forget it." Pat Matterson, also from Burlington, expressed that observing the procession was "good for the children so that they can get to learn the story of Jesus," adding, "The Spanish people are very religious and spiritual people. It's more real to them this way."[70]

Crystalizing that distinction, Kalbacker reinterpreted his civic position after seeing the ritual performance, telling a reporter: "The interesting thing is that Americans, as a nation, are very optimistic people, and therefore we focus a lot on the Easter celebration. Many Third World countries realize that there's a lot of sacrifice and suffering. It gives us the opportunity to refocus our thinking."[71] Kalbacker also described the worship style of Hispanic Catholics as expressing a "demonstrative feeling." He said white Catholics would sing just a few verses, but Hispanic Catholics "sang with their hearts." Comparing changes in worship style at St. Julia since the arrival of Spanish-speaking Catholics to his experiences attending services at other area churches, he said that the feeling is the "same when I go to an African American church. There's life."[72] Through their encounter with Good Friday processions, white Catholics became conscious of a perceived difference between their own historical experiences and theological practices and those of their Latino neighbors.

In their interpretations, white observers associated Hispanic Catholics with an imagined "culture of suffering," the kind of culture that Reverend McGregor had referenced in his sermon, and viewed the physical pain displayed in the Good Friday processions as a physical sign of proximity to the sacred. Their association of bodily suffering with spiritual purity resonated with a generalized public perception that Hispanics were more familiar with everyday pain and hard labor and, therefore, were culturally different from other Americans. Observers often coded that perception in the axiom "They take jobs that Americans don't want." Or they expressed it as romanticized admiration of an unspoiled work ethic. A Greensboro police officer, for example, described his encounter with Hispanic construction workers by saying, "I was talking to a builder the other day, and he was saying you can't get them off the roof. They don't understand you have to stop for lunch. They don't want to stop."[73] Those observations assumed a cultural difference that formed the basis for romanticized projections of spiritual sincerity and uncompromising work ethic, but the same perceived cultural difference also could be used to make a condemning contrast. At a public forum, a Siler City police officer said that Hispanic gang activity was not a "racial thing" but a "cultural thing," adding that "just like Martin Luther King is part of our culture, so are gangs part of theirs."[74] Both of these seemingly oppositional commentaries operated on a shared premise that Hispanic workers were cultural primitives. In the first, Hispanic workers had not yet been spoiled by the knowledge of labor laws and mandatory lunch breaks, like other Americans. In the second, Hispanics were uncivilized and they were not entitled to the same promises and protections of the law given to responsible citizens. In both interpretations, the diligence of new migrants, for roofing or for crime, could be harnessed for productive purposes with proper supervision. White observer responses to the processions located the religious marker for that secular distinction in the perceived difference between suffering migrants and transcendent Americans, between Good Friday observers and Easter celebrants.

Conclusion

By the end of the twentieth century, Latino migrants had transformed Siler City. Latinos have been present in that subregion of the American South, from Mississippi to Georgia through the Carolinas, since the early twentieth century, as itinerant farmworkers.[75] At the end of the twentieth century, though, those seasonal work patterns increasingly gave way to year-round residency, as corporations directly recruited laborers from Mexico while other Latinos, connected through networks of technology and travel, settled in manufacturing towns like Siler City and major cities like Raleigh-Durham along or near the I-85 corridor that runs from Atlanta to Washington DC.[76]

Amidst the rapid demographic and spatial changes in Siler City, Mexican American parishioners of St. Julia Catholic Church brought Good Friday processions to the city streets. In their processional performances, they adapted ritual traditions that they had previously practiced in Mexico (and which other members had practiced in Central America) to their new destination. While those on the St. Julia parish committee rejected or redirected other requests from Mexican American members, such as a request to process a coffin on the Day of the Dead, they strongly supported efforts to organize a Good Friday procession. For white parishioners and clergy, those performances displayed an acceptable form of public Catholic presence in the context of a historically Protestant town; one that they believed would bring positive attention to St. Julia Church and its Latino members. Overall, white observers, Catholics and Protestants alike, interpreted the Good Friday processions as evidence that

Latino Catholics were inherently different than non-Latino Christians; that they were, as one observer put it, part of a "culture that understands suffering." With those kinds of statements, white observers located a religious performance as a locative placeholder for secular distinctions between migrants and other Americans.

Postscript: Silence

SOUTHERN SECULARISM WAS not David Duke on the steps of City Hall. At the end of the twentieth century, it was subtle and silent, not blatant and loudmouthed.

Duke was readily recognizable, a collective symbol of white supremacy. He was not vague or misunderstood. He was easy to catch. While he used secular means to chase his goals—he was, after all, a legislator—he pursued a bullhorn theocracy. He did not separate, by any degree, his Christianity from his political and cultural society.[1] His politics did not leave room for anyone other than white Protestants of his persuasion. Unlike southern progressives, he offered no promises of paternalistic protection for racial, ethnic, or religious minorities.

When Duke visited Siler City in February 2000, town officials dismissed him as a spokesman of hate.[2] They distanced themselves from him and his shadow, much like their civilized forebears distanced themselves from the lynch mob and their spectacle. But as Ilana Dubester, director of the Hispanic Liaison, noted, most Latinos assumed that local leaders had sponsored the anti-immigration rally, because it took place on the steps of Town Hall. Mayor Charles Turner issued a disclaimer stating that the town government neither invited nor supported Duke's presence or his positions, but it did little to assuage fears of INS raids and deportation. Nor did it help matters that, earlier in 1996, the Hispanic Task Force, organized by white resident and City Commissioner Pem Hobbs, partnered with the town council to publish a brochure in Spanish suggesting to newcomers that they "not keep goats in the yard, beat your wife, or watch T.V. after 10 p.m." John Herrera, president of El Pueblo Incorporated in Chapel Hill, said the pamphlet was racist.[3] Father Quakenbush, who ministered to Latino Catholics in Siler City, said the pamphlets were "misguided," explaining that "there's a fear that is often expressed by politicians that these people are somehow a threat to our way of life [but] that's not based on fact. They're working, paying taxes; even if they're working under a false name, they're paying taxes."[4] Against those reactions, city officials defended the good will of the citizens who published the pamphlets. Joel Brewer, Siler City's town manager, said the pamphlets were "poorly worded, but the task force had only good intentions."[5] Regardless of their intent, it was clear that the strategies of southern civility that progressive whites had used for a century were now lost in translation.

Four years after those pamphlets were published, Duke's presence in Siler City further strained local tensions, and outside observers took notice. In a short span of time, social activists, journalists, and academics descended upon the southern town. Some had visited before, such as journalist Paul Cuadros, who had come to town to cover the first wave of migrant arrival and ended up staying, coaching soccer at Jordan-Matthews High School, and later writing a book about his experiences.[6] But most, including me, came later.[7] The investigative pace escalated after 2003, when PBS aired a piece on Siler City titled *The Divide*, part of the series called *Matters of Race*, directed by John Valadez.[8] The film provocatively portrayed a high level of racial tension in the town.[9] It featured an interview with Will Williams, a member of the National Alliance, who took dead aim at new migrants in Siler City, and it flashed an image of a group of high school boys holding a noose while posing for a yearbook photo.

Despite its attention to important matters—to events that *did* happen—*The Divide* did not sit well with residents. Locals argued that it skewed the facts. For one thing, Williams lived in Raleigh, not Siler City, and the film never clarified that point. *The Divide* also implied that the students holding the noose attended Jordan-Matthews, but those students were actually enrolled at Chatham Central High School, outside of Siler City. When a racially and ethnically diverse group of faculty and students at Jordan-Matthews gathered in the auditorium to revisit *The Divide*, they disagreed over the dynamics of their school, but they expressed a shared concern that the film "didn't show Siler City."[10]

The Divide ultimately misrepresented the southern town. The majority of white residents in Siler City performed a more refined etiquette of race relations than did David Duke or the other white supremacists portrayed in the film.[11] They did, however, need some time after the earliest migrant arrivals to recalibrate their methods. The Spanish-language brochure about goats, wives, and television suggested that town leaders' initial reactions were just a step removed from Duke's stride, but once the public called their actions racist, as John Herrera did, they quickly refined their approach. They wanted to show, as Brewer described, that they only had good intentions, so they set out to revitalize their civic image, dampening the ritual mechanics of southern secularism to offer more muted responses to the Latino presence.

A New Day

In 1997, the year following the first public performance of the Good Friday procession, an aging contingent of white leaders renewed the Fourth of July parade on Chatham Avenue.[12] Promoting it as the "Rag Top Parade," organizers invited residents and out-of-towners to enter old-timey and classic cars. The event drew sixty-two vehicles, ranging from a 1922 Ford Model T to a 1975 Granville Pontiac. There were no floats or bands, just cars. Walter Allen of Ramseur entered his 1966 Buick Special, Harley Hinshaw of Randleman drove his 1939 Ford coupe race car, and Thurman Walters of Siler City drove his "immaculate '57 Chevy, just 'cause everyone else did.'" He told reporter Milburn Gibbs that it "sorta brought back memories." Tim, Dee Dee, and Kara Brown rode together in a 1968 Fairlane. Ralph Yarborough of Sanford said he was born the same year as his 1931 Oldsmobile. Polly McLaurin yelled from the rumble seat of a 1934 Ford Roadster, "We were married sixty years [ago] Monday. This car is three years older than our marriage. We used to court in one of these." Margaret and John Rodgers of Siler City drove a 1934 Chevrolet and a 1938 Chevrolet pickup. Margaret told Gibbs, "We'd like to see Siler City get a parade going again. We just like old cars and parades."[13]

Old cars, though, were not a longstanding part of the "old time" Fourth of July tradition. Their association with the parade was a shared memory that white residents constructed after the racial integration of parade participation in the 1970s. A black resident, who participated in the parades in the 1960s as a member of the Chatham High School marching band, told me, "They [parade sponsors and participants] weren't into restoring cars then."[14] Confirming her account with newspaper reports, I did not find evidence of old cars in the downtown parade before 1975. Of course, a '68 Fairlane was not that old by then. But a '57 Chevy was getting there. And the earlier models from the 1930s that appeared in the Rag Top Parade were old enough. The inclusion of cars made before 1970 (most of them from the 1950s and earlier) in the parades after the racial integration of 1972 offered nostalgic white residents a symbolic vehicle for remembering the town before that integrationist moment.

The organizers of the Rag Top parade renewed a post-integrationist ritual innovation of the Fourth of July parade tradition to respond to the ritual display of Good Friday processions, which white residents had observed, as I described in Chapter Five, as a religious performance of Latino presence in Siler City.[15] Though any historical reference point prior to the 1990s would have displaced that Latino presence, they did not claim to recreate the period of the 1970s and 1980s, when they first included old cars in the parades and when parade participation was racially integrated. Rather, they referenced, with their pristine time machines, the grand parades of the Establishment period of the 1930s through the 1960s. Those were the days that white residents remembered the town was "alive"—when "they didn't roll up the sidewalks at dark" and "the Fourth was an all-day affair." For Gibbs, the Rag Top parade "was the first Fourth in a long time when townsfolk could witness—and participate in—their very own parade." He said it harkened to "the days when Siler City regularly produced state-class Fourth of July parades."[16] Former Siler City Mayor Earl Fitts, a deacon at First Baptist Church who drove his own entry in the inaugural Rag Top parade, declared it "the start of a new day." Given that the last time the city produced state-class parades was in the 1950s and 1960s, and that the parade fizzled in the 1970s, the start of that new day began, historically speaking, in the pre-integrationist era.

Though the Rag Top Parade was not officially segregated, photographs printed in the *Chatham News* showed only white participants and observers. Added to that, the captions and arrangement of the images used in that coverage connected the public performance on Chatham Avenue to a semi-private performance at the Siler City Country Club. The arrangement of photographs in the newspaper coverage created a visual bridge that moved from the Rag Top Parade downtown to white children in "their own parade" at the country club. The caption read, "From the big kids' version ... to the little kids' version."[17] The caption implied that the little kids imitated the big kids; the big kids drove old cars, while the little kids rode on bikes and in Radio Flyer wagons. The visual movement of those images, though, also inversely connected the racialized setting of the little kids' version at the club, where whites exercised complete control, to the multiethnic space of Chatham Avenue, where the big kids struggled to retain their cultural dominance. Those photographs connected, without intent or malice, downtown Siler City to the de facto segregated space of the Club that traced its genealogical roots, as I noted in the Introduction, to the early-twentieth-century religious performances of those southern white Methodists on that legally segregated Hill.

Commissioner Hobbs, the key organizer of the Rag Top Parade, had previously worked in other contexts to maintain control of public space in the midst of migrant arrival. The parade was his and Commissioner Robert White's "brainchild."[18] Residents, though, credited Hobbs as the major force behind the renewal. A former Marine and World War II veteran, Hobbs was born in Wilmington and raised in Raleigh. He graduated from North Carolina State in 1952 with a degree in agricultural engineering. In the late

1960s, he moved to Siler City and sold real estate in the area. In the 1980s and 1990s, he served as a member of the Siler City Town Board, the Siler City Rotary Club, and the Chatham County Board of Commissioners. He ran twice, unsuccessfully, for Siler City Mayor. Locals knew Hobbs as "a natural salesman who drove a little red sports car" and they remembered him as someone who dealt directly with the challenges posed by the Hispanic arrival in the 1990s. Bill Lail, director of the Family Resource Center, "a nonprofit agency that provides counseling, child care and other services to immigrants," said, "Pem didn't put his head in the sand. He was the one who saw what was happening, who was saying we needed to recognize certain realities and have the courage to deal with them." Partnering with the Siler City Town Council, Hobbs organized the Hispanic Task Force, which published the controversial brochure for new Hispanic residents in 1996. Publicly engaged and an avid volunteer, he worked for what he considered to be civic improvement. Among his list of activities, Hobbs organized the Optimist Club for Youth, mentored with Chatham Together, and volunteered with the American Heart Association. Mayor Charles Turner, who defeated Hobbs in his two mayoral campaigns, said, "Pem was just the kind of guy who liked to see good things happening in the community and was willing to make them happen."[19]

In 1998, commissioners Hobbs and White enlisted the Chatham Optimist Club to sponsor a second Rag Top Parade. That effort drew seventy-one entries.[20] Hobbs stated that "they hoped to solidify it into a real July Fourth celebration next year." The 1999 parade also included US soldiers—"the Veterans of Foreign Wars Color Guard led the parade, followed by Siler City Police Chief Lewis Phillips"—and the requisite "Siler City and Silk Hope fire trucks." Photographs from both years show only white participants and observers.[21]

In the 2000 parade, organizers added additional elements of "a real July Fourth celebration" to the Rag Top theme. The parade expanded from just "Rag Tops" to "include vintage trucks and tractors, local fire trucks, bicycle clubs, go-carts, and motorcycles," for a total of seventy-six entries. The VFW led the parade and Hobbs and White served as grand marshals. Congressman Howard Coble and North Carolina House Representative Arlie Culp rode as special guests. Mayor Turner also participated, and so did "Karo" the clown. Vernon Chrisco walked the route on three-foot-high stilts. With these additions, Hobbs and other residents tried to recreate the feeling of the "old-time" parades. Ultimately, though, they could not recover what they had lost. After the parade that year, the Siler City Fire Department sold hot dogs, gesturing to the days when parade enthusiasm spilled over to barbecue dinners and athletic contests. But the games scheduled at Paul Braxon Field were canceled at the last minute, and in an unintentionally symbolic event that foreshadowed the imminent passing of the parade, the Lions Club and VFW held "a ceremony honoring our old American flags," advertising ahead of time that "flags that are worn and need to be properly discarded will be burned in a special ceremony."[22]

The 2001 parade was the last year of the renewal efforts by Hobbs, White, and the Chatham County Optimist Club. That final Rag Top Parade included old cars and tractors, motorcycles and Mayor Turner, cowboys and a rodeo.[23] As with previous years, photographs show only white participants and observers. In 2002, the Chatham County Optimist Club canceled the Fourth of July parade, explaining that "it was a lot of hard work," "it was expensive," and "there hasn't been enough interest from Siler City residents in the past that would warrant having another parade this year."[24] Running from 1997 to 2001, the Rag Top parade renewal lasted as long as the Good Friday processions were performed within sight of downtown. In 2002, members of St. Julia Catholic Church moved the processions to the new church building located six miles east of Siler City.

Unlike David Duke, organizers of the renewed parade never publicly verbalized a desire to rid the town of Latino migrants, to my knowledge. No one I read about or talked with acknowledged that the parade renewal was a strategic attempt to recover downtown in the midst of demographic shifts. Nor did they say they used the Fourth of July parade to ritually respond to the Good Friday processions. But the timing of events was suggestive. Even if it were coincidence, the renewal effort demonstrated the ritual contestations of civic space and the importance of Chatham Avenue and the downtown business district for white residents during a period of rapid change. But assuming it was not an adventitious sequence, then white residents drew on their most enduring ritual tradition, the secular parade, to respond to the public performance of a religious procession.

Memorializing Chatham Avenue

Those who promoted the parade were also involved in another effort to project their memories of the town—the place that they remembered before the desegregation of public space and the arrival of Latinos—onto the city streets. In the late 1990s, Pem Hobbs founded the Siler City Mural Society to raise money for "historically themed murals" in the downtown business district. In its first few years, the society had at least eight board members, including commissioners Hobbs and White, local historian Wade Hadley, retired attorney Jack Moody, Ace Hardware owner Dennis Sawyer, and loan officer Sam Adams. In its later years, several of its key members passed away: Hadley in 2002, Hobbs in 2006, and White in 2011. When I spoke with a former member in 2011, he declared the organization "dead." Before its dissolution, the society commissioned and completed three murals. It worked with the Rotary Club to raise funds for a mural on South Birch Avenue, the main street for the black business district before desegregation, located one block west of Chatham Avenue. That mural depicted the Chatham Hospital buildings in Siler City. Sawyer sponsored a mural on the side of Ace Hardware, half a block east of Chatham Avenue, with three scenes of the store through the years. Ruth Smith, who owned stock in the Farmers' Alliance Store in Siler City, donated $20,000 for a mural on the side of the Alliance building, at the south end of the business district on Chatham Avenue. The Alliance mural, the last of the three, was dedicated in August 2006, four month after the downtown immigration rally and seven months after Hobbs passed away. To memorialize his life and his contributions to the society, a portrait of Hobbs was included in the bottom right-hand corner of the mural.

Adams remembered Hobbs as the "dynamo" behind the murals. Hobbs had gotten the idea for the society after visiting Lake Placid, Florida, with Sawyer. The Lake Placid mural society, which two of its residents organized, worked to "beautify the town, preserve its heritage, and educate its citizens," while attracting tourists to the downtown area.[25] The Siler City Mural Society replicated that model, working, as Adams explained, "to keep the murals historical" in order to preserve local history and revitalize the downtown business district.[26] Like the Lake Placid Mural Society, the Siler organization was entirely funded through private donations. Sawyer told me that the society did not want any government money. Without external constraints from federal or state funding, the society exercised complete control over the subject, location, and presentation of the murals.

As Latino migrants transformed downtown, the Siler City Mural Society used the visual displays of the murals to memorialize their own self-selective history. Adams told me, "The murals had to be—how do I put this—pre-'50s." He said that they had to depict times from the founding of Siler City to the 1950s. Moody told me that the society perused old photographs to determine mural scenes. Speaking to the likeness of the murals to the photographs, he added, "It's amazing how realistic those things are."[27]

The material markers of that "pre-'50s" history already were deteriorating in the 1970s, yet white residents did not make much of an effort to restore or memorialize those buildings until after Latino arrival. In 1978, a year without a Fourth of July parade, residents watched a demolition crew tear down First Union Bank on Chatham Avenue to make way for new construction. One observer described the destruction as "better than a parade." Another said, "I don't see why they are tearing it down; it's the best-looking building in downtown Siler City." Describing the scene, a reporter wrote that as "the front panels of the building were pulled down, exposing old marble slabs inscribed with 'The Chatham Bank' across the front," those who saw the building constructed in the 1890s crumble to the ground "felt a sadness creeping over them as they watched something from their past being reopened and then destroyed."[28] Other buildings were vacated in the 1970s, and by the time the parades stopped in 1988, Chatham Avenue was no longer a thriving business district. Despite the downtown decay that preceded migrant arrival, locals did not organize any significant revitalization or preservation efforts, at least not any with the visibility of the mural society, until after Latinos moved into its empty spaces.

Measured solely on the basis of economic impact, though, the arrival of Latino migrants already had "revitalized" the downtown business district before the organization of the Siler City Mural Society. If one of the purposes of the society was to attract visitors to the downtown area to spend money, then its members were not looking to invite customers to Latino businesses; those stores already had customers. Beginning in the late 1990s, storefront Spanish-language Protestant churches and Latino-owned shops filled vacated spaces on Chatham Avenue and its cross streets. When I walked those streets in 2006, for example, the Tabernáculo de Adoración Alfa y Omega was a few blocks from First Baptist Church. The Tienda el Centro was a few steps from the Farmers' Alliance store, and just around the corner from Regal Furniture, which displayed a political sign supporting the reelection of Tommy Emerson for county commissioner in the corner of its storefront window, along with several bean bag chairs: a pink Barbie one, a green camouflage one, and two purple and white ones with the phrase "Our God Is an Awesome God" on them. And the signage of Estética Ángeles, which advertised waxing and facials among its services, contrasted that of Style and Grace, a local hair salon, with a logo that had a cross through the "c" in "Grace" with a motto beneath the logo that read, "You can have both."

In the midst of that multiethnic landscape, the society's murals displayed a narrative of southern progress, persistence, and presence. The Chatham Hospital mural, one block west of Chatham Avenue on the corner of West Raleigh Street and South Birch Avenue, depicted three stages of development,

FIGURE 6.1 Tienda El Centro on Chatham Avenue, 2006. Photo by Author.

from its original home in the 1930s, to a new building of the 1950s, to a new addition in 1969. It staged a historical progression of architectural design around a manicured lawn. On the far left, a circular image of a white male doctor treating a younger white woman hovered above the 1930s hospital. On the far right, positioned at the roofline of the 1969 addition, another circular image in crisper and lighter hues depicted a female medical provider, possibly an African American doctor, treating someone who looked like an older white woman. In the center of the mural, a bright yellow and blue Rotary International emblem descended from the sky, a yellow comet-like tail trailing behind it and wrapping around a large tree. Directly to the right appeared an unnamed portrait, likely that of white Siler City resident and hospital benefactor Thomas Murdock Brooks, of a man in a suit and tie, surrounded by the emanating yellow light of the emblem. Imbuing the symbolic representation of a racially segregated Rotary Club with supernatural force, the hospital mural positioned white male benevolence at the center of medical progress in the southern town. The society also placed that mural within the former black business district without recognizing the history of that space.

The mural on the side of the Ace Hardware building, within sight of Chatham Avenue on East Raleigh Street, displayed the persistence of southern whites across three periods of town history. Like the hospital mural, the scenes moved from left to right, though more distinctly than the hospital mural scenes. The mural positioned white men at the center of each historical stage of the store and presented them as welcoming and friendly to all

FIGURE 6.2 Chatham Hospital Mural on South Birch Avenue, 2006. Photo by Author.

customers: white, black, and Latino. The first scene depicted the building in the early twentieth century, with the law offices of Siler and Milliken on the top floor and the Elder Hardware Company on the bottom floor. Seven white men dressed in tan suits stood in front of the building, near a telegraph or electrical pole and a horse.

The second scene depicted the inside of the store. The exact time period was unclear. Wood-burning stoves were displayed for sale in the front window, and antique brass fire extinguishers lined a top shelf. An employee, an older white man with gray hair and glasses, helped a gray-haired customer wearing a long purple dress. To the right was another customer: a black man wearing overalls, a long-sleeved shirt, and a hat, smiling patiently while waiting at the counter. In the foreground, in front of the cash register, a young white girl in a red shirt sifted through a barrel of nails. By positioning the black customer among the visual markers of a "pre-'50s" history, this second scene conflated pre- and post-segregation history, locating the presence of racial cooperation within a spatial moment that preceded it.

The third scene depicted the store in its present state. Painted in pastels, it portrayed an employee, an older white man with gray hair wearing a blue, short-sleeved Ace Hardware shirt, helping a customer, an African American woman wearing glasses and a pink blouse and carrying a purse on her shoulder. Another employee, also an older white man with gray hair, stood near the top of a ladder. Below him, a Latina woman with braided hair, wearing overalls and a mauve shirt, looked toward the upper shelf. She appeared to be asking

FIGURE 6.3 ACE Hardware Mural on East Raleigh Street, 2006. Photo by Author.

him about an item beyond her reach. A Latina girl walked with her and held her hand. A young white girl dressed in pink overalls, a pink shirt, and with a pink ribbon in her hair stood nearby at the counter, smiling in her direction. In this final scene, the mural offered viewers a narrative of white persistence in the midst of demographic change, displaying that persistence as amenable to, and even promoting, racial and ethnic harmony. Historical progress, implied in this narrative, was the persistent presentation, or promise, of the inherent goodwill of southern white men. And all of those scenes, while sequential, appeared to the observer at the same time. This was the visual narrative of the modern South for Mural Society members, of racial harmony as an eternal moment.

The mural on the Farmers' Alliance store on the south end of Chatham Avenue displayed that perpetual presence. The scene was based on a photograph of Chatham Avenue from around 1906. The photograph depicted a horse and buggy on a dirt street, leading to the town well. The street was lined with wooden and brick buildings. In the photograph, several women stood on the right side of the street. Opposite them, on the left side of the street, an African American man leaned against a post in front of a store. This person was, I was often told, Tod Edwards, the only black businessman in the white business district, in front of his jewelry story. The mural extended the field of vision in the photograph by including several buildings beyond its borders. In the bottom right corner, it added the First Methodist Episcopal Church South, dedicated in 1887 and located at 121 South Chatham Avenue.[29] On the far left side, it showed the Farmers' Alliance buildings. The panorama included the front brick Farmers' Alliance building, which was completed in 1907, as well as the back wooden building built in 1888, which faced the railroad tracks and was attached to the front building by an elevated walkway.[30] In the gap between the front and back buildings, the mural included

FIGURE 6.4 Chatham Avenue around 1906. Source: Hadley, *Town of Siler City*.

FIGURE 6.5 Alliance Store Mural Dedication on Chatham Avenue, August 25, 2006. Credit: Jeff Davis, *Chatham News*, August 31, 2006, 1A.

an empty space with a tree line and blue sky behind it. The black business district on South Birch Avenue, which ran parallel to Chatham Avenue and was directly behind the Farmers' Alliance, would have filled that empty space. It would have been visible between the old and new stores, and would have blocked out part of that horizon—but it was not in the mural. Instead, the mural featured Tod Edwards in the center of its frame, while excluding those buildings—but not the space they would have occupied—from its view.

When I asked about the mural scene, several white residents, including Siler City Mural Society members, identified Edwards as the man on the left side of the street leaning against a post in front of his store. But when I asked about the absence of the black business district, they simply told me the mural does not depict Birch Avenue. The commissioned muralist—who was not from Siler City but rather a resident of the Blue Heron Farm Intentional Living Community in Pittsboro—was, apparently, unaware of that oversight. When I spoke with her at the Farmers' Alliance store on the day of the dedication, she told me that she wanted to help residents of Siler City "project who they remember onto the mural."[31] The memories of those whom she helped only included other white residents and the only black man working in the white business district.

Visual Silence and Religious Difference

What the murals hide, the secular cannot reveal. "The inability to speak, the lack of promise of revelation," writes J. Heath Atchley, is a "defining mark of the secular." Because the secular is silent, we assume it has something to tell us. We grasp for it, trying to get it to say just what we should know in order to live rightly. But we can never know for sure what the secular hides, or if there is anything to discover, after all, and that is frustrating. "Our favorite secrets," Atchley suggests, "are the open kind, and silences are their momentary obstacles. If this be the case, then the kind of silence that is an inability to speak, rather than an unwillingness, must be all the more difficult. This latter version of silence betrays an inadequacy instead of a temptation; hence, it does not appear to hold the promise of a silence that can reveal a secret."[32] If the kind of silence that cannot reveal defines the secular, then a kind of silence that promises to reveal distinguishes religion. Secrets are the currency of the religious trade.[33] "Without secrets," writes Paul Christopher Johnson, "religion becomes unimaginable."[34] This is why the secular cannot do without religion: because lonely is the world without the promise of shared secrets.

Religion fills the silent spaces of the secular.[35] More precisely, our communities—the "we" that we create—fill the silence with religion. We sustain ourselves through the spectacles of collective life, through the ritual performances that promise to reveal. Parades, processions, and pulpit pronouncements share a secret that is nothing more and nothing less than the reiteration of the community to itself: the premise of a present that can withstand whatever may come. This is an impossible promise. Religious ecology entails organizational death.[36] As we have seen in Siler City, no community can keep all of its promises of continuance. Local organizations—the Jaycees, the mural society—eventually pass away. And yet, through religions, communities do this, again and again. They promise to persist.

But the capacity to make promises, Nietzsche wrote, demands forgetfulness, "an active ability to suppress," an ability to "shut the doors and windows of consciousness for a while."[37] An active forgetfulness is what the sponsors of the renewed parade and downtown murals displayed, as they attempted to create the community they promised themselves against the sociological and anthropological forces that threatened its persistence. They shut the *tienda* (shop) doors and *tabernáculo* (tabernacle) windows on Chatham Avenue to make room in their collective consciousness for a little tabula rasa: a clean street, an unmarked wall. Against that blank slate, they renewed the promise that their forbears made to Tod Edwards: the promise of racial harmony, a promise that allowed them to live in a moment detached from its surrounding immediacies. The capacity to make that promise demanded an active forgetfulness of the racial segregation that surrounded it. Without that active forgetfulness, their community, as they know it, would be anomic. Their relationships, as they perceive them, would be dissolute. This "is the benefit of active forgetfulness," Nietzsche proffered, "There could be no happiness, cheerfulness, hope, pride, *immediacy*, without forgetfulness."[38] For those residents, the clean world of moral community is an opportunity, a chance to project a collective will to disremember, in order that they may occupy the present and offer it a future.

In the early twentieth century, southern secularism was a greasy pig. A century later, it is a vehicle of forgetfulness. Without its silent carriage, its inability to speak of itself, there would not be religion in the new millennium. There would not be the capacity to make promises. Religion does not need to speak on behalf of the secular; the secular asks not to be spoken for. Religion just needs to speak. Then the locative naming, the game, begins, with each player, each partner, made in the inverse of its likeness. Like the rag tops on Main Street, patrons of secularism use it to "hide and to unveil, to contain and release" the rhythmic engines of "secrets and the sacred."[39] But their medium can never reveal the revelator. When in motion, secularism is marked by visual silence. We cannot see what is under the hood, what is in the glove box, what is under the seats, what is in the trunk. Those visually silent parts are unveiled before or after the secular parade. If we can survey the machine, count its cylinders and tally its horses, before it moves toward us, if not this time then the next, we may see the sound and hear the sight. Visual hearing, though, demands not just willingness but ability. It requires access, not just proximity. And secularism closes the hood of history, says nothing of before or after. If there is a whisper, it is only of the present, the place where we remember we always were willing but unable. Guilt, remorse—moral forces of remembrance—all rise with thoughts of freedom. We, I, you, were able but unwilling. Secularism squelches those signals of agency, even as it broadcasts the agentive "I." It thwarts the will by disabling the spirit, even as it distributes a corporate science of personalized spirituality. Forgetfulness is the benefit of secularism: a spatial rupture of selves from self, of bodies from body.

Visual silence is the temporal arrangement of those spatial disjunctions. It is inculcated in religious pedagogy, in the "art of silence" transmitted in Candomblé, for example, "through the injunction to see but not speak."[40] It is conveyed in text, in the empty spaces between and within words in modern visual poetry.[41] And it is "heard" in visual arts, such as in René Magritte's painting *Man with a Newspaper*. While all three types of visual silence are instructive, this last example is most useful for interpreting the commissioned murals in Siler City. Linguistics scholar Alina Kwiatkowska argues that Magritte's painting conveys a "visual silence that resembles closely that of the auditory mode."[42] The painting extends that silence temporally in its spatial arrangement of four frames of the same picture. In the first, a man reads a newspaper. In the other three, he is absent. The momentary presence of the man acts as a placeholder that codes the adjacent frames in "negative terms." Kwiatkowska suggests that visual silence is rare in paintings, which more often depict a singular temporal frame. But, she adds, it is common in "everyday-life situations," when "we do not see what we expect to see, and register this absence against the less important ground."[43]

Kwiatkowska's definition of visual silence as a sequential movement of brief presence to prolonged absence helps me make sense of my reaction to the Farmers' Alliance mural. I expected to see South Birch Avenue in the empty space behind Chatham Avenue because I had read in Hadley's history that there were buildings on that street as early as 1888, though he never wrote that they were part of the black business district.[44] But several months prior to the mural dedication, two other white residents, Milo Holt and Tommy Edwards, showed me the ruins of the buildings on that street and told me they were the remains of the former black business district. Upon seeing the mural, I decided that those who commissioned it intentionally omitted the buildings on South Birch Avenue. I felt this was a willing neglect, a failure to make good on a promise to depict the town's history. But now, I am not so sure. Members of the mural society knew about that street, and despite Hadley's omission, they knew it was the black business district. I am fairly certain they knew that because two of their peers knew that, and told me as

FIGURE 6.6 Ruins of Buildings on South Birch Avenue, Site of Former Black Business District, 2006. Photo by Author.

much. But did they remember it? When I asked them, they said the mural does not "depict" Birch Avenue. I already knew that. What I wanted to know was *why* they did not depict it. I wanted them to tell me their secret, tell me why they had excluded it. Yet, they were silent. Birch Avenue, I concluded, was not *their* memory. They had set it apart, along with the black residents who patronized that block.

Forgetting their memories of segregated black bodies, white residents occupied the present and imagined a future that carried that present with it into a new day, a future in which their presence would not be displaced, a future in which even after death, they would endure. To Nietzsche, there is no present without active forgetting, but there is equally no future for the present without the act of remembering. The muscular caretaker of broken blossoms must "think causally, to view the future as the present and anticipate it…to become *reliable, regular, necessary*, even in his own self-image, so that he, as someone making a promise is, is answerable for his own *future*!"[45] To forget Birch Avenue but remember Tod Edwards is to anticipate racial integration, to consider it as having been always present, to control its harmonious presentation. "Precisely here, *promises are made*; precisely here, the person making the promise has to have a memory *made* for him: precisely here, we may suppose, is a repository of hard, cruel, painful things."[46]

Religious differences are made in the secular spaces of visual silence. In the American South, those spaces are the repositories for hard, cruel, and painful memories. Historically, those are racially segregated spaces. Progressive whites in Siler City used secularism to hide the histories of those spaces from the present space in which they reside. They set aside the moments when they set apart black bodies and promised them protection. In doing so, they make the revelation of those memories, of someone else's memory, an imminent possibility, an inevitable unveiling of a segregated past. Against that history, they seek to control the containment and release of that which they made sacred. They need the appearance of black bodies to define their own whiteness, just as the secular needs the noise of religion to locate itself. But they are obliged to include only one marker of difference at a time, and even just one may be enough. They made black bodies powerful in the absence of their memory, so that when they see them in their presence, they are stunned with a type of silence that reveals. Secularism is an opportunity for them to forget not just the memory, but also the very act of forgetting, to mute the power of their sacred with a type of silence that conceals. In the presence of the first type of silence, they are "dyspeptic," because their "apparatus of suppression" has been damaged.[47] They are left to gaze into the face of their sacred, the religious voice to their secular whiteness. In that moment, their memory is *their* memory. The infinite regression, the inability to forget, is nauseating. In the presence of the second type of silence, they retain consciousness, steady themselves, and find their voice. But they speak not of secrets, not of the mysterious, but of the familiar, of friends and family, of faces with names. I close with such an example.

The day of the mural dedication, after the ribbon-cutting ceremony on the side street, the small crowd gathered inside the store to watch Milo Holt screen black-and-white film reels of Siler City from the 1930s through the early 1950s. In previous conversations, Milo explained to me that these films were at one point common in southern towns. Companies traveled from town to town, filmed white and black residents, and then showed the films in local theaters. Those same residents paid to see themselves on the silver screen in a shared but segregated theater. That day at the Farmers' Alliance store, white residents observed that kind of film. As scenes of white students at the high school flashed on the screen, the audience called out the names of those whom they recognized and remembered. This was a collective task; one person said a name, and another person confirmed or suggested that it was someone else. Senior residents settled all debates. When the crowd saw images of black students at a separate school, however, they stopped naming. No one spoke until white residents in other scenes around town appeared again on the screen. Edwards was the exception. When they saw him, several audience members immediately said, "There's Tod Edwards."

The bounded space for that screening, the Farmers' Alliance store, has been a historical placeholder of material cultures of racial segregation, a space historically limited to members of the "Anglo-Saxon race." The store no longer discriminates against certain customers but welcomes all, particularly Latino shoppers, who generally pay in cash.[48] But legacies of segregation persisted in its ownership of stock, passed down within white families and among relatives. More significant for understanding the mural, the Farmers' Alliance store is a place where white residents come to remember their past. The store displays numerous photographs dating from the 1920s through the 1960s—almost all of them of white residents. There is, however, one exception: Landrus Siler, the janitor of Siler City High School. His photograph is placed in the middle of the photographs of white students.

Nancy Tysor, a longtime store operator, explained to me that the former principal of Paul Braxton Elementary School, which occupied the school building after the desegregation of Siler City High School, donated most of the photographs on display in the Farmers' Alliance store. Braxton Manor, a senior living community in the former Siler City High School building, still keeps a collection of the Siler City High School annuals in its office. Only locals know that they are there, and they are not available in the public library. I asked about them, and a staff member suggested I try Braxton Manor. In that collection, I found a yearbook from the 1950s that contained a photograph of students in blackface for Halloween, as seen in Figure 2.3. Many of the photographs displayed at the Farmers' Alliance store came from that school collection, along with others of white baseball teams, including the 1949 Siler City Millers, and images of white soldiers in uniform. Absent from the display, however, were any photographs of residents in blackface. As with their ritual memories of old-time Fourth of July parades, white residents filtered the public display of their pictorial memories through a lens of racial harmony, keeping visual memories that evoked good feelings—classmates, teammates, soldiers and the high school janitor they all knew and treated kindly—while discarding evidence of collective shame associated with their performances of blackface and racial segregation. After the 1970s, if they displayed those images, they risked accusations of racism—and they were determined to never be characterized by that unfitly spoken term.

The visual displays at the Farmers' Alliance store were charged with the racialized codes of southern history.[49] Some outsiders did not immediately recognize the latent meanings of those displays. Or if they did, they did not say anything about them. At the mural dedication, a white newspaper reporter covering the event introduced me to a local nonprofit advocate who coordinated the volunteer efforts for the mural construction. She was, to my surprise, an African American woman. When we spoke, she told me that she had moved from Connecticut a few years prior to work in a hosiery mill. She eventually left the mill and took a position at a local nonprofit. As part of her new job, she coordinated activities for at-risk youth in Siler City. She told me that she saw the Farmers' Alliance mural as an opportunity to connect those kids to an artistic project. In her appropriation of the mural construction as a service project and in her presence at the dedication ceremony, she demonstrated the multiplicity of meanings that observers attached to the Farmers' Alliance mural.[50] She was able to connect her communal efforts to that historical projection, because she did not share the memories of those who commissioned its construction. That day, she was the only African American present, although organizers had tried to get another black resident to appear. I heard someone say that Elizabeth Edwards, the daughter-in-law of Tod Edwards, had been invited, but she could not attend, although it was not made clear why she was unable.

The Farmers' Alliance was historically "Anglo-Saxon" property, but those who protected its history imagined it as universal. A town commissioner and society member stated at the dedication, "We really appreciate the Farmers' Alliance for their presence in the community for all these years. I am glad to have a mural on their building that depicts our rich history."[51] On the side of the store, in the proximity of Spanish-language signage, that history erased the material markers of racial segregation within its view. Inside the store, its curators displayed photographs of white students and Landrus Siler from the 1950s, while excluding images of the same white students in blackface that were part of the school collection. In the presence of those images, white residents watched a film of their past and called out the names of their friends, family, and Tod Edwards as the voiceless images moved across the screen. Then they stopped, abruptly and without murmur, collectively silenced by the flickering spectacle of black bodies. And there, in that moment, was their response: the shared secret of southern secularism.

Notes

INTRODUCTION

1. Martin Luther, "The Fourteen of Consolation," in *Pastoral Care in Historical Perspective*, ed. William A. Clebsch and Charles R. Jaekle (New York: Harper and Row, 1975 [1967]), 223.
2. *Siler City Grit*, July 1911.
3. Wade Hampton Hadley, *The Town of Siler City, 1887–1987: A History of the Town's Centennial Anniversary on March 7 of 1987* (Siler City, NC: Caviness Printing Service, Inc., 1986), 48.
4. Isaac London, ed., *Grit*, December 23, 1914.
5. Milo Holt, interview with the author, September 13, 2004.
6. Milo Holt, interview with the author, October 9, 2006.
7. Altha Cravey, "Latino Labor and Poultry Production in Rural North Carolina," *Southeastern Geographer* 37 (November 1997): 295–300.
8. Twelfth Census of the United States, 1900: Chatham County, Population Schedule.
9. US Bureau of the Census, 1950.
10. As of 1990, the city population of 4,955 was 68 percent white, 27 percent African American, 3 percent Hispanic, and 2 percent other. US Bureau of the Census, 1990.
11. US Bureau of the Census, 2000. In 2010, the town's population of 7,887 residents was 49.8 percent Hispanic or Latino. US Bureau of the Census, 2010. It is important to note that ethnic categories used to identify migrants from Latin America have a contested history. Many scholars prefer the term *Latino* instead of *Hispanic*, because it implies Iberian origins. Anthony Stevens-Arroyo and others argue that the category "Latino or Latina" better describes persons from Latin America who migrate to or reside in the United States. For that reason, I try to use the terms *Latino or Latina* when I can. This is not always possible, though. Older census data, many surveys, nonprofit agencies, and social activists often use the term *Hispanic*. To complicate matters further, a migrant is more likely to identify with his or her country of origin than to refer to himself or herself as Hispanic, Latino, or Latina. See Marcelo M. Suárez-Orozco and Mariela M. Paez, eds., *Latinos: Remaking America* (Berkeley: University of California Press, 2002), 2–5; Anthony M. Stevens-Arroyo,

"Introduction," in *Old Masks, New Faces: Religion and Latino Identities*, ed. Anthony M. Stevens-Arroyo and Gilbert R. Cadena (New York: Bildner Center for Western Hemispheric Studies, 1995).

12. Andres Viglucci, "Hispanic Wave Forever Alters Small Town in North Carolina," *Miami Herald*, January 2, 2000.

13. Fieldnotes, February 20, 2006.

14. For Clebsch, that "turnabout" was not a "strictly Protestant phenomenon." He maintained that, "if the pattern was established by Calvinistic religion, by it was cut the cloth of American Catholicism." William A. Clebsch, *From Sacred to Profane America: The Role of Religion in American History* (Ann Arbor, MI: Scholars Press American Academy of Religion, 1981), ix, 2. Despite that gesture, historians of public religion and civic life have worked primarily with Protestant textiles. For a notable exception, see Thomas A. Tweed, *America's Church: The National Shrine and Catholic Presence in the Nation's Capital* (New York: Oxford University Press, 2011).

15. William R, Hutchison, ed., *Between the Times: The Travail of the Protestant Establishment in America, 1900–1960* (Cambridge: Cambridge University Press, 1989), xi.

16. Dorothy Bass, "Ministry on the Margin: Protestants and Education," in William R. Hutchison, ed., *Between the Times: The Travail of the Protestant Establishment in America, 1900–1960* (Cambridge: Cambridge University Press, 1989), 66.

17. R. Stephen Warner, *A Church of Our Own: Disestablishment and Diversity in American Religion* (New Brunswick, NJ: Rutgers University Press, 2005); Phillip E. Hammond, *Religion and Personal Autonomy: The Third Disestablishment in America* (Columbia: University of South Carolina Press, 1992).

18. David Sehat argues that the "moral establishment" of liberal Protestantism in its public form was not merely an "informal religious establishment," but rather it "had a connection to law that was sometimes more forthright in connecting morality and religion and sometimes less so." In other words, the de facto status of liberal Protestantism as public religion depended upon certain formal expressions of legal mandates and state control. David Sehat, *The Myth of American Religious Freedom* (New York: Oxford University Press, 2011), 4, 286. Catherine Albanese uses the term *public Protestantism*, arguing that it had its roots in "the Calvinist Christianity of the early Puritan settlers." Catherine L. Albanese, *America, Religions, and Religion* (Belmont, CA: Wadsworth Publishing, 1999), 399.

19. Secularization narratives of public religion in the United States emphasize legacies of Protestant revivalism and its organizational forms of voluntary association, connecting them to the formation of the nation-state, and following institutional expansion from the colonies outward. For many American religious historians and sociologists of religion, secularism promoted organizational convergence of increasing religious diversity, particularly after 1965, to congregational models of earlier Protestantism even after its historical moment passed. On legacies of revivalism, see Timothy L. Smith, *Revivalism and Social Reform in Mid-Nineteenth Century*

America (New York: Abingdon Press, 1957); Nathan Hatch, *The Democratization of American Christianity* (New Haven, CT: Yale University Press, 1989); William G. McLoughlin, *Modern Revivalism: Charles Grandison Finney to Billy Graham* (New York: Ronald Press Co., 1959); and Mark Noll, *American Evangelical Christianity: An Introduction* (Malden, MA: Blackwell Publishers, 2001). On de facto congregationalism as an innovation of Protestant organizational forms, see R. Stephen Warner, "Work in Progress Toward a New Paradigm for the Sociological Study of Religion in the United States," *American Journal of Sociology* 98 (March 1993): 1044–1093.

20. Tracy Fessenden, *Culture and Redemption: Religion, the Secular, and American Literature* (Princeton, NJ: Princeton University Press, 2007), 4.

21. Talal Asad, *Formations of the Secular: Christianity, Islam, Modernity* (Palo Alto, CA: Stanford University Press, 2003), 5.

22. Holt interview, October 9, 2006.

23. Asad argues that "the secular is neither continuous with the religious that supposedly preceded it (that is, it is not the latest phase of a sacred origin) nor a simple break from it (that is, it is not the opposite, an essence that excludes the sacred)." Asad, *Formations of the Secular*, 25.

24. Historian Rhys Isaac observed that, "in many houses below the gentry level, matched individual place settings of china and cutlery began to replace the small stock of communal vessels and utensils that formerly had to do duty for everyone." Rhys Isaac, *The Transformation of Virginia, 1780–1790* (New York: W. W. Norton, 1982), 305.

25. Michel Foucault described governmentality as "at once internal and external to the state, since it is the tactics of government which make possible the continual definition and redefinition of what is within the competence of the state and what is not, the public versus the private, and so on; thus the state can only be understood in its survival and its limits on the basis of the general tactics of governmentality." Michel Foucault, Graham Burchell, and Colin Gordon, *The Foucault Effect: Studies in Governmentality* (Chicago: University of Chicago Press, 1991), 103. Or, as Bratich, Packer, and McCarthy explain in their reading of Foucault, "Governmentality addresses a formation of power that differs from disciplinarity and sovereignty. This formation is derived from the recognition that the strength of the state is dependent upon the proper disposition of humans and things. But, this recognition is not the state's alone. It is not so much that the state's reach is all-consuming; instead, the techniques of governmentality emanate from numerous sources and without them the state would not be what it is." Jack Z. Bratich, Jeremy Packer, and Cameron McCarthy, *Foucault, Cultural Studies, and Governmentality* (New York: SUNY Press, 2003), 5. Employing the term *governmentality*, I consider the Club, for example, as a site of power for the local formation of governmental control, even though it is outside the boundaries of official government. It is a site for the disciplining of dispositions that favor those in civic positions of social regulation.

26. I agree with Giles Gunn's assessment that "The religious and the secular have not only coexisted in their modern formation…but actually adjusted to, and profited from, the rearrangements and adjustments required for coexistence with the other." Giles Gunn, "Cultural Models and Rethinking Secularism," *The Immanent Frame* (blog), March 13, 2012, http://blogs.ssrc.org.

27. Asad argues against the notion that the secular is just religion in another form. He writes, "I simply want to get away from the idea that the secular is a mask for religion." Asad, *Formations of the Secular*, 26. I am influenced by this assessment, although I do think, as I argue later, that secularism can mask religion as secularity during liminal moments akin to minstrelsy. But these moments only reinforce divisions of those two categories, of religion as distinct or set apart from the secular.

28. My invocation of a haunted landscape echoes John Lardas Modern's characterization of secularism as "unseen somethings haunting the day." John Lardas Modern, *Secularism in Antebellum America* (Chicago: University of Chicago Press, 2011), 7.

29. *Revision Context 2003: First United Methodist Church–Siler City, North Carolina*, (Rancho Santa Margarita, CA: Percept, 2003), in the collection of First United Methodist Church, Siler City.

30. Sydney Verba et al. argue that education, which is tied to socioeconomic status, determines public political participation; that this process privileges those with Anglo-white civic skills, measured primarily in organizational habits and the ability to speak English; and that "only religious institutions provide a counterbalance to this cumulative resource process." Sidney Verba, Kay Lehman Schlozman, and Henry E. Brady, *Voice and Equality: Civic Voluntarism in American Politics* (Cambridge, MA: Harvard University Press, 1995), 18. While I disaffirm the qualification of civic skills in those racialized terms, I do consider religious congregations a site for the formation of civic tools needed for political participation. For a critique of the descriptive category "Anglo-white civic skills," see Frederick C. Harris, *Something Within: Religion in African-American Political Activism* (New York: Oxford University Press, 1999), 38.

31. Clifford Geertz, "Religion as a Cultural System," *Interpretation of Cultures* (New York: Basic Books, 1973), 94–98.

32. Max Weber, *The Protestant Ethic and the Spirit of Capitalism*, trans. Talcott Parsons (Mineola, NY: Courier Dover Publications, 2003 [1958]), 36.

33. Fessenden, *Culture and Redemption*, 4.

34. Ibid.

35. E. P. Thompson, *The Making of the English Working Class* (New York: Vintage Books, 1966).

36. Christian Smith argues that "a distinct and important group of players in the secularization of American public life were the many liberal Protestant leaders who capitulated early to the basic assumptions and standards of the secularizers and so helped pave the way for their eventual success." Christian Smith, *The Secular Revolution: Power, Interests, and Conflict in the Secularization of American Public*

Life (Berkeley: University of California Press, 2003), 35. James Davison Hunter claims that the "liberal Protestant worldview functions as a deeply secularized cosmology." James Davison Hunter, "Conservative Protestantism," in *The Sacred in a Secular Age: Toward Revision in the Scientific Study of Religion*, ed. Phillip E. Hammond (Berkeley: University of California Press, 1985), 150. Smith and Hunter represent opposing approaches to secularization and its relationship to evangelicalism, with Smith considering evangelicals "embattled but thriving" in public life and Hunter considering them as likely to become more privatized and removed from public life. Yet both use liberal Protestantism to locate secularism as something evangelicals encounter and adapt to, rather than something evangelicals use in differing ways to their own advantage, just as liberal Protestants have done, or attempted to do.

37. Kathleen Sands has proposed that liberal Protestantism won the culture war in the 1920s, concerning religious feminism, and "fundamentalist Protestantism retreated for decades from public life." She writes, "What was left to dominate the public sphere was a liberal Protestantism comfortable with modernity and quite at home in the secular landscape." Continuing, she claims that, "the cultural provenance of second-wave secularism was therefore Protestant, albeit meaning a Protestantism of a particular kind. Soon after this, feminism emerged, and partly in response to it, evangelical Protestantism burst back into public life. In direct contrast to the nineteenth century, when religion reentered public life in the name of feminist and other progressive causes, the religion that asserted itself in the 1970s was that of a revitalized patriarchalism. This evangelical patriarchalism looked religious in a way that secularized liberal Protestantism did not, so religion appeared to be reentering a public sphere from which it long and unjustly had been banished." Kathleen Sands, "Feminisms and Secularisms," in *Secularisms*, ed. Janet R. Jakobsen and Ann Pellegrini (Durham, NC: Duke University Press, 2008), 318. Again, this all makes sense from the point of view that begins with liberal Protestantism. But looking at it from the vantage point of the South, patriarchal uses of secularism by evangelicals were well established in the first half of the twentieth century and never fully retreated from public life in the following decades. To understand the apparent surprise of their public emergence in the 1970s is to see the ways in which they were institutionalized in public life throughout the region in earlier periods.

38. Historian George Rable has noted that southern "preachers and politicians drew a sharp contrast between the Confederate Constitution and the godless United States Constitution that failed to acknowledge divine sovereignty." George C. Rable, *God's Almost Chosen Peoples: A Religious History of the American Civil War* (Chapel Hill: University of North Carolina Press, 2010), 62–63. Michael Warner has cited the preamble to the Confederate Constitution, which he describes as "designed to counteract the godlessness of the Union counterpart," as evidence of "rivalry between Southern and Northern versions of religious nationalism." That rivalry, he argues, illustrates how "different parties of religious struggle might have

shared elements of a secular metaphysics, but they certainly put competing spins on its political implications." Michael Warner, "Rethinking Secularism: Was antebellum America secular?" *The Immanent Frame* (blog), October, 2 2012, http://blogs. ssrc.org.

39. On the notion of proximal distance, Georg Simmel wrote, "Relationships of an intimate character, the formal vehicle of which is pyscho-physical proximity, lose the charm, and even the content, of their intimacy, unless the proximity includes, at the same time and alternately, distance and intermission." Georg Simmel, "The Sociology of Secrecy and of Secret Societies," *American Journal of Sociology* 11, no. 4 (1906), 448.

40. Fessenden, *Culture and Redemption*, 12. On regionalism, see Jerald C. Brauer, "Regionalism and Religion in America," *Church History* 54 (1985): 366–378. See also Edwin S. Gaustad, "Regionalism in American Religion," in *Religion in the South*, ed. Charles Reagan Wilson (Jackson: University Press of Mississippi, 1985), 155–172. On varieties of secularism, see Winnifred Fallers Sullivan, *Prison Religion: Faith-Based Reform and the Constitution* (Princeton, NJ: Princeton University Press, 2009), 229–230; Michael Warner, Jonathan VanAntwerpen, and Craig J. Calhoun, *Varieties of Secularism in a Secular Age* (Cambridge, MA: Harvard University Press, 2010).

41. I am persuaded by Kathryn Lofton, who writes in another context regarding the relationship between the method of history and the study of religion that, "history is not just a single strategy of organizing thought, but also a description of thinking itself." Kathryn Lofton, "Religious History as Religious Studies," *Religion* 42, no. 3 (2012), 383–394. Translating Lofton's statement to this context, I contend with affirmative likeness that southern secularism is not just a single strategy of organizing regional difference but also an epistemological conception of that difference and its relationship to American pluralism and diversity. Some readers may interpret my call for a regionalization of secularism as echoing a similar claim made by Charles Reagan Wilson (in *Baptized in Blood)* regarding civil religion. In 1980, Wilson argued that there is "a Southern civil religion, based on Christianity and regional history." Charles Reagan Wilson, *Baptized in Blood: The Religion of the Lost Cause, 1865–1920* (Athens: University of Georgia Press, [1980] 2009), 8. This would be a generous comparison; however, in my invocation of southern secularism as not just a descriptive difference but also as a competing mode of thinking *about* difference, I want to resist certain readings of geographic difference, religious pluralism, or ethnic diversity as sufficient explanations for various formations of secularism and their varied productions of difference, plurality, and diversity.

42. I borrow the term *extended case* from Michael Burawoy, who uses it to describe a methodology that moves back and forth from theory to local ethnographic case studies. Michael Burawoy, *The Extended Case Method: Four Countries, Four Decades, Four Great Transformations, and One Theoretical Tradition* (Berkeley: University of California Press, 2009).

43. Modern, *Secularism in Antebellum America*, 74.

44. Modern believes that "antebellum America secularism moved across a number of sites—evangelicalism and liberal Protestantism, burgeoning fields of mental science, spiritualism, ethnographic inquiry, moral reform, etc." Modern, *Secularism in Antebellum America*, 12.

45. Modern, *Secularism in Antebellum America*, 54. Charles Taylor has used a continuum to describe the range of views of a supreme being with agency to an indifferent or nonexistent God. Charles Taylor, *A Secular Age* (Cambridge, MA: Belknap Press of Harvard University Press, 2007), 270. Continuum models have varied in scale and have been broadly applied. Alfred Stepan, for example, has calibrated a continuum with a "four-point scale for eleven variables concerning state control of majority religions" and a "continuum for state control of minority religions," adding ranges of composite scores to those continuums for nation-states such as Denmark, Norway, Bangladesh, Pakistan, and Egypt. Alfred Stepan, "The Multiple Secularisms of Modern Democratic and Non-Democratic Regimes," in *Rethinking Secularism*, ed. Craig Calhoun, Mark Juergensmeyer, and Jonathan VanAntwerpen (New York: Oxford University Press, 2011), 121. In the same collection of essays, Elizabeth Shakman Hurd has argued against continuum models that carry with them a "developmentalist teleology." Hurd, "A Suspension of (Dis) Belief: The Secular-Religious Binary and the Study of International Relations," in Calhoun, et al., *Rethinking Secularism*, 171. To argue this point, Hurd cites Jillian Schwedler, who has proposed that "scholars should abandon the notion that the 'space' between authoritarianism and democracy is characterized by a continuum of stages from primitive, traditional, or patriarchal systems of rule (authoritarianism) to modern, rational-legal systems of rule (democracy)." Jillian Schwedler, *Faith in Moderation: Islamist Parties in Jordan and Yemen* (Cambridge: Cambridge University Press, 2006), 6. For other uses of continuum models, see Markus Dressler, "The Religio-Secular Continuum: Reflections on the Religious Dimensions of Turkish Secularism," in *After Secular Law*, ed. Winnifred Fallers Sullivan, Robert Yelle, and Mateo Taussig-Rubbo (Palo Alto, CA: Stanford University Press, 2011), 221–241. See also Peter L., Berger, Grace Davie, and Effie Fokas, *Religious America, Secular Europe? A Theme and Variation.* (Burlington, VT: Ashgate Publishing, Ltd., 2008), 24, 56, 100.

46. Fessenden, *Culture and Redemption*, 5. Ann Braude, "American Religious History Is Women's History," in Thomas A. Tweed, ed., *Retelling U.S. Religious History* (Berkeley: University of California Press, 1997), 87–107.

47. Thomas A. Tweed, *Crossing and Dwelling: A Theory of Religion* (Cambridge, MA: Harvard University Press, 2006), 13.

48. This book offers a theoretical sighting of secularization and secularism from a Durkheimian tradition of social performativity—proposing that the performance of religion is a secular spectacle—while looking back at that sighting from a southern town where white residents used secularism as an institutional

mechanism for religious and racial purification. The book, however, rejects the Durkheimian claim that society is sui generis and that the soul of religion, its essence, is unchangeable, even as it evolves into malleable forms. Instead, it maintains that ritual performances of essential difference are monuments, a term that land surveyors use to designate arbitrary but fixed points that establish location, for sightings of modernity, secularization, and secularism. Itinerant cartographers of secularization and secularism in the United States have typically referenced the Protestant Reformation as their major historical and conceptual monument, connecting it to those of the French Enlightenment and constitutional disestablishment. Henry May, *The Enlightenment in America* (New York: Oxford University Press, 1976). Admittedly, the Reformation is more foundational to Weberian than Durkheimian readings, but Durkheim too considered Protestantism a key source of individualism in modern life. J. A. Hughes, Wes W. Sharrock, and Peter J. Martin, *Understanding Classical Sociology: Marx, Weber, Durkheim* (London: Sage, 2003), 171. Further, Durkheimian theories of American religion feature individualism as their central normative category of sociological analysis. See Robert Bellah, Richard Madsen, William M. Sullivan, Ann Swidler, and Steven M. Tipton, *Habits of the Heart: Individualism and Commitment in American Life* (Berkeley: University of California Press, 1996).

49. Tweed, *Crossing and Dwelling*, 13.

50. On depictions of the South in northern print media, see Mary Beth Swetnam Mathews, *Rethinking Zion: How the Print Media Placed Fundamentalism in the South* (Knoxville: University of Tennessee Press, 2006). On the WPA, see Colleen McDannell, *Picturing Faith: Photography and The Great Depression* (New Haven, CT: Yale University Press, 2004). On the Scopes Trial, see Edward J. Larson, *Summer for the Gods: The Scopes Trial And America's Continuing Debate over Science and Religion* (New York: Basic Books, 2006).

51. Jeffrey P. Moran, *The Scopes Trial: A Brief History with Documents* (New York: Palgrave Macmillan, 2002), 53–55.

52. Thomas Tweed has used the homophonous terms *sight*, *cite*, and *site* when considering narratives of religion in the United States. Thomas A. Tweed, ed., *Retelling U.S. Religious History* (Berkeley: University of California Press, 1997), 6.

53. Southern varieties of secularism entailed feelings of difference and similarity, and those feelings were recognizable as common sense. Modern has proposed that secularism refers to "that which conditioned not only particular understandings of the religious but also the environment in which these understandings became matters of common sense." Modern, *Secularism in Antebellum America*, 8. Applying this description of a particular characteristic of secularism to the study of Siler City, I see it as contrary to Durkheimian claims that categorical similarities are recognizable solely in rational terms. Durkheim made a point of saying that "the feeling of similarities is one thing and the notion of genus another." Émile Durkheim, *The Elementary Forms of Religious Life*, trans. Carol Cosman (New York: Oxford

University Press, 2001), 114. Classical versions of secularization theory perpetuated the view that reason and rationality were the dominant modes of organizing civic life into differentiated spheres, relegating emotive perceptions to privatized domestic and religious spaces. Nancy Fraser has challenged those approaches, noting that they operate primarily by a Harbermasian notion that reason is the organizing principle of the public sphere. Fraser argues against that limited understanding, proposing that feeling and emotion are viable sources of civic participation. Nancy Fraser, *Justice Interruptus: Critical Reflections on the "Postsocialist" Condition* (New York: Routledge, 1997). Building on that argument, Marie Marquardt finds expressions of overlooked civic participation among those at "the margins of society" in the "counterpublics" of their religious congregations. Marie Marquardt, "A Continuum of Hybridity: Latino Churches in the New South," in *Globalizing the Sacred: Religion Across the Americas*, ed. Marie Marquardt and Manuel Vásquez (New Brunswick, NJ: Rutgers University Press, 2003), 124, 145–170. Influenced by those approaches, I contend that southern secularism institutionalized emotive perceptions of normative civility, projecting it as a rationalized whiteness. Contestations within southern secularism pitted the feelings of those who experienced the brute force of racial segregation against the feelings of those who swung its gavel and walked away. White progressives with a heavy hand steeled their facial expressions, framing their feelings as reasonable while reframing the feelings of those who had been struck by their anonymous blows, those who dared disagree with them, as irrational. In southern secularism, they excluded any disagreeable "counterpublics," particularly those of African Americans, from their public sphere by charging them with the civil violation of emotional intoxication. They could issue that charge at any time under the name of civic protection. Thus, the so-called "rational" exercises of public authority in Siler City, particularly in its law and commerce, hinged on restraining feelings of those associated with honor, respect, and submission.

54. Commonsense views of religion as essentially different from secularity have permeated scholarly distinctions. Samuel S. Hill considered it likely that as southerners became "modern men" they would become less swayed by the proposition of a heaven and a hell and "they may reject a God who is represented as not free to accept men until some need of his own has been satisfied; or they may take the road of avowed secularism." The assumption offered in that assessment is that the road to modernity leads away from religious convictions and that secularism facilitates religious decline. Samuel S. Hill, *Southern Churches in Crisis Revisited* (Tuscaloosa: University of Alabama Press, 1999), 196. Christine Heyrman writes in plain terms that, "Baptists were obliged to work at secular occupations as well as preach." That statement assumes commonsense knowledge that preaching is not a secular occupation. Christine Leigh Heyrman, *Southern Cross: The Beginnings of the Bible Belt* (Chapel Hill: University of North Carolina Press, 1998), 288. Neither of these assessments necessarily makes a theoretical claim regarding secularization

or secularism. Rather, they demonstrate the pervasive notion that southern evangelicalism is easily recognizable, in its beliefs and its practices, as essentially religious and not secular.

55. My approach replicates Durkheim's claim that social organizations, as the groupings of like kind, or genus, begin with public display. In the "panorama of collective life" or "spectacle of collective life," as the phrase reads in two different translations, Durkheim found the "indispensable model" for the "idea of genus." Collective life, then, is a site to observe the formation of categorical schemes and classification systems premised on distinctions between the sacred and the profane. Durkheim contended that the "dramatic performance" of religion initiated those schemes and systems. Émile Durkheim, *The Elementary Forms of Religious Life*, trans. Karen E. Fields (New York: The Free Press, 1995), 148, 376. Durkheim, *The Elementary Forms of Religious Life*, trans. Carol Cosman, 114. That insight can be applied to the study of secularism, which begins with the dramatic performance of religion. But as I noted earlier, I jettison Durkheim's idea that religion is unique in its ability to construct moral communities, or that religion contains within itself an essence (the idea of society) that can pass between "pure" and "impure" forms of the sacred without changing its nature. Alexander T. Riley, " 'Renegade Durkheimianism' and the Transgressive Left Sacred," in *The Cambridge Companion to Durkheim*, ed. Jeffrey C. Alexander and Philip Daniel Smith (Cambridge: Cambridge University Press, 2005), 296. Secularism, I argue, does not reveal an impartial religious essence in its attempts to form collectivities such as nation-states or sporting nations, like the "Gator Nation," a reference to the collegiate collectivity of the University of Florida, whose identity is based in the totemic rites of Southeastern Conference football performed in "The Swamp," even as that identity, branded and marketed with a reptilian logo, encompasses the broader academic reputation of the university as a whole. Scholars who use the categories of "civil religion" and "quasi-religion" to describe the shared rituals of patriotic pomp or stadium fever perpetuate that Durkheimian premise that the secular may possess like-abilities (or like-essence), but never the same-ability (or same-essence) as religion. For the purposes of this study, I do not use that configuration of a continuum of religion to secularity, which positions secular rites with social power along its linear scale using those labels of "civil" or "quasi." The notion of secular mimicry is an intellectual device for dealing with the uncomfortable notion that religion is not unique and there are other social sources, which secularism proliferates, for the formation of moral communities. Secularism, though, makes religion in its sightings of it as recognizable performances. And there is nothing (or nothingness) beyond what is made. Within that void we project meanings that we consider essential. To this point, I reiterate Catherine Bell's criticism of performance studies. Ritual actions performed in secular sites do not reveal a preexisting behavioral script written within religion. Catherine Bell, "Performance," in *Critical Terms for the Religious Studies*, ed. by Mark C. Taylor (Chicago: University of Chicago Press, 1998),

205–224. Echoing Bell, I do not use *spectacle* to designate a "specious form of the sacred," as Guy Debord applied the term. See Guy Debord, *Society of the Spectacle*, trans. Donald Nicholson-Smith (New York: Zone Books, 1994 [1967]), 20. See also Jonathan Crary, *Suspensions of Perception: Attention, Spectacle, and Modern Culture* (Cambridge, MA: MIT Press, 1999), 184. Rather, I use the term *spectacle* to describe publicly observable ritual performances, such as Fourth of July parades or Good Friday processions, which include visual displays—the material objects and bodily movements that can be seen, such as flags, crosses, clowns, and soldiers—and illocutionary acts, meaning the production of statements made by participants and performers that can be heard or read, such as speeches delivered by politicians or preachers, descriptions of the Stations of the Cross recited by a priest, or the words of Christ spoken from the cross. Further, I use the phrase *illocutionary act* to gesture toward the notion that public speech acts that are part of observable ritual performances "do things" beyond merely conveying ideas or meanings. They too make, rather than solely reveal. Catherine Bell, *Ritual: Perspectives and Dimensions* (Oxford: Oxford University Press, 2009), 69. Categorical distinctions between the religious and the secular are made in the spectacle of collective life. The secular spectacle, then, is the sighting of religion as an observable performance that positions both the religious and the secular relationally as things set apart. That is its locative function.

56. Michel Foucault, "The Subject and Power," in *Michel Foucault: Beyond Structuralism and Hermeneutics*, ed. Huber L. Dreyfus and Paul Rabinow (Chicago: University of Chicago Press, 1982), 208.

57. Honi Fern Haber has argued that Foucault's conception of the self that is at war with its own values, of the self as "sub-individuals," makes it impossible to "admit consensus and community." Honi Fern Haber, *Beyond Postmodern Politics: Lyotard, Rorty, Foucault* (New York: Routledge, 1994), 105. I read Foucault not to comment on those politics, but to claim that striving for consensus entails social violence, seen and unseen. Southern progressives regulated public spaces in such a way that they made latent within them the present absence of what Foucault described as "heterotopia," or spatial otherness, by the very process of purifying the space of its otherness. Blacks were always present within "white-only" spaces even in their silent absence, even as whites excluded them, because the very definitional distinction of that spatial difference depended on the proximal distance of performative blackness. On striated space, see Gilles Deleuze and Félix Guattari, A Thousand Plateaus: Capitalism and Schizophrenia, trans. Brian Massumi (Minneapolis and London: University of Minnesota Press, 1987), xiii, 370.

58. *Mount Airy Times*, July 5, 1900.

59. This book contributes to interdisciplinary conversations on the social construction of whiteness for the study of American religions. With notable exceptions, American religious historians have neglected the construction and maintenance of whiteness in their discussions of racial difference. For a survey of studies of

whiteness in relation to studies of religion, see Judith Weisenfeld, "Forum on 'Whiteness' and American Religion," *Religion and American Culture 19* (Winter 2009), 27–35. This disciplinary trend, in part, reflects an overarching presumption in public racial discourse that whiteness is a taken-for-granted "fact" against which all racial and ethnic difference is defined. Richard Dyer has argued that, "As long as race is something only applied to non-white peoples, as long as white people are not racially seen and named, they/we function as a human norm. Other people are raced, we are just people." Richard Dyer, *White* (London: Routledge, 1997), 4.

60. In Siler City, most white Protestants have taken "being white" for granted, without question and without defense. But that racial difference required ritual repetition. There, as in other southern towns, spatial order was predicated on a racial essence, even though its boundary markers were never clearly manifested. Those boundaries demanded constant upkeep and increasingly complex rules for bodily interaction. In the segregated South, biological explanations of racial and gendered differences were ideological justifications of social order. But contrary to prevailing opinion, social difference was not natural law. Identity, difference, and status were never given facts. As Evelyn Brooks Higginbotham has proposed, "the recognition of racial distinctions emanates from and adapts to multiple uses of power in society," and a "metalanguage of race" masks the "construction and representation of other social and power relations." Evelyn Brooks Higginbotham, "African-American Women's History and the Metalanguage of Race," *Signs* 17 (Winter 1992): 252, 253. Racial identities, then, are social propositions, contingent on the persistent performance of the "structuring structures of everyday practice." Pierre Bourdieu, *The Logic of Practice* (Palo Alto, CA: Stanford University Press, 1990), 52–57. My understanding of practice also has been influenced by the work of Michel De Certeau. See Michel De Certeau, *The Practice of Everyday Life* (Berkeley: University of California Press, 1984). For a discussion of theories of practice, including Bourdieu and De Certeau, as they relate to the study of American religious history, see Laurie F. Maffly-Kipp, Leigh E. Schmidt, and Mark Valeri, eds., *Practicing Protestants: Histories of Christian Life in America, 1630–1965* (Baltimore, MD: The Johns Hopkins University Press, 2006).

61. Amy Robinson, "Forms of Appearance of Value: Homer Plessy and the Politics of Privacy," in *Performance and Cultural Politics*, ed. Elin Diamond (New York: Routledge, 1996), 237–262.

62. Resident A, Phone interview with the author, June 28, 2011.

63. In the Mississippi Delta during the early twentieth century, Mexican and Mexican American laborers were classified for census records using a racial binary according to their domestic associations with blacks or whites. Julie M. Weise, "Mexican Nationalisms, Southern Racisms: Mexicans and Mexican Americans in the U.S. South, 1908–1939," *American Quarterly* 60 (September 2008): 749–777.

64. African Americans, particularly African Methodist Episcopal and African Methodist Episcopal Zion missionaries to the South, also expressed concerns

about "excessive emotionalism." William E. Montgomery, *Under Their Own Vine and Fig Tree: The African-American Church in the South, 1865–1900* (Baton Rouge: Louisiana State University Press, 1993), 84. Whites leveraged such concern to their advantage, citing it as another reason why they should control civic life and regulate public commerce. For a discussion of the manner in which black business confounded white perceptions, see Walter B. Weare, *Black Business in the New South: A Social History of the North Carolina Mutual Life Insurance Company* (Urbana: University of Illinois Press, 1973), 180–181.

65. Paul Harvey has argued that southern whites were fearful of the ability of blacks to use their own mechanisms against them. He describes such a fear in relation to African American configurations of a white Jesus as what Edward Blum phrased a "trickster of the trinity, able to enter the world of whiteness, defy it, and sometimes dismantle it." Harvey explains that in the antebellum South, "Slaves thus embraced a Jesus that the whites around them feared and tried to repress, for Jesus's own life and message were a trickster tale of how the powerless might overcome the powerful through parable and poetry." Paul Harvey, *Moses, Jesus, and the Trickster in the Evangelical South* (Athens: University of Georgia Press, 2012), 36.

66. On the notion of "passing back," see Tracy Fessenden, "The Sisters of the Holy Family and the Veil of Race," *Religion and American Culture: A Journal of Interpretation* 10 (Summer 2000): 209.

67. Judith Weisenfeld has argued that, "One of the fictions that invests whiteness with its social power and its sense of immutability is white Americans' security in their own racial identity and their belief, or at least hope, that they can easily recognize those who are not white." Judith Weisenfeld, *Hollywood Be Thy Name: African American Religion in American Film, 1929–1949* (Berkeley: University of California Press, 2007), 212.

68. I am influenced by Victor Turner's classical description of "liminal entities" as "neither here nor there" or as "betwixt and between the positions assigned and arrayed by law, custom, convention, and ceremonial." In brief moments, southerners conflated secular and religious differences as liminal entities, as betwixt and between the designations made by law, custom, and ceremony. Yet there was seldom, contrary to Turner, a sense of *communitas* in those moments. They were never free of structural mechanisms that upheld distinctions of categorical difference. Rather, they reinforced the impossibility of such conflation, even as they conflated them. This difference was evidenced in the mock weddings sponsored by white Protestant churches, which I discuss in Chapter Two. Turner notes that liminality was frequently likened to bisexuality. But when young southern men dressed as young southern women to be married, they did not testify to that experience in those terms. That ritual performance did not include any opportunity to share private feelings. Instead, it offered a spectacle intended to humor the audience and invite them to laugh at what they considered the impossibility of the sight. Thus, the liminal conflation offered a structural, rather than anti-structural, statement on the proper

divisions of gendered binaries. Victor W. Turner, *The Ritual Process: Structure and Anti-Structure* (Chicago: Aldine Publishing Company, 1995), 95.

69. Within the context of North Carolina, following the disenfranchisement campaigns at the end of the nineteenth century, John Haley writes, "The political terrain had shifted dramatically. Now a 'progressive' was a white supremacist who favored black disenfranchisement and even minimal public support for black schools; a conservative was a white supremacist who favored black disenfranchisement but did not believe public funds should support black schools." John Haley, "Race, Rhetoric, and Revolution," in *Democracy Betrayed: The Wilmington Race Riot of 1898 and Its Legacy*, ed. David S. Cecelski and Timothy B. Tyson (Chapel Hill: University of North Carolina Press, 1998), 216–217. I discuss the disenfranchisement campaigns and their impact on Siler City in more detail in Chapter Two.

70. On this point concerning the relationship of unclean spaces to the idea of civil society, the book diverges from Durkheimian traditions that manufacture "good religion" as that which inherently generates a positive force in modern societies through its functional integration of individuals, atomized by increasingly complex divisions of labor, into more expansive moral communities. Such assumptions are recast in depictions of world polity that attempt to purify a global public sphere of "bad religion" by subjecting it, from the late twentieth century forward, to the standards of modernity born out of a rationalized Enlightenment impulse. José Casanova has argued "that only a religion which has incorporated as its own the central aspects of the Enlightenment critique of religion is in a position today to play a positive role in furthering processes of practical rationalization." José Casanova, *Public Religions in the Modern World* (Chicago: University of Chicago Press, 1994), 233. On the production of good religion, see Robert Orsi, "Snakes Alive: Resituating the Moral in the Study of Religion," in *Face of the Facts: Moral Inquiry in American Scholarship*, ed. Richard Fox and Robert Westbrook (Cambridge: Cambridge University Press, 1998), 210–211. Religion does function in so-called positive integrationist ways, as does secularism. But religion and secularism also function *at the same time* in negative exclusionary ways. As Jonthan Crary notes, Foucault argued that Durkheim did not consider the ways in which societies exclude certain persons and groups. Crary, *Suspensions of Perception*, 184. With every spatial expansion of civil society, there are related but unseen contractions of civil rights in separate or segregated spaces. There is a "dark side" of democracy, theorist Michael Mann proposes, that hides logics of coercion and cleansing underneath the ideals of freedom and equality. Michael Mann, "Dark Side of Democracy: The Modern Tradition of Ethnic and Political Cleansing," *New Left Review* 235 (May/June 1999): 18–45.

71. Religious ministers like D. L. Moody blessed the white republic on their tours of the South, by accepting race-based segregation in their revivals and "praying for the Confederate dead, and by paying homage to the Lost Cause." Edward J. Blum, *Reforging the White Republic: Race, Religion, and American Nationalism, 1865–1898* (Baton Rouge: Louisiana State University Press, 2005), 15, 124.

72. Hatch writes that, "the democratization of Christianity, then, has less to do with the specifics of polity and governance and more with the incarnation of the church in popular culture." Nathan Hatch, *The Democratization of American Christianity* (New Haven, CT: Yale University Press, 1989), 9. Fessenden has claimed that "what Nathan Hatch calls the 'democratization of American Christianity' and literary historian Cathy Davidson the 'democratization of the written word' proceeded together, less toward the end of generalized equality than toward particular distributions of knowledge, mobility, and cultural authority." Fessenden, *Culture and Redemption*, 90.

73. William H. Chafe, *Civilities and Civil Rights: Greensboro, North Carolina and the Black Struggle for Freedom* (Oxford: Oxford University Press, 1981), 8.

74. In his study of Gastonia, North Carolina, Liston Pope described how mill owners gave large donations directly to churches in the 1920s and 1930s, and, in return, clergy preached a conservative message of worker obedience and restraint. Liston Pope, *Millhands and Preachers* (New Haven, CT: Yale University Press, 1942), 36–48, 143–186.

75. Mill owners and other upper-class southerners considered seersucker a "fancier" urban fabric than that woven with less-refined rural simplicity. George Calvin Waldrep, *Southern Workers and the Search for Community: Spartanburg County, South Carolina* (Urbana: University of Illinois Press, 2000), 205–206n68. Describing the travels of Fred Beal, a Communist organizer in the early twentieth century, from Charlotte to Gastonia, North Carolina, historian Glenda Gilmore writes, "If capitalism wore seersucker suits, white bucks, and panama hats in Charlotte, in Gastonia it didn't bother to dress up." Glenda Elizabeth Gilmore, *Defying Dixie: The Radical Roots of Civil Rights, 1919–1950* (New York: W. W. Norton & Company, 2008), 75.

76. Building on the work of historians David Roediger and Grace Hale, the book contributes to those conversations on race and class by examining the role of southern religion and secularism, with its heightened concern for sacred place and segregated space, in the formation of "racial class" and the spatial expression of that social difference. My attention to the formation of a "racial class" of white Protestants is indebted to Roediger, who has called for "historical studies that focus on the racism of class as well as of society." Drawing on a tradition that emerged from the work of W. E. B. Du Bois, Roediger has skillfully linked the "wages of whiteness"—a psychological wage based on phenotype that is associated with social status—with working-class racism. David R. Roediger, *The Wages of Whiteness: Race and the Making of the American Working Class* (New York: Verso, 1999), 7. In her discussion of segregated consumptive spaces in the Jim Crow South, Hale shows how social differences are expressed through spatial arrangements. Hale notes that "Segregation attempted to counter a world in which people increasingly moved beyond the local and thus the known by creating racial identity anonymously as well, through spatially grounded signifiers of black difference and white belonging.

With the color line, whites literalized the metaphor of keeping blacks 'in their place.' Whether an individual white was superior to an individual black did not matter so much in a world in which the qualities of the spaces within which cross-race contact occurred materially spelled out racial hierarchy." Grace Elizabeth Hale, *Making Whiteness: The Culture of Segregation in the South, 1890–1940* (New York: Pantheon Books, 1998), 136.

77. Donald G. Mathews, "Lynching Is Part of the Religion of Our People: Faith in the Christian South," in *Religion in the American South: Protestants and Others in History and Culture*, ed. Beth Barton Schweiger and Donald G. Mathews (Chapel Hill: University of North Carolina Press, 2004), 157.

78. The restrained body alone, as civic men said with their silence, could physically perform blackness, extract the sacred essence from its natural state, and transform it into the transcendent presence of whiteness. That racial essence was observable, according to this logic, in the religious performances of segregated churches. Citizens fit to govern, by this logic, worshipped calmly and with orderly control, while believers unfit for public service were prone to emotional outbursts.

79. On the dialogical construction of textual sources, see James P. Spradley, *The Ethnographic Interview* (Belmont, CA: Wadsworth, 1979). See also Robert M. Emerson, Rachel I. Fretz, and Linda L. Shaw, *Writing Ethnographic Fieldnotes* (Chicago: University of Chicago Press, 1995). I assume that ethnographers produce "texts" through observation and interviews. James Clifford and George Marcus refer to this process as "textualization." James Clifford and George Marcus, eds., *Writing Culture: The Poetics and Politics of Ethnography* (Berkeley: University of California Press, 1986). The meaning of this textual production, however, is not as static as Clifford and Marcus suggest, as Lila Abu-Lughod has argued. Lila Abu-Lughod, "Writing Against Culture," in *Recapturing Anthropology: Working in the Present*, ed. Richard G. Fox (Santa Fe, NM: School of American Research Press, 1991), 137–161. The dialogical encounter between ethnographer and subject is fraught with ambiguity, but no more or less than other textual productions that qualify as historical sources, for example, memoir, sermons, letters, and institutional records. In my use of oral sources, I recognize, with a number of other ethnographers, that these sources, and subsequent readings of them, "reconstruct" the past. Each reconstruction, though, is tied to collective histories, and as such is not reducible by deconstruction to isolated signifiers. For an example of this argument, see John Comaroff and Jean Comaroff's "neomodern historical anthropology." John Comaroff and Jean Comaroff, *Ethnography and the Historical Imagination* (Boulder, CO: Westview Press, 1992).

80. I conducted fieldwork and face-to-face interviews from December 2003 to April 2007. In 2011, I conducted informal phone interviews and carried out e-mail correspondence to supplement those sources. I recorded and transcribed face-to-face interviews, which all took place in Siler City, unless otherwise indicated. In-person and phone interviews ranged between a half hour to one and a half hours in length.

Phone interviews were not recorded. I took handwritten notes during those conversations. All persons I spoke with granted me permission to use their statements. When quoting statements, I have chosen to list only the names of public figures and residents who requested that I directly reference them. In some cases, I do not cite the names of interviewees because I feel that their statements may impact their relationship with other residents. In those instances, I do not use pseudonymns, since I am not using them consistently throughout the book. Instead, I cite those sources by a generic designation and letter, such as "Resident A," that corresponds to my interview records. Added to interview sources, I compiled notes from participant observation at services at Corinth AME Zion Church, First Baptist Church, First United Methodist Church, First Missionary Baptist Church, Loves Creek Baptist Church, Siler City Presbyterian Church, and St. Julia Catholic Church. I also observed three Good Friday processional performances, an Our Lady of Guadalupe celebration, and an Easter Vigil service at St. Julia Catholic Church. I attended Easter sunrise services at FBC and FUMC, a Christmas cantata at FBC, a drive-through Easter pageant, and a communion service at Rocky River Baptist Church. I also attended the Martin Luther King, Jr., annual birthday celebration and two community panels at Jordan-Matthews High School, the April tenth immigration rally downtown, the Emerson Fourth of July celebration, a historic tour of homes and businesses, and a downtown Christmas parade.

81. Examples of documents include Siler City High School annuals, public information pamphlets and literature from the Town of Siler City and local nonprofits such as The Hispanic Liaison, as well as occasional memoirs and biographies. I referenced L. L. Wren, *My Church: A History of Springfield Methodist Protestant Church—Organized in 1873* (Kathryn B. Rees Collection, Siler City, NC) and H. F. Seawell, Jr., *Sir Walter: The Earl of Chatham* (Charlotte, NC: Heritage House, 1959). I utilized the records of the four oldest congregations in Siler City: Corinth AME Zion Church (1884), First Baptist Church (1887), First Missionary Baptist Church (1919), and First United Methodist Church (1968), which resulted locally from the merger of the Methodist Episcopal Church South (1886) and the Methodist Protestant Church (1894). Wade Hampton Hadley, ed., *Church History: 1887–1980, the First United Methodist Church Siler City, North Carolina and Its Predecessors: First Methodist Episcopal Church, South 1886-1940, the Methodist Protestant Church 1894-1940, First Methodist Church, 1940-1968* (Siler City, NC: FUMC, 1978); Wade Hampton Hadley, Jr., *Historical Buildings of the Central Business District, Siler City, North Carolina* (Pittsboro, NC: Chatham County Historical Association, 1996); and Murray M. Andrew, *First Baptist Church 1889–1989* (Winston-Salem, NC: Hunter Publishing Company, 1989).

82. Although I affirm a methodological shift "from text to territory," I maintain that the importance of texts is not lost. Rather, there is a heightened awareness of the conditions and locality of textual production. For a survey of the spatial turn "from text to territory" in religious studies, see Thomas A. Tweed, "On Moving

Across: Translocative Religion and the Interpreter's Position," *Journal of the American Academy of Religion* 70 (June 2002), 253–277. Every text comes from somewhere, even as it is carries within itself an infinite regression of beginnings. See Michel Foucault, *The Archeology of Knowledge*, trans. A. M. Sheridan Smith (New York: Pantheon Books, 1972).

83. When I first visited the *Chatham News* office in 2006, I was escorted to the back to the printing area, where the original print issues from 1961, bound with large hard covers, were opened on a long wooden table. The issues that would have covered the Fourth of July events were missing. But I did find in a September issue of that year a story on Tod Edwards with the quote, "For the past 66 years the Edwards Jewelry Store in Siler City was proof that whites and Negro people can live side by side without hatred and violence and with respect for each other." *Chatham News*, September 21, 1961.

84. Wade Hadley used the archival collection of the *Chatham News* for his history of Siler City and his coauthored history of Chatham County. Hadley, *Town of Siler City*. Wade Hampton Hadley, Doris Goerch Horton, and Nell Craig Strowd, *Chatham County, 1771–1971* (Durham, NC: Moore Publishing Company, 1976). As part of the county bicentennial celebration, North Carolina governor Robert (Bob) Scott was given a "complimentary copy of 'Chatham County, 1771–1971,' the recently published history book of the county." *Chatham Record,* July 1, 1971, 6. In both his county and local history, Hadley never mentioned any evidence of racial conflict or contestation. Yet, as I discuss in Chapter Two, the *Grit*, which he cites, described instances of blackface performances in Fourth of July parades in the early twentieth century. Hadley does not mention those. Nor did he write about the public events that followed the shooting of Melvin White in 1962, which the *Chatham News* covered.

85. Hadley, *The Town of Siler City*, 26–27.

86. The printed photographs of parade participation helped me confirm the racial integration of local bands and parade floats during the 1970s, which I discuss in more detail in Chapter Four. It is important to note that I employ a flawed methodology in my interpretation of visual sources. By categorizing persons in the newspaper photographs by the appearance of phenotype, rather than by their self-identification or the classification of other residents, I risk applying an essentializing standard of race. But that was, I feel, unavoidable, since I was not able to copy the photographs and show them to residents. Even if I could have done that, though, it would not have resolved the methodological truism that I observe and code phenotype in my use of visual sources and in my techniques of participant observation. Using historical and ethnographic methods to locate, define, and interpret sources in order to study social constructions of race, I may unwittingly reproduce the very essence I work to deconstruct. This is a dilemma, it seems to me, without any resolution other than silence. In this book, I try to interrupt that silence by speaking as I am able. In doing so, I take that risk.

87. Each one of these themes, for example, appears in Charles Taylor, *A Secular Age*.

88. "Incorporation," *Oxford English Dictionary* (New York: Oxford University Press, 1989).

89. Wilson, *Baptized in Blood*, ix, x.

90. William H. Chafe, *Civilities and Civil Rights: Greensboro, North Carolina, and the Black Struggle for Freedom* (Oxford: Oxford University Press, 1981), 8.

91. Ibid.

92. The intellectual position that religious and racial identities are socially constructed runs counter to the beliefs of many of the Baptists and Methodists I interviewed. By default, humanist inquiry is a dangerous and potentially subversive enterprise. While I try to let persons speak in their terms, using quotes to represent their interpretation, I cannot help but reconfigure their "voice" in my interpretations. I recognize this problem, though I can never be fully aware of its reach. I do not claim to collect narrative accounts and chronicle them for the reader. Rather, I provide a theoretical interpretation based on what I heard persons in Siler City say, what I saw them do, and what I read about in articles, newspapers, and other printed sources.

CHAPTER I

1. Atticus G. Haygood, "The New South: Gratitude, Amendment, Hope. Thanksgiving Sermon for November 25, 1880" (Oxford, GA: n.p., 1880), 16.

2. Hadley, *The Town of Siler City*, 50. It is important to note that Hadley wrote the only local history of Siler City, and his work is a valuable reference; his own personal reflections on town life are especially useful. However, Hadley chronicles names and events in the town's history without providing a historical narrative or any discussion of race. In this chapter, I attempt to organize churches, businesses, and residents into a coherent narrative structure that takes into consideration the social construction of racial difference.

3. Observers of the American South tend to view the relationship between southern religion and industrial development as antagonistic and cite that relational caricature as a marker of difference between southern evangelicalism and northern liberalism. I discuss those historiographical accounts in more detail in an article on indoor baptisteries in the American South. See Chad E. Seales, "An Old Love for New Things: Southern Baptists and the Modern Technology of Indoor Baptisteries," *Journal of Southern Religion* 13 (2001), np.

4. Haygood, "The New South," 12.

5. These antebellum legacies may include what Jonathan Daniel Wells has described as the development of a discernible middle class in the Old South. Jonathan Daniel Wells, *The Origins of the Southern Middle Class, 1860–1861* (Chapel Hill: University of North Carolina Press, 2004). Beth Barton Schweiger has argued that Wells overstates the influence of northern middle-class culture on its southern counterpart,

as well as the perceived antagonism between industry and agriculture, urban and rural. Beth Barton Schweiger, "Review of *The Origins of the Middles Class 1860–1861* by Jonathan Daniel Wells," *Arkansas Historical Quarterly 64* (Winter 2005): 442–445. Still, Wells makes an important point concerning the economic opportunities for merchants and ship owners—opportunities generated by institutional slavery. Following the end of slavery and the acceleration of industrialization, those opportunities for upward mobility multiplied in the New South. But the expanding middle class in the early-twentieth-century South was not always the economic or cultural descendant of the antebellum middle class. Although Wells argues that the middle class in the New South was not new at all, it really was "new" in places like Siler City. Members of the middle class in Siler City were often either from the elite or lower agrarian classes. They were plantation masters-turned-mill owners, such as the Hadley family, or farmers-turned-merchants, such as Daniel G. Fox, who was listed as a farmer in the 1880 census and who opened a general merchandise store in Siler City in 1897. Tenth Census of the United Sates, 1880: Chatham County, North Carolina, Population Schedule, National Archives, Washington D.C.; Hadley, *The Town of Siler City*, 3.

6. John Randolph Lane, "Address at Gettysburg," July 5, 1903, John Randolph Lane Papers, #411, Southern Historical Collection, Manuscripts Department, Wilson Library, University of North Carolina at Chapel Hill.

7. For a discussion of the role of head of household on antebellum plantations and its impact on urban society, see Edward J. Cashin, "Paternalism in Augusta: The Impact of the Plantation Ethic upon an Urban Society," in *Paternalism in a Southern City: Race, Religion, and Gender in Augusta, Georgia*, ed. Edward J. Cashin and Glenn T. Eskew (Athens: University of Georgia Press, 2001), 19. For a discussion of the role of head of household in the paternalistic social order of a mill town, see Leeann Whites, "Paternalism and Protest in Augusta's Cotton Mills: What's Gender Got to Do with It?" in *Paternalism in a Southern City*, 77.

8. Wade Hampton Hadley, Jr., born 1910, is listed as the grandson of F. Mint Hadley. Fourteenth Census of the United States, 1920: Chatham County, Population Schedule. F. M. Hadley's full name was Franklin Minter Hadley, 1855–1940. Grave marker: Chatham County North Carolina Cemeteries, http://cemeterycensus.com/nc/chat/cem196.html. The 1860 census lists Minter Hadley, born approximately 1856, as the son of Wm. P. Hadley, born about 1810, and residing in Middle Division, Chatham, North Carolina. Eighth Census of the United States, 1860: Chatham County, Population Schedule. In the 1960 US Federal Census Slave Schedules, Wm. P. Hadley is listed as the owner of two slaves, a male, age 19, and a female, age 12. Eighth Census of the United States, 1860: Chatham County, Slave Schedule. On the National Register of Historic Places, William P. Hadley is listed as a former owner of the Hadley House and Grist Mill, northwest of Pittsboro, North Carolina, on current State Road 2165. The site includes 462 acres and three buildings. National Register of Historic Places, www.nationalregisterofhistoricalplaces.com/NC/Chatham/vacant.html.

9. Hadley, *Town of Siler City*, 4. F. M. Hadley also helped organize the Chatham Bank and served as its president for twenty years. Judith Williams, producer, *A Photographic Journey of a Chatham Native Son: Wade Hampton Hadley, Jr., December 23, 1909–April 7, 2002*. VHS tape prepared for the funeral services of Wade Hampton Hadley, Jr., 2002, copy held at First United Methodist Church, Siler City.

10. As economic classes further solidified, a group of white elites formed an Episcopal congregation to further distinguish themselves from upwardly mobile Methodists and Baptists. In 1951, white businessmen and mill owners organized the Church of the Holy Cross, which first met at the Hadley-Peoples Manufacturing Company. Two years later, they relocated the Saint Mark's Episcopal Church building from Gulf, North Carolina, where it had been abandoned, to Siler City, about sixteen miles away. Constructed in 1847, the church was a material marker of antebellum prestige. It originally served as the private chapel on the plantation of John Haughton and included a slave gallery. During the height of their public power, during the period of Establishment in the 1950s and 1960s, the church building symbolized white elite social status. As that power declined in the 1970s, so did the congregation. In 1979, the chapel was moved to Raleigh, North Carolina, where it now stands in the historic district. Hadley, *The Town of Siler City*, 15.

11. Joel Williamson, *The Crucible of Race: Black/White Relations in the American South Since Emancipation* (New York: Oxford University Press, 1984), 43.

12. Two key works by Don Mathews and Christine Heyrman provide wonderful surveys of the Old South. See Donald G. Mathews, *Religion in the Old South* (Chicago: University of Chicago Press, 1977) and Christine Leigh Heyrman, *Southern Cross: The Beginnings of the Bible Belt* (Chapel Hill: University of North Carolina Press, 1998). But less is known about religion in the New South. For a notable exception, see Paul Harvey, *Redeeming the South: Religious Cultures and Racial Identities among Southern Baptists, 1865–1925* (Chapel Hill: University of North Carolina Press, 1997).

13. Hadley, *The Town of Siler City*, 1; M. M. Fox, "Historical Sketch of Siler City Methodist Church." n.d., Kathryn B. Rees Collection, Wren Memorial Library, Siler City, North Carolina, hereinafter cited as Rees Collection. For a detailed history of the Siler family, see A. O. Siler, *The Siler Family: A Compilation of Biographical and Historical Sketches Relating to the Descendants of Plikard Dederic and Elizabeth Siler, with Genealogical Chart* (A. O. Siler: Marfork, Raleigh County, WV, 1922).

14. Prior to incorporation, the town was known as Matthews Crossroads, named after William W. Matthews, the man who bought the Siler house and 140 acres of land in 1842. Hadley, *The Town of Siler City*, 1.

15. Hadley, *The Town of Siler City*, 1, 2, 9; fieldnotes, December 15, 2003.

16. Members of the Siler family would later join the Springfield Methodist Church, toward the end of the nineteenth century. L. L. Wren, "My Church: A History of Springfield

Methodist Protestant Church, Organized in 1873." n.d., p. 1, Rees Collection. The term "Separate Baptists" generally refers to a subset of evangelical Protestants that trace their organizational roots to the proselytizing work of individuals influenced by the revivals of George Whitefield in the eighteenth century. Shubal Stearns was one of those individuals and historians note his efforts, along with Daniel Marshall's, to organize Sandy Creek Baptist Church in 1755 as a catalyst for the spread of Separate Baptists in the American South. Separate Baptists also are often grouped with "New Lights," who broke away from "Old Light" Congregationalists in New England. New Lights were distinguished by their vibrant evangelical spirit, their experiential emphasis on mood over doctrine, and their theological loosening of Calvinist strictures. See John R. Woodard, "North Carolina," in Samuel S. Hill, ed., *Religion in the Southern States: A Historical Study* (Macon, GA: Mercer University Press, 1983), 220. See also Samuel S. Hill, Charles H. Lippy, and Charles Reagan Wilson, eds., *Encyclopedia of Religion in the South* (Macon, GA: Mercer University Press, 2005), 717, 742, 762.

17. The Sandy Creek Baptist Association was founded in 1758. See George W. Purefoy, *A History of the Sandy Creek Baptist Association: From Its Organization in A.D. 1758 to A.D. 1858* (New York: Sheldon and Co., 1859); and Author unknown, *Rocky River Baptist Church, 1756–1996* (Siler City, NC: Rocky River Baptist Church, 1996, unpaginated). On the influence of Shubal Stearns and Separate Baptists in the South, see Rhys Isaac, *The Transformation of Virginia, 1780–1790* (New York: W.W. Norton, 1852), 159. See also Harvey, *Redeeming the South,* 5.

18. M. M. Fox, "Historical Sketch of Siler City Methodist Church," 1.

19. West End Methodist Church was organized with help from First Methodist Episcopal Church members.

20. Baptists have the oldest roots in the area, but Methodists who moved to Siler City quickly established themselves within the dominant business class. In the New South, Methodists did not necessarily make better business leaders than Baptists, or for that matter, Presbyterians or Episcopalians. The emergence of a managerial class in a particular town was shaped by its own local history. In Siler City, at least, particular characteristics of Methodist theology—an expectation of self-perfection through disciplined method and a relatively structured polity that institutionalized authority more efficiently than Baptist churches—were better suited for business and financial management.

21. By 1920, there were at least five churches in the downtown area, and as far as I can tell they all chimed their bells. I found no evidence to suggest otherwise. Hadley, though, counted only four. Those he remembered were probably white congregations: three Methodist churches and First Baptist Church. But he never mentions exactly which churches he counted, so it is difficult to know for sure.

22. For an account of frontier liminality followed by the emergence of a local Protestant establishment, see Thomas A. Tweed, "An Emerging Protestant Establishment: Religious Affiliation and Public Power on the Urban Frontier in Miami, 1896–1904," *Church History* 64 (September 1995), 412–437.

23. Sunday school at FBC–Siler City was called the Philathea for women and Baraca class for men, at least during the early 1900s. Murray M. Andrew, *First Baptist Church of Siler City, North Carolina, May 17, 1889–May 17, 1989* (Winston-Salem, North Carolina: Hunter Publishing Company, 1989), 13–14.

24. Andrew, *First Baptist Church of Siler City*, 11.

25. Wren, "My Church," 12.

26. Annie Fox, "The Story and History of First Baptist Church," in *First Baptist Church, 75th Anniversary, 1919–1994* (history compiled by and in the collection of the First Baptist Church Siler City, Martin Luther King Jr. Blvd., n.d.), unpaginated. I obtained a copy of this document from the manager of the Town of Siler City. The original name of the congregation was First Baptist Church. The name was later changed to North Sixth Avenue. But, First Baptist Church then changed back to First Baptist Church, after North Sixth Avenue was renamed Martin Luther King Jr. Blvd. in 1991. In 2005, the church marquee read "First Missionary Baptist Church."

27. Fox, "Historical Sketch of Siler City Methodist Church," 2.

28. Fox, "The Story and History of First Baptist Church." Despite the difference in spelling, Annie Fox is referring to the same L. L. Wren mentioned above. Both the Wren and Wrenn families were influential Methodists in Siler City.

29. Hadley, *The Town of Siler City*, 2.

30. Ibid., 29.

31. Ibid., 6, 39.

32. Ibid. Twelfth Census of the United States, 1900: Chatham County, Population Schedule. According to the 1920 U.S. Census, none of the 3,639 residents of Matthews Township were foreign born. Of the 1,057 blacks listed, none were born outside of North Carolina, fifteen of the 2,565 whites listed were born outside the state: one from Mississippi, one from Pennsylvania, two from New Jersey, three from Kentucky, one from Indiana, one from Iowa, four from Virginia, one from New York, and one from Texas. Fourteenth Census of the United States, 1920: Chatham County, Population Schedule.

33. Jacquelyn Dowd Hall, James Leloudis, Robert Korstad, Mary Murphy, Lu Ann Jones, and Christopher B. Daly, *Like a Family: The Making of a Southern Cotton Mill World* (Chapel Hill: University of North Carolina Press, 1987), 127.

34. In the early twentieth century, agrarian patterns of plantations and family farms gave way to factory towns with denser populations. Although many towns like Siler City never became large-scale cities, the division of religious and economic labor that developed in such places resembled, on a smaller scale, more metropolitan counterparts. Such divisions distinguished those industrialized communities from surrounding rural counterparts. Pittsboro, founded in 1787 and one of North Carolina's oldest towns, is also located in Chatham County. After 1887, though, Siler City quickly grew to overtake Pittsboro in size. Another century later, Siler City remains the largest town in one of the fastest-growing counties in North

Carolina. Twenty-Second Census of the United States, 2000: Chatham County, Population Schedule.

35. C. Vann Woodward, *Origins of the New South, 1877–1913* (Baton Rouge: Louisiana State University Press, 1951), 139, 294.

36. Don H. Doyle, *New Men, New Cities, New South: Atlanta, Charleston, Mobile, 1860–1910* (Chapel Hill: University of North Carolina Press, 1990), 34.

37. While conducting fieldwork in Siler City, I saw chickens running around dusty yards of smaller homes and trailers on the outskirts of town, but never in the middle-class, country club neighborhood.

38. Hadley, *The Town of Siler City*, 50.

39. Ibid., 44.

40. Ibid., 23.

41. *Siler City Grit*, April 8, 1914. In 1976, Siler City resident John W. Snipes told University of North Carolina interviewer Brent Glass that Chatham County was "the only county in the world that I've ever heard tell of (and the records bear this out) that ever shipped a solid carload of rabbit to New York. Chatham rabbits; we were known for Chatham rabbits. They caught them in hollows and boxes. And you could go in New York seventy-five years ago and call for Chatham rabbit on the menu in New York City [Laughter]." Oral History Interview with John W. Snipes, September 20, 1976. Interview H-0098-1. Southern Oral History Program Collection (#4007) in the Southern Oral History Program Collection, Southern Historical Collection, Wilson Library, University of North Carolina at Chapel Hill.

42. The term *grit*, used for the local newspaper and a popular southern dish, grits, called "Georgia ice cream" around Atlanta, was also a racial reference to the general white population in the South. As Joel Williamson describes, conservative elites placed blame for resistance to social change on white masses, referred to as "The Grits." According to this "Grit" thesis, democracy in the South ran counter to freedom of thought and speech, and if masses would listen to elites then the south would be a happier racial place. Joel Williamson, *The Crucible of Race: Black/White Relations in the American South since Emancipation* (New York: Oxford University Press, 1984), 292.

43. *Siler City Grit*, October 6, 1909.

44. On the cultural influence of chickens in the New South, focusing on the rise of Chick-fil-A in suburban life, see Darren E. Grem, "The Marketplace Missions of S. Truett Cathy and Chick-fil-A," in *Sunbelt Rising: The Politics of Place, Space, and Region*, ed. Michelle Nickerson and Darren Dochuk (Philadelphia: University of Pennsylvania Press, 2011), 293–315.

45. Thirteenth Census of the United States, 1910: Chatham County, Population Schedule; *Siler City Grit,* July 24, 1912.

46. In his study of Greensboro, North Carolina, William Chafe found that patterns of racism and segregation were directly related to the town's industrialization and emergence as a New South city. He observed, "In 1880, on seven of nineteen streets,

black and white households existed side by side.... Yet by 1900, Greensboro had rejected these potentially egalitarian patterns and had moved sharply toward a system of rigid racial and economic discrimination." Even though Greensboro, organized in 1808, is older than Siler City, it, too, was transformed by industrialization in a brief time. Greensboro's major growth was concurrent with Siler City in the late nineteenth century, but was accomplished on a larger scale. Chafe notes that, "between 1880 and 1900 Greensboro's population increased fivefold, from 2000 to 10,000. The three decades after the turn of the century witnessed an even more spectacular population boom, with the city growing to 53,000 residents by 1930, almost a third of them black." William H. Chafe, *Civilities and Civil Rights: Greensboro, North Carolina, and the Black Struggle for Freedom* (Oxford: Oxford University Press, 1981), 14–16.

47. Douglas Egerton has argued that Denmark Vesey organized a plot, not a revolt. Douglas R. Egerton, *He Shall Go Out Free: The Lives of Denmark Vesey* (Lanham, MD: Rowman & Littlefield, 2004), xiv.

48. Donald Mathews noted the significance of bodily proximity for the policing of social norms in Protestant congregations: "The fact the every Virginian, for example, was required by law to attend church services each week was designed to reinforce the moral policing of the church-wardens by bringing people together within sight and touch of each other to hear the moral precepts of the community explained." Mathews, *Religion in the Old South*, 4.

49. Visit to Rocky River Baptist Church cemetery, January 29, 2006. On contact between blacks and whites in religious spaces in the Old South, see Donald G. Mathews, *Religion in the Old South* (Chicago: University of Chicago Press, 1977); John B. Boles, *The Irony of Southern Religion* (New York: P. Lang, 1994); Sylvia R. Frey and Betty Wood, *Come Shouting to Zion: African American Protestantism in the American South and British Caribbean to 1830* (Chapel Hill: University of North Carolina Press, 1998); and H. Richard Niebuhr, *The Social Sources of Denominationalism* (Gloucester, MA: Peter Smith, 1987), 236–263. On cultural contact, see Mechal Sobel, *The World They Made Together: Black and White Values in Eighteenth-Century Virginia* (Princeton, NJ: Princeton University Press, 1987).

50. Hadley, *The Town of Siler City*, 50–51.

51. Ibid., 53.

52. Ibid., 16, 49–51.

53. Building on the work of Whitney Cross, Paul Johnson argues that revivals occur most often in manufacturing towns. Paul E. Johnson, *A Shopkeeper's Millennium: Society and Revivals in Rochester, New York, 1815–1837* (New York: Hill and Wang, 1978); Whitney R. Cross, *The Burned–Over District: The Social and Intellectual History of Enthusiastic Religion in Western New York, 1800–1850* (New York: Harper and Row, 1965 [1950]).

54. Wren, "My Church," 7; E. B. Craven, entry on June 22, 1912. Quarterly Conference Records, First Methodist Episcopal Church, South, Siler City, North Carolina.

55. This revival, held on September 8, 1915, added close to one hundred new local church members. *Siler City Grit*, September 1915, cited in Hadley, *The Town of Siler City*, 48. The phrase "iceberg church members" is evangelical vernacular for those who attend services and profess belief, but do not demonstrate what other members consider a sufficient amount of emotional expression through either personal testimony or proselytizing efforts. It is another way of saying that their hearts have "grown cold" and therefore they are in need of revival.

56. *Siler City Grit*, October 14, 1914.

57. Daniel Sack, *Whitebread Protestants: Food and Religion in American Culture* (New York: St. Martin's Press, 2000), 33.

58. First Baptist Church of Siler City also had a Ladies Aid Society. Andrew, *First Baptist Church of Siler City*, 27.

59. Wade Hampton Hadley, *Church History: 1887–1980, the First United Methodist Church Siler City, North Carolina and Its Predecessors: First Methodist Episcopal Church, South 1886–1940, the Methodist Protestant Church 1894–1940, First Methodist Church, 1940–1968* (Siler City, NC: First United Methodist Church, 1978), 18.

60. Andrew, *First Baptist Church of Siler City*, 74.

61. Haygood, "The New South."

62. Hadley, *The Town of Siler City*, 48.

63. Ibid.

64. By the mid-twentieth century, white Protestants had sanitized their public places and private homes, making them, as they saw it, fit for good Christians. Their purification efforts, though, did not always keep out unpleasant smells that drifted into downtown from surrounding industrial farms. For all the work they put into cleaning their bodies, streets, homes, churches, and congregations, they could not keep factory filth entirely outside city limits. Depending on the winds, odors from the poultry plants sometimes drift into town, as I discovered while attending the downtown Christmas parade in 2005.

65. L. L. Wren, *A History of the Chatham Bank* (Siler City, NC: Chatham Bank, 1953).

66. Suellen Hoy, *Chasing Dirt: The American Pursuit of Cleanliness* (New York: Oxford University Press, 1996), 3–4.

67. Wren, *A History of the Chatham Bank*, 132.

68. Proverbs 18:24 (New International Version).

69. Wren, *A History of the Chatham Bank*, 132. Wren's "ten commandments" highlight the practices of pecuniary emulation (modeling a social status that is associated with monetary wealth) and conspicuous consumption (modeling a social status that is associated with material consumption) that were hallmarks of the Gilded Age. The terms *pecuniary emulation* and *conspicuous consumption* were developed by Thorstein Veblen, who emphasized a moral connection between religious discourse and economic practice. For Veblen, religion "reflects the character of economic institutions in a naïve and truthful manner." As a scholar trained to be suspicious

of any nineteenth-century talk of historical causality and social evolution, I am not fond of this language of religious reflection, especially when described as naïve and truthful. But I do find Veblen's emphasis on religion as a measure of economic institutional character methodologically useful, even if theoretically lacking. Joseph Dorfman, *Thorstein Veblen and His America* (New York: The Viking Press, 1934), 298.

70. "Pay as you go" was also a financial habit practiced by Protestant congregations. In the first half of the twentieth century, congregations like First Baptist Church in Siler City did not finance construction of new church buildings. Rather, they completed stages of their church buildings as they could afford to do so: the foundation today, the walls in a few months, the roof later, and so on. Murray M. Andrew, *First Baptist Church, 1889–1989* (Winston-Salem, NC: Hunter Publishing Company, 1989), 26.

71. "Tod Edwards, the Jeweler," *North Carolina State* magazine, February 11, 1950, 22.

72. In the Jim Crow South, though, any displays of conspicuous consumption, even those associated with this strand of pecuniary emulation, were regulated within a racially segregated social order. Historians like Grace Hale have noted how the rise of the black middle class at the turn of the century threatened southern racial order. Hale, *Making Whiteness*, 121–151. With slavery removed, and blacks able to afford the same products as whites, old markers of racial order were not as clearly defined. Enforcing Jim Crow laws, southern whites attempted to retain racial order by regulating consumptive spaces, such as stores, theaters, train cars, and neighborhoods.

73. The Siler City Farmers' Alliance Store is the oldest "surviving member of a large group of mercantile businesses started throughout the nation during the 1880's by Farmers' Alliance groups." It was organized "by a group of farmers from the surrounding area" in 1888 at Loves Creek School House, "a one-room building located on the ground of the present Loves Creek Baptist Church on Highway 64 outside [the] eastern limits of Siler City." Ruth R. Smith, *History of the Farmers' Alliance Store, Inc.* (Siler City, NC: Caviness Printing Service, Inc., 1988), unpaginated.

74. Hadley, *The Town of Siler City*, 20; *Siler City Grit*, December 18, 1924.

75. American religious historian Leigh Schmidt has proposed that the neo-Gothic architecture of Catholic and Episcopal churches in New York City influenced the development of holiday window displays in fashionable stores, particularly during the Easter and Christmas seasons. Advertisements, combined with window displays, suggest that buyers and sellers in Siler City shared similar economic habits— the "consumer rites" that Schmidt describes—with other American Protestants, further illustrating the integration of the town of Siler City into a modern economy of consumption and production. Like their northern counterparts, American Protestants developed those habits, as merchants and marketers intentionally used religious language to promote their products. In Siler City, those habits were expressed in southern style. Leigh Eric Schmidt, *Consumer Rites: The Buying and Selling of American Holidays* (Princeton, NJ: Princeton University Press, 1995), 195; *Siler City Grit*, April 8, 1914.

76. For an interpretation of modern advertising techniques and the "making of modern objects," including soda biscuits, soaps, and candles, see Kathryn E. Lofton, "Making the Modern in Religious America, 1870–1935" (PhD diss., University of North Carolina, 2005), 37–78.

77. For a historical and theoretical interpretation of the phenomenon of mass-produced authenticity, see Miles Orvell, *The Real Thing: Imitation and Authenticity in American Culture, 1880–1940* (Chapel Hill: University of North Carolina Press, 1989).

CHAPTER 2

1. George C. Underwood, *History of the Twenty-Sixth Regiment of the North Carolina Troops in the Great War, 1861–1865* (Goldsboro, NC: Nash Brothers Printers, 1901), 47.

2. Hadley, *The Town of Siler City,* 26.

3. Lillian White, "An Essay on a Distinguished Countyman," date unknown, John R. Lane Papers, 1890-1903, in Southern Historical Collection, University of North Carolina at Chapel Hill.

4. In the eyes of his admirers, Lane also demonstrated one of the highest of Christian virtues by forgiving his enemies. At a reunion of Blues and Grays, Lane met the man who shot him at Gettysburg. He responded to the Chicago barber by shaking his hand, a gesture that symbolized his resolve to let go of the "temper of war" and embrace the "gentle tones of brotherhood and peace." Lane, "Address at Gettysburg," July 5, 1903. For Lillian White, Lane took the moral high ground, imitating Jesus, who forgave his enemies, even in the face of death. Lane had been sanctified through suffering. In his attempts to reconcile with the enemy, Lane modeled the valor and heroism of the Confederate soldier that southerners like White hoped would soon "be regarded as the common heritage of the American nation." White, "An Essay on a Distinguished Countyman."

5. Lillian White is one example of the influence of white women on public spaces and collective memory in the New South. As historian Fitzhugh Brundage has pointed out, white women played an important role in shaping the memory of a Confederate past in the New South. According to Brundage, "The historical memory promulgated by white women…shaped the civic spaces of the cities and towns of the New South, now increasingly important to southern life, as well as the lessons that those spaces taught." W. Fitzhugh Brundage, "White Women and the Politics of Historical Memory in the New South, 1880–1920," in *Jumpin' Jim Crow: Southern Politics from Civil War to Civil Rights,* ed. Jane Dailey, Glenda Elizabeth Gilmore, and Bryant Simon (Princeton, NJ: Princeton University Press, 2000), 131.

6. Elizabeth Fox-Genovese and Eugene D. Genovese, "The Divine Sanction of Social Order: Religious Foundations of the Southern Slaveholders' World View," *Journal of the American Academy of Religion* 55 (Summer 1987): 211–233.

7. William Faulkner, *Absalom, Absalom* (New York: Random House [1936] 1993), 5.

8. My interpretation of the ritual performance of Fourth of July parades in twentieth-century Siler City is informed by the historical work of Susan Davis on Fourth of July parades in nineteenth-century Philadelphia. Davis argues that parades are political actions; they are "rhetorical means by which performers attempted to accomplish practical and symbolic goals." In short, parades are public dramas of communal life. Susan G. Davis, *Parades and Power: Street Theatre in Nineteenth-Century Philadelphia* (Philadelphia: Temple University Press, 1986), 5. For another interpretation of parades as sites of social disputes, see Dominic Bryan, *Orange Parades: The Politics of Ritual, Tradition, and Control* (London: Pluto Press, 2000). See also T. G. Fraser, ed., *The Irish Parading Tradition: Following the Drum* (New York: St. Martin's Press, 2000).

9. "Frederick Douglass: Independence Day Speech at Rochester," in *The American Reader: Words That Moved a Nation*, ed. Diane Ravitch (New York: HarperCollins, 2000), 207.

10. W. E. B. Du Bois, *Black Reconstruction: An Essay Toward a History of the Part Which Black Folk Played in America, 1860–1880* (New York: Russel & Russel, 1935); Leon F. Litwack, *Been in the Storm So Long: The Aftermath of Slavery* (New York: Knopf, 1979); and Eric Foner, *Reconstruction: America's Unfinished Revolution, 1863–1877* (New York: Harper & Row, 1988).

11. After the Civil War, when whites had forsaken their public Independence Day celebrations, blacks in the South annually celebrated Emancipation Day, the day that the news of freedom reached their town. For example, the US government officially announced the Emancipation Proclamation on January 1, 1863, but in a place like Hickman, Kentucky, Emancipation Day is celebrated on August 8. In Siler City, though, I could not find any evidence of an Emancipation Day, likely because there were very few slaves in the area (most were in the eastern part of the county). Hadley, *Chatham County*, 319.

12. Historian Richard Gowers describes how "in Atlanta [between 1880 and 1900], in the uncertainty over the social meaning of 'white' and 'black' after Reconstruction, different Fourth of July celebration patterns emerged whereby white Atlantans fled from the city into the surrounding resorts and the black community was drawn into the city. As Jim Crow descended, however, the 'black' Fourth was removed from the city so that urban centers could mark the 'white' Fourth and demonstrate which race would prosper in the industrial and urban future of the New South." Richard James Gowers, "Contested Celebrations: The Fourth of July and Changing National Identity in the United States" (PhD diss., University of New South Wales, 2004), 360. For additional examples, see Brian D. Page, "'Stand by the Flag': Nationalism and African-American Celebrations of the Fourth of July in Memphis, 1866–1887," *Tennessee Historical Quarterly* 58, no. 4 (1999): 284–301; Philip S. Foner, "Black Participation in the Centennial of 1876," *Phylon* 39, no. 4 (1978): 283–296. There is a long tradition of American patriotism, of proclaiming

the ideals of human rights and liberty, among African Americans. For a few examples, see the writings of Martin Delany, John Chavis, and Anna J. Cooper. Martin Robinson Delany, *The Condition, Elevation, Emigration, and Destiny of the Colored People of the United States* (New York: Arno Press, 1968); Helen Chavis Othow, *John Chavis: African American Patriot, Preacher, Teacher, and Mentor, 1763–1838* (Jefferson, NC: McFarland & Company, 2001); Charles Lemert and Esme Bhan, eds., *The Voice of Anna Julia Cooper: Including A Voice from the South and Other Important Essays, Papers, and Letters* (Lanham, MD: Rowan and Littlefield, 1998). See also Benjamin Quarles, "Antebellum Free Blacks and the 'Spirit of '76,'" *Journal of Negro History* 61, no. 3 (1976): 229–242.

13. Edward J. Blum, *Reforging the White Republic: Race, Religion, and American Nationalism, 1865–1898* (Baton Rouge: Louisiana State University Press, 2005), 149–150.

14. Noel Ignatiev, *How the Irish Became White* (New York: Routledge, 1995), 173.

15. A. H. Merritt, ed., "A Good Move," *Pittsboro Weekly*, October 27, 1887.

16. John Dollard argued that in the New South, "Caste has replaced slavery as a means of maintaining the essence of the old status order in the South." John Dollard, *Caste and Class in a Southern Town* (New York: Harper & Brothers, 1949), 62. Donald Mathews proposed that white Protestants in the New South viewed segregation as a "sacred order." Donald G. Mathews, Samuel S. Hill, Beth Barton Schweiger, and John B. Boles, "Forum: Southern Religion," *Religion and American Culture* 8 no. 2 (Summer 1998): 144–177.

17. Donald G. Mathews, *Religion in the Old South* (Chicago: University of Chicago Press, 1977), xvii.

18. Ibid.

19. Southern Protestants imagined themselves descendants of what they considered the purest of European stock, the Anglo-Saxons. When their ministers adapted theology to fit the cultural and social changes of the early twentieth century, they "stressed that the Lost Cause had been concerned, in essence, with liberty." Wilson, *Baptized in Blood*, 164. Baptist minister Victor I. Master proclaimed the southern white race champions of liberty, stating that "in America the love for freedom of this [Anglo-Saxon] race found its fullest expression, and in the South their blood has remained freest from mixture with other strains." Wilson, *Baptized in Blood*, 167. When white Protestants embraced the American flag during Siler City's Fourth of July parades, literally wrapping themselves in its colors, they did not concede regional ground. Rather, they ritually performed their sacred place. My understanding of the ritual constructions of "sacred patriotic space" is influenced by the work of Edward Linenthal. See Edward T. Linenthal, *Sacred Ground: Americans and Their Battlefields* (Urbana: University of Illinois Press, 1991). On the streets of Siler City, in full public view, they sanctified the United States flag with the blood sacrifice of their highest-ranking Christian soldier, Colonel John Randolph Lane. For a Durkheimian survey of the relationship between blood sacrifice and

the American flag, see Carolyn Marvin and David W. Ingle, *Blood Sacrifice and the Nation: Totem Rituals and the American Flag* (New York: Cambridge University Press, 1999).

20. Gregory A. Schneider, *The Way of the Cross Leads Home: The Domestication of American Methodism* (Bloomington: Indiana University Press, 1993), 167, 197–198.

21. Rhys Isaac, *The Transformation of Virginia, 1780–1790* (New York: W. W. Norton, 1982).

22. Schneider, *The Way of the Cross Leads Home*, xxv.

23. Ibid., 154.

24. Ibid., 155.

25. Prior to World War II, Fourth of July festivities in Siler City were interrupted only for sewer and water construction in 1925 and 1926, and at the onset of the Great Depression in 1933. Hadley, *The Town of Siler City*, 26–27.

26. *Siler City Grit*, July 1911.

27. "Colonel Lane of the Famous 26th North Carolina Regiment, C.S.A., Operated Mill and Store in County," in the Southern Historical Collection, University of North Carolina at Chapel Hill.

28. John Randolph Lane, "Address at Gettysburg," July 5, 1903, John R. Lane Papers, 1890–1903, in the Southern Historical Collection, University of North Carolina at Chapel Hill.

29. Lloyd Hunter argues that proponents of the Lost Cause, in terms of protecting their way of life, never really conceded defeat; that "the cultural faith was the Confederates' belief that the Lost Cause was never genuinely lost." Lloyd A. Hunter, "The Immortal Confederacy: Another Look at Lost Cause Religion," in *The Myth of the Lost Cause and Civil War History*, ed. Gary W. Gallagher and Alan T. Nolan (Bloomington: Indiana University Press, 2000), 208.

30. Lane, "Address at Gettysburg."

31. Ibid.

32. White, "An Essay on a Distinguished Countyman."

33. I did not find any other record of Lane's participation in Siler City Fourth of July parades after 1901. Lane did make dedicatory public appearances in Chatham County after his participation in the 1901 parade in Siler, and he served as chief marshal for the dedication of a Confederate monument in Pittsboro in 1907. A story reprinted in the bicentennial issue of the *Chatham News-Record* described the scene: "Col. John R. Lane...aroused the enthusiasm of the multitude, and shout after shout arose as the imposing spectacle was passing in review." Similar to his appearance in the 1901 Fourth of July parade, Lane was described as "clad in his wartime uniform, bearing evidence of fire and shell." "Confederate Monument in Pittsboro Unveiled," *Chatham News-Record*, bicentennial issue, July 1976, D5.

34. Lane lived long enough to witness the memorials that preceded his own. In his 1903 speech at Gettysburg, Lane called out to his deceased soldiers, "O, my noble comrades! You poured your life blood for a cause you loved. But you are not reckoned

among the dead. In the affectionate remembrance of your comrades you still live!"
Remembering the past in the light of the present, Lane let the dead know that living southerners moving in their "old haunts" were "baptized in the same baptism as
you." Lane, "Address at Gettysburg." Shortly after his death in 1908, a monument
was erected at Brush Creek Baptist Church cemetery, near Siler City, "to honor
[Lane's] bravery and service to the Confederacy." This memorial is still maintained
by the Colonel John Randolph Lane Society of Chatham County, see http://cha-
thamhistory.org/archiverandolph.html.

35. Hadley, *The Town of Siler City*, 25; Isaac London, "July 4th," *Siler City Grit*, July 9,
    1913; July 8, 1914; July 7, 1915.

36. According to Census data, the town population was 895 in 1910 and 1,253 in 1920.
    US Bureau of the Census, 1910 and 1920.

37. Isaac London, "July 4th," *Siler City Grit*, July 10, 1918.

38. The key period of reconciliation between the North and South after the Civil War
    was between 1900 and 1920. The rise of the Fourth of July parade in the early 1900s
    in Siler City supports in part Wilson's assessment that "after 1900 the American
    civil religion began fully functioning in the South for the first time since the Civil
    War." Wilson notes that the symbols, rituals, and myths of the Lost Cause consti-
    tuted a southern variant of the national civil religion. Yet he contends that, "the
    Southern civil religion failed after 1900 to perform a prophetic function in regard
    to the American civil religion." Charles Reagan Wilson, *Baptized in Blood: The
    Religion of the Lost Cause, 1865–1920* (Athens: University of Georgia Press, 1980),
    16, 100, 161. If that is the case, then the Fourth of July parades in Siler reconfigured
    that vision of the United States. It resembled but did not reflect what Wilson and
    other scholars have described as a coherent "American" civil religion. For a classic
    account of American civil religion, see Robert Bellah, "Civil Religion in America,"
    Daedalus 96, no. 1 (1967): 1–21. As noted in the Introduction, I prefer not to use the
    term "civil religion" because of categorical limitations and its implied consensus.
    I interpret Fourth of July parades in Siler City not as revealing a cultural consensus
    of shared symbolism, even in its regional difference, but as contested constructions
    of nationalism, which exemplify the process by which observers project meaning
    onto ritual performances and material artifacts.

39. For a historical account of the influence of Confederate tradition on the New
    South, see Gaines Foster, *Ghosts of the Confederacy: Defeat, The Lost Cause, and the
    Emergence of the New South, 1865 to 1913* (New York: Oxford University Press, 1987).

40. As Noel Ignatiev describes, Irish Catholic immigrants, most of whom were aboli-
    tionists in their home country, quickly learned that on American soil, "to enter the
    white race was a strategy to secure an advantage in a competitive society." Defining
    themselves as not black, Irish Catholics were able to collectively compete for jobs
    as an upwardly mobile class of ethnically white Americans. In an effort to elevate
    their status in an imagined white America, they strategically associated themselves
    with a pan-European identity. For example, Irish American labor unions, such as

the Longshoremen's Benevolent Society in Philadelphia, would often attach the flags of European countries to their union banners. According to Ignatiev, the 1852 Longshoremen's banner, for instance, was "decorated with flags from France, Germany, Sweden, Ireland, Denmark, Hungary, and Italy." But, as Ignatiev points out, there were no French, German, Swedish, Danish, Hungarian, or Italian members. The labor union was exclusively Irish. Noel Ignatiev, *How the Irish Became White* (New York: Routledge, 1995), 1–3, 120–121.

41. Eric Lott, *Love and Theft: Blackface Minstrelsy and the American Working Class* (New York: Oxford University Press, 1993), 3–6.

42. Ignatiev, *How the Irish Became White*, 42.

43. Michael Gomez, *Exchanging Our Country Marks: The Transformation of African Identities in the Colonial and Antebellum South* (Chapel Hill: University of North Carolina Press, 1998).

44. James Barrett has argued that blackface performances in the mid-nineteenth century "allowed Irish Americans to separate their own collective persona from that of African Americans and, in the process, earn a more secure place in the racial hierarchy." James R. Barrett, *The Irish Way: Becoming American in the Multiethnic City* (New York: Penguin, 2012), 159.

45. Annemarie Bean, "Presenting the Prima Donna: Femininity and Performance in Nineteenth-Century American Blackface Minstrelsy," *Performance Research: On Illusion* 1 (Autumn 1996): 32.

46. Davis, *Parades and Power*, 106. Michael Rogin, *Blackface, White Noise: Jewish Immigrants in the Hollywood Melting Pot* (Berkeley: University of California Press, 1996), 73–120. Roediger argues that immigrants used blackface minstrel shows to become white, noting how Sophie Tucker's "racy blackface act, for example, ended with her removing a glove to 'prove' her whiteness" and referencing Michael Rogin's interpretation of *The Jazz Singer*. David R. Roediger, *Working Toward Whiteness: How America's Immigrants Became White: The Strange Journey from Ellis Island to the Suburbs* (New York: Basic Books, 2006), 125.

47. For a textual reading on the production of whiteness for performance in staged plays, see Mary Brewer, *Staging Whiteness* (Middletown, CT: Wesleyan University Press, 2005).

48. Isaac London, ed., *Siler City Grit*, July 10, 1912.

49. Isaac London, ed., *Siler City Grit*, July 10, 1918.

50. Isaac London, ed. "July 4th," *Siler City Grit*, 1913–1915.

51. Isaac London, ed., *Siler City Grit*, April 1, 1920.

52. Daniel Lee has argued that after the Civil War, white evangelicals used Christian practices to "incorporate non-White others into the hierarchical order of White society." Daniel B. Lee, "A Great Racial Commision: Religion and the Construction of White America," in *Race, Nation, and Religion in the Americas*, ed. Henry Goldschmidt and Elizabeth McAlister (Oxford: Oxford University Press, 2004), 85–110.

53. Isaac London, ed., *Siler City Grit*, July 10, 1918.

54. For the purposes of my argument here, I assume that blackface performances illustrate how the construction of whiteness is bound up in the production of blackness. The history of this relationship in Siler City is rooted in the racial worlds of antebellum institutions. For a ranging survey of the cultural expressions of blackface minstrelsy, see Dale Cockrell, *Demons of Disorder: Early Blackface Minstrels and Their World* (Cambridge: Cambridge University Press, 1997). For an argument that blackface minstrelsy is potentially subversive, see W. T. Lhamon, Jr., *Raising Cain: Blackface Performance from Jim Crow to Hip Hop* (Cambridge, MA: Harvard University Press, 1998). For a study of the musical performances of blackface minstrels in the mid-nineteenth century, see William J. Mahar, *Behind the Burnt Cork Mask: Early Blackface Minstrelsy and Antebellum American Popular Culture* (Urbana: University of Illinois Press, 1999).

55. Milo Holt, interview with the author, June 30, 2005. According to another resident, white Protestants also performed blackface minstrel shows in the high school gym into the 1950s. Tommy Edwards, interview with the author, June 23, 2005.

56. The *Sanford Express* (Sanford, North Carolina), February 23, 1917.

57. Clifford Geertz, "Religion as a Cultural System," in *Interpretation of Cultures* (New York: Basic Books, 1973), 90.

58. In that southern order, virtuous white women were bodily placeholders of religious and racial purity, signified in their spiritual innocence and their physical beauty. As Colonel Lane expressed to his soldiers at Gettysburg and as admirers like Lillian White recounted, Confederate soldiers upheld a gendered code of southern conduct in their defense of Christian homes. In those Christian homes, white women were the heart of hearths. White masculine sacrifice on behalf of white women modeled the New Testament description of the relationship between Jesus and the church. In Ephesians, Paul confirmed that the "husband is the head of the wife as Christ is the head of the church, his body, of which he is the Savior." He instructed wives to "submit to their husband in all things." But he also commanded husbands to "love your wives, just as Christ loved the church and gave himself up for her." For Paul, this Christlike sacrifice was intended "to make her holy, cleansing her by the washing with water through the word." The husband was "to present [his bride] to himself as a radiant church, without stain or wrinkle or any other blemish, but holy and blameless." Ephesians 5:22–26 (New International Version).

59. Fourth of July parades in New South towns like Siler City were public ritual expressions of what historian Christine Heyrman has called "ministerial efforts to meld the South's regional mores of masculinity and martial honor with the evangelical ethos." Christine Leigh Heyrman, *Southern Cross: The Beginnings of the Bible Belt* (Chapel Hill: University of North Carolina Press, 1998), 205, 259. The ethos that demanded white masculine protection of white feminine purity was racially sharpened in the New South. It entailed purification of sexual contact between white women and black men. Relationships tolerated by some in the antebellum period

were not prohibited in the segregated South. Martha Hodes, *White Women, Black Men: Illicit Sex in the Nineteenth-Century South* (New Haven, CT: Yale University Press, 1999). Juxtaposing the southern soldier with the southern beauty, while excluding black men from its segregated space, the Fourth of July parades ritual displayed and socially reinforced that racial norm. Diane Miller Sommerville, "The Rape Myth in the Old South Reconsidered," *The Journal of Southern History* 61 (1995): 481–518.

60. Ephesians 5:26–27 (King James Version).

61. Such comedic rites were tools of class formation and social solidarity. Davis writes of "neighborhood bands of young male peers" who performed masking and burlesque practices in nineteenth-century Philadelphia parades: "by creating hilarity through the delineation of deviant characteristics (blackface, women's dress), young men laughingly drew their social circle tighter." Davis, *Parades and Power*, 110.

62. Joe Creech, *Righteous Indignation: Religion and the Populist Revolution* (Urbana: University of Illinois Press, 2006).

63. "To Exclude Negro Voters: Proposed Amendment to the North Carolina Constitution," *New York Times*, March 19, 1899: 8.

64. Author unknown, *The Messenger*, May 3, 1900.

65. Author unknown, *The Messenger*, June 28, 1900.

66. H. Leon Prather, "The Red Shirt Movement in North Carolina, 1898–1900," *The Journal of Negro History* 62, no. 2 (April 1977): 174–184.

67. *Siler City Leader*, August 8, 1900.

68. Most fans believe Andy Griffith modeled the show after his hometown of Mount Airy, and they often visit the town in search of the real Mayberry. But white Siler residents claim that Griffith based Mayberry on Siler City, citing that he visited the town as a younger man and it is often referenced on the show. They also point out that the actress Frances Bavier, who played Aunt Bee on the show, retired in Siler City. Locals remember her as a reclusive woman who lived with her cats in a nice home on the hill, the same neighborhood once known as Palestine. In the late 1980s, Joe McKeever, self-described as a "preacher, cartoonist, and the director of missions for the Baptist Association of greater New Orleans," recalled that when he worked in Charlotte, North Carolina, he once set out for Siler City in search of Eden. The Baptist minister heard that Frances Bavier had retired to the small North Carolina town. Arriving at Siler, McKeever "aimed at the tall white spire of the First Baptist Church." Once inside, he introduced himself to the secretary "as pastor of the First Baptist Church of Charlotte." She told the minister where Miss Bavier lived, but warned, "She's a recluse. Stays inside with a houseful of cats." Upon finding Bavier's residence, a "two-story brick-and-rock façade house…a dozen blocks away," McKeever reflected, "So this is where a Hollywood star retires. The house would have fit in any middle-class neighborhood in the country." He knocked but there was no answer. Leaving his business card, McKeever headed to the local newspaper office, hoping for information. There he was met with more

disappointment. From the woman working at the paper, he learned that Miss Bavier had grown tired of strangers "walking all over her lawn and peeking in her windows." Her need for privacy explained her elusiveness. She came to Siler City in search of the "idyllic place to live," in pursuit of "the Mayberry myth." Once there, she found herself burdened by fame. Everyone expected her to be like Aunt Bee. But as Joe concluded, "Apparently, Frances Bavier was no Aunt Bee....Maybe that's why she did not answer the door. To leave us with our illusions." Joe McKeever, July 10, 2008, "In Search of Eden," July 13, 2004, http://www.joemckeever.com/mt/archives/000046.html. For a further discussion of that kind of Mayberry effect, see Allison Graham, *Framing the South: Hollywood, Television, and Race During the Civil Rights Struggle* (Baltimore: The Johns Hopkins University Press, 2001), 157–160.

69. *Mount Airy Times,* August 9, 1900.

70. Reconciliation did not necessarily erase southern memory or dissolve its racial order. David Blight has outlined three visions of Civil War memory, one of which included a "white supremacist vision that...locked arms with reconciliationists of many kinds, and by the turn of the century delivered the country a segregated memory of the Civil War on Southern terms." David W. Blight, *Race and Reunion: The Civil War in American Memory* (Cambridge: Harvard University Press, 2001), 2.

71. There is evidence that black residents in the Siler City area gathered independently on the Fourth of July in the neighboring town of Pittsboro in the 1950s. Kermit DeGraffenreidt of Pittsboro, who graduated from Horton High School in 1956, said that he never went to the parades in Siler City. Nevertheless, Fourth of July was a big day for the family. In the early 1950s, his family would gather at an old house with a three-acre pond. They had a baseball park, he said, and baseball was the main activity for the Fourth. His grandmother ran a store that supplied the community, all of whom would come for the game. Though less than twenty miles, Siler, he said, seemed so far away. Kermit DeGraffenreidt, phone interview with the author, June 27, 2011.

72. *Mount Airy Times*, July 4, 1901. The previous year, the newspaper announced what was likely an invitation for the white Odd Fellows, since racial identity was not designated: "The Odd Fellows of this city will picnic at The Flat Rock, July 4th, and invite all Odd Fellows and friends to bring baskets and join in and help make the occasion one of real pleasure." *Mount Airy Times,* June 29, 1899. Black Odd Fellows are members of the Grand United Order of Odd Fellows, which differs from the historically white Independent Order of Odd Fellows. The split between the two organizations dates to the late nineteenth century in Louisville, Kentucky. According to George C. Wright, "Several members of the Center Street AME church formed Louisville's first order of black Odd Fellows in June 1867. They first called themselves United Sons of Independence but changed their names to Odd Fellows after receiving literature and aprons from white Odd Fellows. The white Odd Fellows, however, refused to accept blacks as members in their order. Therefore, with the

aid of black Odd Fellows from Cleveland, Louisville blacks organized eight Odd Fellows lodges, which formed the Grand United Order of Odd Fellows in order to pool their resources to purchase property. George C. Wright, *Life Behind a Veil: Blacks in Louisville, Kentucky, 1865–1930* (Baton Rouge: Louisiana State University Press, 1985), 132–133. For a historical survey of the Grand United Order of Odd Fellow in the United States, see Charles H. Brooks, *The Official History and Manual of the Grand United Order of Odd Fellows in America* (New York: Books for Libraries Free Press, 1971 [1902]).

73. *Mount Airy Times*, July 11, 1901.

74. Ibid.

75. *Mount Airy Times*, July 5, 1900.

76. *Mount Airy Times*, July 20, 1904.

77. *Mount Airy Times*, July 10, 1913.

78. *Mount Airy Times*, July 6, 1911.

79. Rebecca J. Fraser, *Courtship and Love Among the Enslaved in North Carolina* (Jackson: University Press of Mississippi, 2007), 29. Elizabeth Fox-Genovese, *Within the Plantation Household: Black and White Women of the Old South* (Chapel Hill: University of North Carolina Press, 1988), 208.

80. Ralph Ellison, *Shadow and Act* (New York: Random House, 1995 [1953]), 54–55.

CHAPTER 3

1. On the character of Latino protestors, Tommy added that when he went downtown the day after the April 10 rally to clean up on Chatham Avenue and around First Baptist Church (where he is a member), "there wasn't any trash." He said, "They [the immigrant rights supporters] had cleaned up good." Tommy Emerson, interview with the author, February 9, 2006.

2. Ibid. Tommy described another lynching, at Harper's Crossroads, of a black man he said was guilty of raping and killing a white woman. He said they put him behind a buggy and dragged him to a tree.

3. On the point of reconfiguring violence, I have in mind Michelle Alexander's work on the incarceration of African Americans in the twenty-first century. Michelle Alexander, *The New Jim Crow* (New York: The New Press, 2010). See also Jennifer Graber's narrative of incarceration in the United States, which is part of the introduction to her history of Protestant reformers and prison experiments in antebellum America. Jennifer Graber, *The Furnace of Affliction: Prisons and Religion in Antebellum America* (Chapel Hill: University of North Carolina Press, 2011), 1–4. In 1998, the Siler City police staged a drug sting in Lincoln Heights and forty of the forty-four persons arrested were black males. Todd Nelson, "Critic Says Siler City Sting Targeted Blacks," *News and Observer*, April 30, 1998, B3. Of the seven mainline churches I visited—the historically white congregations of FBC, FUMC, Rocky River Baptist, Loves Creek Baptist, and Siler City Presbyterian and the historically

black congregations of Corinth AME Zion and First Missionary Baptist—only First Missionary Baptist asked for prayers for "all of our incarcerated brothers and sisters" and listed in their bulletin contact information for church members and related persons held in prison. The bulletin for February 22, 2004 listed thirteen persons. Fieldnotes, February 22, 2004.

4. In his sweeping historical survey, Charles Taylor notes that "civility" has been used for centuries in Europe to distinguish the civilized from the savages. The distinguishing marker of the civilized, as it was in seventeenth-century France, was "what we think of as a modern state, a continuing instrument of government in whose hands was concentrated a great deal of power over society, so that it was capable of remoulding this society in important ways." This, he says of the French, was what they considered "sauvages" or "natural man" lacked. Taylor further distinguishes a modern civility, that which characterizes the mode of government in the modern state, as assuring "some degree of domestic peace." The "feeling" of that peace is what makes us—those whom he refers to as "we"—feel that we live in a "civilization." Southern progressives adeptly produced this type of feeling in their configurations of modern civility. They offered a feeling of civic harmony for their white constituents and then acted as if it that feeling had universal affect, even among blacks in the South. But there were two sides of civility in the American South that William Chafe documented in his study of Greensboro and which I work through in this chapter: the type of civic feeling produced by progressive whites and the type of civil distress that resulted from the violence it legitimated and the justice it distorted. Taylor, in my reading of his narrative, does not adequately account for the racial mechanics of civility that impact how those living within the same communities feel civility in differing ways. When he does mention race, he uses it to illustrate its disruption of a homogenized public who share the same civic emotions: "A race riot at home may disturb our equanimity, but we revert rapidly." Charles Taylor, *A Secular Age*, 100.

5. On the institutional diffusion of liberal Protestantism, William Hutchison argued that the "distinguishing attitudes of the liberal theology did spread widely among the missionaries and mission boards of the mainline Protestant denominations after the turn of the century and were transmitted through such undenominational agencies as the Student Volunteer Movement and the YMCA." William R. Hutchison, *The Modernist Impulse in American Protestantism* (Durham, NC: Duke University Press, 1992), 155. On the institutional role of Catholicism in inculcating "the habits of civic participation," Thomas Tweed writes, "Continuing efforts that predated the turn of the twentieth century, Catholic educators promoted American virtues, such as 'industry and application,' and taught 'lessons of a patriotic and national character.' Civics textbooks, courses, and clubs also presented the same 'patriotic' messages." Thomas A. Tweed, *America's Church: The National Shrine and Catholic Presence in the Nation's Capitol* (New York: Oxford University Press, 2011), 195–196.

6. Samuel S. Hill and Charles Lippy, eds., *Encyclopedia of Religion in the South*, 2d ed. (Macon, GA: Mercer University Press, 2005), 180, 701. For a discussion of immigration in the American South, see Charles Reagan Wilson, *Southern Missions: The Religion of the American South in Global Perspective* (Waco, TX: Baylor University Press, 2006), 36–38.

7. David Goldfield, "Unmelting the Ethnic South: Changing Boundaries of Race and Ethnicity in the Modern South," in *The American South in the Twentieth Century*, ed. Craig S. Pascoe, Karen Trahan Leathem, and Andy Ambrose (Athens: University of Georgia Press, 2005), 19–20.

8. To use Joel Williamson's phrase, the South was the nation's "crucible of race," within which the idea of racial difference was forged. Williamson, *The Crucible of Race*.

9. Donald G. Mathews, "Lynching Is Part of the Religion of Our People: Faith in the Christian South," in *Religion in the American South: Protestants and Others in History and Culture*, ed. Beth Barton Schweiger and Donald G. Mathews (Chapel Hill: University of North Carolina Press, 2004), 161.

10. Mathews, "Lynching Is Part of the Religion of Our People," 166.

11. Leigh Anne Duck notes that Willis Weatherford and Charles Johnson's *Race Relations* associated lynching with "primitive communities," and Gunnar Myrdal's *An American Dilemma* (1944) "described lynching as one element in the South's broader resistance to modernity." Leigh Anne Duck, *The Nation's Region: Southern Modernism, Segregation, and U.S. Nationalism* (Athens: University of Georgia Press, 2006), 189.

12. On the Wilmington riot, see David S. Cecelski and Timothy B. Tyson, eds., *Democracy Betrayed: The Wilmington Race Riot of 1898 and Its Legacy* (Chapel Hill: University of North Carolina Press, 1998).

13. Nineteenth-century sociologist Thorstein Veblen proposed, "The basis on which good repute in any highly organized industrial community ultimately rests is pecuniary strength." Thorstein Veblen, *The Theory of the Leisure Class* (New York: Macmillan Company, 1912 [1899]), 84. At least in the historical context of the early-twentieth-century American South, where a reputation of racial progress was key to investment and exchange, the opposite of Veblen's formulation may have been the case: that pecuniary strength equally depended upon good repute. In either arrangement, both variables are mutually dependent, rather than singularly causal.

14. W. Fitzhugh Brundage, *Lynching in the New South: Georgia and Virginia, 1880–1930* (Urbana: University of Illinois, 1993), 124, 186, 212.

15. Ibid.

16. Here, I am translating Asad's oft-cited formulation that the "concept of the secular cannot do without the idea of religion." Talal Asad, "Religion, Nation-State, Secularism," in *Nation and Religion: Perspectives on Europe and Asia*, ed. Peter van der Veer and Hartmut Lehmann (Princeton, NJ: Princeton University Press, 1999), 192. Historian Rosalyn Terborg-Penn has noted that, "the height of the lynching

era in United States history coincided with the Progressive Era, stretching from the mid-1890s to the early 1920s." Rosalyn Terborg-Penn, "African-American Women's Networks in the Anti-Lynching Crusade," in *Gender, Class, Race and Reform in the Progressive Era*, ed. Noralee Frankel and Nancy S. Dye (Lexington: University of Kentucky Press, 1991), 148.

17. Atticus G. Haygood, "The Black Shadow in the South," *Forum*, October 1893, 171, cited in Mathews, *Rethinking Zion*, 18. For an example of a northern argument against lynching that condemned burning someone alive, not because of concern for the victim, but because of concern for the reputation of civilized whites, see what W. G. Sumner wrote from New Haven, Connecticut, in 1905, as part of his foreword to James Elbert Cutler's investigation into lynch law: "it should be a disgrace to us if amongst us men should burn a rattlesnake or a dog.... Torture and burning are forbidden, not because the victim is not bad enough, but because we are too good." James Elbert Cutler, *Lynch-law: An Investigation into the History of Lynching in the United States* (London: Longmans, Green, and Co., 1905), v.

18. Willis D. Weatherford, "Lynching, Removing Its Causes" (Nashville: Southern Sociological Congress, 1916), unpaginated. Briscoe Center for American History Collection, University of Texas at Austin.

19. Weatherford, "Lynching, Removing Its Causes."

20. William A. Link, *The Paradox of Southern Progressivism, 1880–1930* (Chapel Hill: University of North Carolina Press, 1992), 251.

21. It is important to note that Mathews expresses a concern that southerners were "conflicted" in their attempts to meet what she call's the "North's standards [of the Social Gospel]" as they "tried to industrialize rapidly and yet maintain [their] strange version of race relations." Mathews, *Rethinking Zion*, 14–15, 116. That perceived "conflict" between northern promotions of modern progress and southern prescriptions of racial primitivism, is, I argue, a projected historical antagonism. It appears in the historiography when the scholarly observer limits secularism to the North, marks it by liberal Protestantism, and then tracks its appearance in the South. Take, for example, John Carlisle Kilgo, "Methodist minister and President of Trinity College (later Duke University)," who Mathews classifies as a proponent of the Social Gospel. Kilgo indeed denounced lynching. But similar to Weatherford, he also stated, "I have more than ordinary sympathy with the negro, and I am glad to lend my hand to uplift that race of people and bring them to whatever they can attain, but I am not yet ready to dignify them to the place of trying to control and manage government." John Carlisle Kilgo, *Chapel Talks* (Nashville, TN: Publishing House M. E. Church, South, 1922), 113.

22. On educational promotion in the New South, see James L. Leloudis, *Schooling the New South: Pedagogy, Self, and Society in North Carolina, 1880–1920* (Chapel Hill: University of North Carolina Press, 1996). See also Hugh C. Bailey, *Liberalism in the New South: Southern Social Reformers and the Progressive Movement.* (Coral Gables, FL: University of Miami Press, 1969).

23. Donovan E. Smucker, *The Origins of Walter Rauschenbusch's Social Ethics.* (Quebec: McGill-Queens University Press, 1994), 83. Robert Moore-Jumonville, *The Hermeneutics of Historical Distance: Mapping the Terrain of American Biblical Criticism, 1880–1914* (Lanham, MD: University Press of America, 2002), 63. Elizabeth Fox-Genovese and Eugene Genovese have noted about the nineteenth century, "Although Schleiermacher's view of religion deeply penetrated the North, only slowly did Southerners like Thomas Peck and Basil Manly, Jr., single him out for criticism in their reaction to the mounting denial of basic doctrine and the divine inspiration of Scripture." Elizabeth Fox-Genovese and Eugene D. Genovese, *The Mind of the Master Class: History and Faith in the Southern Slaveholders' Worldview* (Cambridge: Cambridge University Press, 2005), 532.

24. William R. Hutchison, *The Modernist Impulse in American Protestantism* (Durham, NC: Duke University Press, 1992), 3–5.

25. Philip Dray, *At the Hands of Persons Unknown: The Lynching of Black America* (New York: Random House, 2002), 277.

26. Ronald C. White, Jr., *Liberty and Justice for All: Racial Reform and the Social Gospel (1877–1925)* (Louisville, KY: Westminster John Knox Press, 2002), 186.

27. Weatherford, "Lynching, Removing Its Causes."

28. Hutchison writes, "Liberalism emphasized the immanence of God in nature and human nature." *Modernist Impulse*, 3.

29. Weatherford, "Lynching, Removing Its Causes."

30. Some readers may apologize for Weatherford, saying he merely used the terminology of his day. If he spoke otherwise, he may have been dismissed. If that is the case, it also is the point. The decision was not his alone. It was made for him as he made it for southern blacks.

31. Weatherford, *Lynching, Removing Its Causes.*

32. Ibid.

33. Ibid.

34. Anti-lynching campaigns resulted principally from the efforts of African American women, as Terborg-Penn has argued, through organizations such as the National Federation of Afro-American Women, the National Association of Colored Women, along with the National Association for the Advancement of Colored People, to pass congressional legislation to make lynching a federal crime. The federal government did not pass such laws during the Progressive Era, when lynching was at its height. "Nonetheless," Terborg-Penn writes, "white public opinion eventually turned against the barbarism of lynch law, as white women like Jessie Ames mobilized to stop the carnage." "African-American Women's Network in the Anti-Lynching Crusade," 148. African American women influential in anti-lynching campaigns were measured against the standards of white "ladies," including those of white women who supported them. Even when African American women championed the same social causes as white women, such as Prohibition, they were segregated within those movements and at their meetings. Glenda Elizabeth Gilmore,

Gender and Jim Crow: Women and the Politics of White Supremacy in North Carolina, 1896–1920 (Chapel Hill: University of North Carolina Press, 1996), 46.

35. Helen Rappaport, *Encyclopedia of Women Social Reformers, Volume One* (Santa Barbara, CA: ABC-CLIO, 2001), 12–13. White women who supported African American women in their efforts to halt lynching were subject to racial insults. According to Jacquelyn Hall, "Ames reported that women who sought to convince officers to guard their prisoners against mob violence 'found themselves in receipt of anonymous letters conveying nauseating threats in slimy words—threats against Southern white women by Southern white men.'" Hall notes that "even the eminent respectability and moderation of the women of the Anti-Lynching Association did not shield them from the charge that only the desire to sleep with a black man could account for their scandalous betrayal of caste solidarity." Jacquelyn Dowd Hall, *Revolt Against Chivalry: Jessie Daniel Ames and the Women's Campaign Against Lynching* (New York: Columbia University Press, 1993), 153–154.

36. Hall, *Revolt Against Chivalry*, 256.

37. Ralph Luker, *Social Gospel in Black and White: American Racial Reform, 1885–1912* (Chapel Hill: University of North Carolina Press, 1998), 315.

38. Ibid.

39. Ibid., 212, 245.

40. Stephen Prothero, *American Jesus: How the Son of God Became a National Icon* (New York: Farrar, Straus and Giroux, 2003), 95.

41. Luker, *Social Gospel in Black and White*, 215.

42. Lindsey Hall, *Swinburne's Hell and Hick's Universalism: Are We Free to Reject God?* (Burlington, VT: Ashgate Publishing, Ltd., 2003), 21–22.

43. Hall, *Swinburne's Hell and Hick's Universalism*, 20. Elizabeth Fox-Genovese and Eugene D. Genovese, *The Mind of the Master Class: History and Faith in the Southern Slaveholders' Worldview* (Cambridge: Cambridge University Press, 2005), 532.

44. Luker, *Social Gospel in Black and White*, 278, 280. Historian Wayne Flynt counts Edgar Gardner Murphy among the "South's liberals." Wayne Flynt, "'Feeding the Hungry and Ministering to the Broken Hearted': The Presbyterian Church in the United States and the Social Gospel, 1900–1920," in *Religion in the South*, ed. Charles Reagan Wilson (Jackson: University Press of Mississippi, 1985), 87.

45. Luker, *Social Gospel in Black and White*, 281–282.

46. Ibid.

47. Ibid.

48. Ibid.

49. Kelly J. Baker, *The Gospel According to the Klan: The Ku Klux Klan's Appeal to Protestant America, 1915–1930* (Lawrence: University of Kansas Press, 2011).

50. Resident A, phone interview with the author, June 28, 2011.

51. Elizabeth Edwards, interview with the author, January 5, 2006.

52. All quotes and summaries contained within my narrative account of the shooting of Melvin White by a Siler City police officer were compiled from the following

sources: The *Chatham News,* July 19 and July 26, and August 2 and August 9, 1962;
the *Chatham Record,* August 9, November 22 and 29, 1962; the *Carolina Times,*
December 1, 1962; the *Carolinian,* October 13, 1962; "July 27, 1962 NAACP Press
Release on Shooting of Melvin White," Box III: A 243 "Police Brutality: North
Carolina, 1956–1965" (NAACP Collection, Library of Congress).

53. Partially confirming Womble's assertion that the shooting of Melvin White was the
fourth incident in which a white officer shot and killed a black resident, I found
two cases involving the police shootings of black men in the Siler City area. In
October 1952, "local police officer" Leroy Pittman shot and killed Ernest Carter, a
"negro assailant." A jury absolved the officer of any blame (*Chatham News,* October
9, 1952). In October 1954, a coroner's jury cleared Siler City deputy C. A. Simmons
in the shooting of a "negro tramp," Odell Hendricks. Chatham County Sheriff
John W. Emerson "pointed out evidence." Based on the official account, resident
Jim Strickland phoned the police saying there was a "strange Negro on the railroad
tracks at Mt. Vernon Springs." The report said "the Negro" had a rock in one hand
and his other hand was in his pocket. The officer shot him twice (*Chatham News,*
October 28, 1954). I also found a third case that occurred after the White shooting. In October 1962, Thomas Earl Paschal, a twenty-one-year-old "Negro [who]
worked for Siler City poultry processing plant [was] found barely alive [with a]
massive fracture head wound" in the middle of the road. The news report questioned whether it was murder or a hit-and-run. It reported that "Paschal had been
drinking earlier in the day, and his movements had been partially traced by officers
working on the case." Paschal's head was the only injured part of his body and he
had no "highway burns" or other signs that a car had hit him. He was found "lying
with his head near the center line of the road. Nearby was a pint bottle of white
liquor." His shoes "were both off, lying neatly by his feet" (*Chatham News,* October
18, 1962).

54. Guytanna Horton was President of the North Carolina Youth Councils and College
Chapters for the NAACP. Program for the North Carolina State Conference of
NAACP Branches, "Freedom Day Celebrations" Raleigh, North Carolina, May 5,
1963, document in Richard B. Harrison Public Library, Raleigh, North Carolina.
According to NAACP records, on "Sunday August 5th at 3:00 p.m. Waldo Means,
a white graduate theology student at Duke University, refused to accept service at
Howard Johnson's restaurant located on US highway #15 and #501 until three other
persons were served. These other persons were Miss Guytanna Horton, President
Chatham County (N.C.) NAACP Youth Council, Miss Joycelyn McKissick,
Durham Youth Council, and Mr. Jon Schaeffer, a member of CORE, Seattle,
Wash." Box III: C112 "Branch File, Durham, NC 1956–63" (NAACP Collection,
Library of Congress). According to Horton's husband, Kermit DeGraffenreidt,
Horton and McKissick were arrested for sitting at the counter. They were given the
option of paying a $25 fine or going to jail for thirty days. They refused to pay the
fine. Kermit DeGraffenreidt, phone interview with the author, June 27, 2011.

CHAPTER 4

1. Roy Key, "July 4th Parade May Be Last One," *Chatham Record*, July 8, 1976, 2, 6.

2. *Chatham News*, July 10, 1958; July 8, 1965; July 6, 1967; July 10, 1969.

3. *Chatham Record*, July 8, 1976.

4. The parade was canceled in 1950 because of "the inability to obtain a baseball game." Dr. Mott Blair, president of the Jaycees, said, "You can't expect people to wait in the middle of the day between parade and evening activities with nothing to do." *Chatham News*, June 22, 1950. The 1973 parade in Siler City was advertised as the twenty-eighth annual celebration. *Chatham Record*, June 28, 1973.

5. I directly asked nineteen different residents in Siler who had lived in the town since at least the 1960s if desegregation had any impact on the Fourth of July parade. Within the local racial binary, six of those residents were considered black, and thirteen were considered white.

6. On a national level, that impulse to reclaim muscular Christianity found its organizational voice in the 1990s, with the Promise Keepers movement. Leaders of that organization blamed the moral decline of the United States on the feminization of men, pointing to the 1970s as the starting point of that decline. And they directed Christian men to reclaim their divine right as the spiritual head of household. Becky Beal, "The Promise Keepers' Use of Sport in Defining 'Christlike' Masculinity," in *The Promise Keepers: Essays on Masculinity and Christianity*, ed. Dane S. Claussen (Jefferson, NC: McFarland & Company, 2000), 156.

7. Kathryn Lofton has noted that "A 'muscular' Christianity arose [within early-twentieth-century Protestant circles] to supply modern men with manly means to renegotiate a public sphere that increasingly included women's presence at the polls, in the office, and behind the pulpit." The rise of the Moral Majority in the 1980s, along with the organizational development of the Promise Keepers in the 1990s, demonstrated a public revival of that strand of muscular Christianity. Kathryn Lofton, *Oprah: The Gospel of an Icon* (Berkeley: University of California Press, 2011), 165.

8. Brett Clifton, "Focus on the Family," in *Encyclopedia of American Religion and Politics*, ed. Paul A. Djupe and Laura R. Olson (New York: Facts on File, 2003), 171.

9. Jane Gurganus Rainey, "Moral Majority," in *Encyclopedia of American Religion and Politics*, 287.

10. Dan Gilgoff, *The Jesus Machine: How James Dobson, Focus on the Family, and Evangelical America Are Winning the Culture War* (New York: Macmillan, 2008), 2.

11. Christian Smith, *American Evangelicalism: Embattled and Thriving* (Chicago: University of Chicago Press, 1998), 89–119.

12. An article on "upward bound students" confirmed that black students attended Northwood High School in 1972. *Chatham Record*, August 10, 1972. Northwood High School, however, does not have copies of yearbooks from the 1970s, therefore, I could not confirm black participation in the 1972 band using that source.

Northwood High School was not officially dedicated until August 20, 1972. Public school integration in Chatham County began in 1965–1966 with the "Freedom of Choice" plan, which was an attempt to comply with the Civil Rights Act of 1964 without fully integrating schools. Under that plan, only a few black students attended formerly all-white schools. According to Hadley and Jane Pyle of the Chatham County Historical Society, "Six black students were assigned to Jordan-Matthews, three chose Chatham Central, and twenty-five selected Pittsboro High School." In 1967, because of the slow pace of school integration, Chatham County was placed on a "deferred list" by the federal government, denying them the option of purchasing federal surplus goods for lunchrooms. That ruling was later overturned with the promise of full integration. Pyle notes, "At a hearing in Washington, the school board was told that the county could forgo federal funds but that total integration would have to occur within two or three years. Federal funds were reinstated after an 11-point plan was approved in mid-February 1968." The "1969–1970" plan called for three integrated high schools: Chatham Central, north of Siler City; Jordan-Matthews, in Siler City; and Northwood, in Pittsboro. According to Hadley, Chatham Central was fully integrated by 1968 and Jordan-Matthews by 1969. Pyle, though, notes that the plan "was disallowed" because the schools that would merge both Northwood High, Pittsboro (an all-white school), and Horton (an all-black school) "were still not integrated." Chatham County had passed a $3.6-million-bond issue in 1969 to construct a new school building for Northwood High School. But, as Hadley writes, it was not scheduled for completion until the "1971–1972 school year." To comply with federal requirements, the county integrated those two schools by placing grades ten to twelve at Pittsboro High and grades five to nine at Horton School. Hadley and Pyle note that full integration of public schools in Chatham County was complete by the fall of 1970, though neither address what happened after construction of Northwood High was completed. Hadley, *Chatham County*, 300–303; Jane Pyle, "A Brief History of the Schools of Chatham County," Chatham County Historical Association website, June 22, 2011, http://www.chathamhistory.org/archiveschools.html.

13. Photo with caption, "The spirit of '72," *Chatham Record*, July 6, 1972, 1.
14. *Chatham Record*, July 4, 1974.
15. *Chatham News*, July 10, 1975.
16. *Chatham News*, July 8, 1976, 7A.
17. Box 105, Folder 5, Records of General Counsel Cases Closed, 1968-1974, ACLU-NC Archives, Duke University, Durham, North Carolina.
18. *Chatham News*, July 8, 1976, 7A.
19. *Chatham Record*, July 1, 1971.
20. *Chatham Record*, July 15, 1971, 3.
21. *Chatham Record*, June 28, 1973
22. *Chatham Record*, June 28, 1973; *Chatham News*, July 12, 1973.
23. Alan D. Resch, phone interview with the author, June 28, 2011.

24. Larry Cheek, phone interview with the author, June 21, 2011.

25. Resident B, phone interview with the author, June 22, 2011.

26. The Supreme Court decided in *Roberts v. U.S. Jaycees* in 1984 that the Jaycees could no longer discriminate based on gender. Leslie Friedman Goldstein, *The Constitutional Rights of Women: Cases in Law and Social Change* (Madison: University of Wisconsin Press, 1988), 540–541.

27. Nelly Cole, interview with the author, January 4, 2006.

28. The Christmas parade was typically sponsored by local businesses and performed on and off since the 1950s. When I asked residents about the parade, they told me it was never as big of a deal as the Fourth of July parade. The Christmas parade never included the all-day festivities that characterized the July Fourth celebrations. While it is an important part of Siler City local history, I do not fully address its development in this book because it did not appear until after 1945 and locals did not describe it with the same enthusiasm that they did the Fourth of July parade.

29. Another former Chatham High band member also told me he marched in the Fourth of July parades from his freshman year in 1965 until he graduated in 1969. Rob Edwards, phone interview with the author, April 11, 2007.

30. Resident C, e-mail message to author, June 29, 2011.

31. Resident B, phone interview with the author, June 24, 2011.

32. Resident D, phone interview with the author, June 21, 2011.

33. Resident C, e-mail message to author, June 28, 2011.

34. Paul Cuadros, *A Home on the Field: How One Championship Team Inspires Hope for the Revival of Small Town America* (San Francisco: HarperCollins, 2007), 31.

35. Resident C, e-mail message to author, June 29, 2011.

36. Resident E, phone interview with the author, June 28, 2011.

37. *Chatham News*, June 26, 1952; June 3 1954.

38. Resident C, e-mail message to author, June 29, 2011.

39. *Chatham News*, July 7, 1977.

40. *Chatham News*, July 6, 1978

41. Lee Moody, informal conversation with the author, July 6, 2011; *Chatham News*, July 6, 1978.

42. *Chatham News*, July 5, 1979.

43. *Chatham News*, July 9, 1981, 12A, 13A.

44. *Chatham News,* July 8, 1982.

45. *Chatham News*, July 7, 1988.

46. There were three small celebrations in the downtown area during this time. In 1990, the local National Guard participated in Operation Patriotism, which involved a handful of people running through downtown with an American flag. That event was held in conjunction with the 150th celebration of the state capitol building in Raleigh. "Local National Guard Member..." (photo caption), *Chatham News*, July 5, 1990. In 1991, the Shriner's organized a "Salute to the Troops" parade in downtown Siler to honor troops who had participated in Operation Desert Storm. The

event "lasted all day and included a chicken fry, parade, games and a make-believe gunfight put on by the Restless Range Gunfighters." This, however, was not an official town function. "Do You See What I See?" (photo caption), *Chatham News*, July 11, 1991. In 1992, the Chatham County Shriners Club sponsored another small parade. "Say Hey!!" (photo caption), *Chatham News*, July 9, 1992. None of these parades, however, were officially sponsored by the town of Siler City.

47. On Tuesday, July 6, 1976, Democratic gubernatorial candidate Jim Hunt visited a barbecue "near Siler City" which was attended by forty people. Town commissioner Charles Turner, who was "Hunt's county campaign manager," organized it. *Chatham Record*, July 8, 1976.

48. According to Mitch Simpson, a self-described progressive white Baptist pastor in Chapel Hill who grew up in Siler City during the 1950s and 1960s, the kids who tried to get the watermelon were most often African American. Simpson explained that because they already did not have status, they had nothing to lose. He remembered seeing black kids slide across the street from the pressure of the fire hoses, and he admitted that this sight made him feel uncomfortable. At the same time, though, white kids, including Tommy Emerson, also participated. Such participation complicates the racial dynamics of the game. Loss of control, more so than a clear racial division, best describes those who chase the prize. But, at least in this case, white men who held the fire hose regulated the degree of personal fun or public humiliation, depending upon the observer's interpretation. Mitch Simpson, interview with the author, Chapel Hill, North Carolina, February 13, 2007.

49. Tommy Emerson, interview with the author, February 9, 2006.

50. For a description of the 2006 Emerson Fourth of July party in Siler City as an old-fashioned display of "hand-over-your-heart patriotism," see Janet C. Pittard, "Old-Fashioned Family Fourth," in *Our State North Carolina*, July 2006, 161.

51. Korie L. Edwards, *The Elusive Dream: The Power of Race in Interracial Churches* (Oxford: Oxford University Press, 2008).

52. In the discourse of the Fourth of July celebration, the concepts of nation-state and patriotic soldier are gendered. In his "patriotic words," Pastor Wall asked those present to "pray for the country and *her* leaders." In prayer, he called on "our heavenly father" and connected the sacrifice of Jesus on the cross to the sacrifices made for the freedom symbolized in the Fourth of July. Fieldnotes, July 4, 2006.

CHAPTER 5

1. Joyce Clark, "Headline: Newcomers Re-create Christ's Passion in Siler City: Holy Drama the Latino Way," *News and Observer*, April 6, 1996, B1.

2. Sam McGregor, Jr., "A Journal of Fastings," Allison Creek Presbyterian Church website, http://www.allisoncreekchurch.com/April_20_2003B.pdf.

3. Ben Stocking, "A Surging Latino Population Calls Siler City 'Home' Challenge of an American Dream," *News and Observer*, January 14, 1996, A1. See Lorrie Elizabeth

Bradley, "Shared Space and Common Faith: Latino Immigrants, Catholicism and Collective Identity in North Carolina" (Honors Thesis, University of North Carolina at Chapel Hill, 2001), 14. "What Does the Future Hold? Piedmont Communities Experiencing Growing Pains as Population Becomes More Diverse," *Greensboro News and Record*, May 7, 1997, A1.

4. Barry Yeoman, "Hispanic Diaspora," *Mother Jones*, August 2000, 39. Poultry companies like Tyson Foods have used intermediaries to illegally transport Mexican workers across the US border to plants in North Carolina. Edward Martin, "Down Mexico Way: Illegal Immigration Is Suppressing Tar Heel Wages, but This Boon to Business also Is Creating a New Underclass," *BusinessNC.com*, May 2006.

5. John J. Valadez, *Matters of Race* (PBS video, 2003).

6. Ben Stocking, "Language Gap Strains Schools," *News and Observer*, September 3, 1997. County schools enhanced their curriculum to assist Spanish-speaking students, including the Migrant Summer Program and the Hispanic Initiative, a collaborative effort with the University of North Carolina, at Jordan-Matthews High School. "Crossing Cultures," *News and Observer*, July 21, 2000, E1. These programs addressed tensions among racial and ethnic groups, including those that existed within migrant subgroups. For a description of Latino experiences at Jordan-Matthews, see Cuadros, *A Home on the Field*, 2007.

7. Leda Hartman, "Voice of America, Siler City," *Chatham Journal Online,* June 14, 2003.

8. Joseph Pardington, "Immigration March Comes to Siler City," *Chatham News*, April 13, 2006. Religion alone was not a singular force for public display of Latino presence in Siler, as secular organizations like the Hispanic Liaison and UNC–Chapel Hill worked in conjunction with religious organizations like St. Julia Catholic Church and the Catholic Diocese of Raleigh to deliver services and organize rallies and protests.

9. Steve Striffler, *Chicken: The Dangerous Transformation of America's Favorite Food* (New Haven, CT: Yale University Press, 2007), 141.

10. Ben Stocking, "Side by Side: Worlds Apart (Part 1)," *News and Observer*, May 4, 1997, A1.

11. Paul Cuadros, "Hispanic Poultry Workers Live in New Southern Slums," *APF Reporter 20* (2001), 32–37.

12. A study sponsored by the Kenan Institute at UNC showed that Hispanics in North Carolina are a significant factor of economic growth in the state. In 2004, Latinos composed 7 percent of the total population in North Carolina. They accounted for 27.5 percent of the state's total population growth from 1990 to 2004 and 57 percent of the total enrollment growth in North Carolina public schools between 2000–2001 and 2004–2005. Hispanics filled one in three new jobs created in North Carolina between 1995 and 2005. Hispanics annually contributed about $756 million in state taxes while costing the state budget about $817 million annually for K–12 education ($467 million), health care ($299 million), and

corrections ($51 million)—for net cost to the state of about $61 million, or $102 per Hispanic resident. But North Carolina Hispanics spent about 80 percent of their total income in the state for a total impact of $9.2 billion to North Carolina businesses. They also lowered labor cost. For example, without Hispanic labor, the construction labor cost was an estimated $1 billion higher. John D. Kasarda and James H. Johnson, Jr., "The Economic Impact of the Hispanic Population on the State of North Carolina" (Frank Hawking Kenan Institute of Private Enterprise, Kenan-Flagler Business School, University of North Carolina at Chapel Hill, January 2006).

13. Cuadros, "Hispanic Poultry Workers Live in New Southern Slums."

14. Valadez, *Matters of Race*.

15. Altha Cravey, "Latino Labor and Poultry Production in Rural North Carolina," *Southeastern Geographer* 37 (November 1997): 295–300.

16. The comment concerning the Latino festival, contrasted with the fact that Latino workers were present at the country club but absent from the surrounding neighborhood, is significant because it illustrates the role that class status played within the segregated order of Siler. As I noted in earlier chapters, racial segregation was a southern white institutional response to the rise of a black middle class in the early twentieth century. The development of a Latino consumer class at the end of the twentieth century similarly threatened southern racial norms. Certain types of spatial proximity were tolerated, such as Latino workers at the country club, whereas a public disruption of that order in parks or streets was not.

17. Ned Glascock, "Town Prepares for Worst from Hate Group," *News and Observer*, February 19, 2000.

18. Ned Glascock, "Rally Divides Siler City," *News and Observer*, February 20, 2000.

19. David Duke, "Siler City and Immigration," David Duke's official website, www.duke.org.

20. Denise Becker and Annette Barr, "Cheers and Jeers Greet David Duke," *News & Record*, February 20, 2000, R1.

21. Patrick O'Neill, "Jubilee: Siler City Residents Reclaim Their Town from David Duke," *Independent* 3 (May 3, 2000): http://www.indyweek.com/gyrobase/Content?oid+oid%3A14289.

22. Joseph Pardington, "Immigration March Comes to Siler City," *Chatham News*, April 13, 2006, A1, A9.

23. Fieldnotes, April 10, 2006. For another description of the event, see Joseph Pardington, "Immigration March Comes to Siler City," *Chatham News*, April 13, 2006.

24. An estimated one hundred officers were present that day and there were no arrests. Joseph Pardington, "Security Tight at Monday's Event," *Chatham News*, April 13, 2006, A9.

25. The organizational development of CITCA, which brought Catholic pilgrims and nonresident progressive activists to the rally, is one example of how multiple

religious histories from across the Americas converged in downtown Siler City. CITCA, a Catholic-led coalition, was organized in 1982 by Gail Phares, an ex–Maryknoll nun. Phares worked in Nicaragua in the 1960s, and moved to the United States in the 1970s to advocate on behalf of the poor in Central America. In the 1980s, she participated in religious protest movements, including Witness for Peace, which resisted United States military involvement in the region. As part of her advocacy work, she accompanied progressive Christians from Raleigh on trips to Nicaragua to see firsthand the effects of American militarism. Christian Smith, *Resisting Reagan: The U.S. Central America Peace Movement* (Chicago: University of Chicago Press, 1996), 71. Sweeping strands of material culture are latent with multiple identities (national, cultural, social, ethnic, colonial, and indigenous); each contains histories within a history, stories within a story. In this chapter, I do not address in sustained detail the pluralities and fractures that developed over years of contact, exchange, and contestation. Nor do I capture the intricacies of transnational patterns of Latino migration, which include complex social networks and economic remittances. Rather, my goal is to contrast the "New" with the "Nuevo" in Siler, while situating both in broader historical patterns. Most Latinos who moved to Siler City in the 1990s arrived from Mexico, though a significant number also came from Central America, as well as from US states such as Texas and California. For an ethnographic account of Guatemalan migration to Siler City, see Susan G. Hicks, "Guatemalan-U.S. Migration and Sending Communities" (2003 CLAS Summer Research Report, Center for Latin American Studies, University of California at Berkeley, http://socrates.berkeley.edu:7001/Research/graduate/summer2003/hicks/index.html). For a descriptive use of the term *contact zone*, see Mary Louis Pratt, *Imperial Eyes: Travel Writing and Transculturation* (London: Routledge, 1992).

26. In her approach to the study of spirituality and "the spiritual," Courtney Bender has argued that scholars consider both as "entangled in various religious and secular histories, social structures, and cultural practices." Courtney Bender, *The New Metaphysicals: Spirituality and the American Religious Imagination* (Chicago: University of Chicago Press, 2010), 182. In the context of the April tenth rally, I use the term to describe the convergence of multiple histories, religious performances, and secular claims in that particular place.

27. In the nineteenth century, some white evangelicals worked for social change as educators and abolitionists. They organized public schools and opposed slavery. In the twentieth century, African American Protestants used speeches and marches to protest racial segregation and achieve suffrage in the civil rights movement. For a brief survey of the historical overlaps between evangelical activism and social movements, see Michael O. Emerson and Christian Smith, *Divided by Faith: Evangelical Religion and the Problem of Race in America* (New York: Oxford University Press, 2000).

28. I use the term *popular Catholicism* to describe the religious practices of lay Catholics that extend beyond the authoritative proscriptions of the clergy and may or may not meet with their approval. For three significant studies of popular Catholicism, see Robert A. Orsi, *The Madonna of 115th Street* (New Haven, CT: Yale University Press, 1985); Daniel Levine, *Popular Voices in Latin American Catholicism* (Princeton, NJ: Princeton University Press, 1992); and Rowan Ireland, *Kingdoms Come: Religion and Politics in Brazil* (Pittsburgh, PA: University of Pittsburgh Press, 1991).

29. For studies that use the term *parallel congregations*, see Paul David Numrich, *Old Wisdom in the New World: Americanization in Two Immigrant Theravada Buddhist Temples* (Knoxville: University of Tennessee Press, 1996), 63. For a usage of that category in another context, see Susan Ridgely Bales, *When I Was a Child: Children's Interpretations of First Communion* (Chapel Hill: University of North Carolina Press, 2005), 46, 177. For a revision of the term in yet another context, see Jeff Wilson, *Dixie Dharma: Inside a Buddhist Temple in the American South* (Chapel Hill: University of North Carolina Press, 2012), 148.

30. By 2000, at least eight Protestant congregations ministered to Spanish speakers. Loves Creek Baptist Church, for example, sponsored the Loves Creek Hispanic Baptist Mission. At an outdoor baptism service at Jordan Lake, Loves Creek member Wilfredo Hernández videorecorded greetings from fellow Baptists, first introducing them by name and then by their respective Salvadoran and Mexican hometowns or sending communities. That day, he recorded greetings to send to Chirilagua, Veracruz, Aguascalientes, and Tránsito, among other towns. The development of Latino Protestantism in Siler, like the congregation at Loves Creek, reflects the interconnectedness of missionary networks across the Americas. Denominationally affiliated Latino preachers also relocated from other parts of the United States to minister in Siler. Israel Tapia, pastor at the Loves Creek mission, was born in Mexico and served as a Baptist minister in the Texas Panhandle before moving to Siler. Migrants like Israel arrived at Siler already affiliated with a particular denomination. Barry Yeoman, "Hispanic Diaspora," *Mother Jones* (August 2000), http://motherjones.com/politics/2000/07/hispanic-diaspora. For a more detailed description of the religious work of Israel and Ruth Tapia, see Gaston Espinosa, Virgilio P. Elizondo, and Jesse Miranda, *Latino Religions and Civic Activism in the United States* (New York: Oxford University Press, 2005), 190–191. Pentecostalism, which has rapidly spread through the Americas since the 1970s, is also visible in Siler. Pentecostals meet in storefront churches in downtown and in abandoned mills nearby. While my fieldwork did not focus on Latino Protestants, I did observe Pentecostal revivals outside of an old mill and in the Walmart parking lot on Highway 64. These, too, were public religious performances that signaled a new ethnic presence in Siler City. Yet, locals I talked with and read about did not associate Protestant congregations solely with migrant arrival, as they did in the case of St. Julia Catholic Church.

31. There is one African American member at Siler City Presbyterian Church. She told me that she was not from Siler City originally. She was already a Presbyterian before she moved to Siler, and wanted to maintain her denominational affiliation. Fieldnotes, January 8, 2006.

32. This description is based on participant observation of a service at Siler City Presbyterian and informal conversations with members after the service at a potluck dinner, January 8, 2006.

33. David Kalbacker, interview with the author, April 22, 2011.

34. Valadez, *Matters of Race*.

35. Andres Viglucci, "Hispanic Wave Forever Alters Small Town in North Carolina," *Miami Herald*, January 2, 2000.

36. Patrick O'Neill, "Jubilee."

37. Melanie R. Wasserman, "Latina Immigrants, Bridge Persons, and Utilization of Preventive Health Services" (PhD diss., University of North Carolina, 2004).

38. Hadley, *Chatham County*, 257–258. Unpublished history of St. Julia Catholic Church. Father Jim Fukes, pastor of St. Julia parish, gave me a two-page copy of that history on April 22, 2011. David Kalbacker, interview with the author, April 22, 2011.

39. David Kalbacker, interview with the author, April 22, 2011.

40. Unpublished history of St. Julia Catholic Church.

41. Unpublished history of St. Julia Catholic Church. During the early years of Latino arrival, Reverend McGregor, who was a friend of Father Quakenbush, offered the Presbyterian Church, which was across the street, as overflow space for Christmas Mass. The congregations also held joint services on Palm Sunday. Reverend Sam McGregor, phone interview with the author, June 25, 2011.

42. Latino members also helped shape ritual life at St. Julia through their participation in church meetings. Kalbacker recalled how during a meeting at the old church location, a woman from Ecuador clearly stated that she wanted a statue of the Blessed Virgin, not Our Lady of Guadalupe. So the church now has a statue of the Blessed Virgin as well as a statue of Our Lady of Guadalupe. In the end, Kalbacker cracked, "St. Joseph got the short stick."

43. Kalbacker works in marketing and public relations, and during the early years of the procession, he called newspapers and television stations to let them know about the Good Friday processions at St. Julia Church. He said that they were glad to hear about it and willingly covered the event. In following years, they continued coverage and contacted him or the church to confirm the time of the processions.

44. Tommy Emerson, phone interview with the author, June 21, 2011. Tommy Emerson, longtime member of FBC Siler, told me he saw the first Good Friday procession while he was landscaping the church grounds. He said the Catholic congregants marched between the church building and the Friendly Florist. Based on what I learned later about the processional route, the Good Friday procession route would not have gone that close to FBC or on the street that passed the Friendly

Florist. It is possible that Tommy witnessed the CITCA march in 2000, and not the Good Friday service. But in either case, the initial procession did come within at least a few blocks of Chatham Avenue, if it did not cross over it. Tommy Emerson, interview with the author, February 9, 2006.

45. Daniel Quakenbush, e-mail message to author, June 22, 2011.

46. Nor did white Catholics ever ask in private conversation how to translate their prayers into English. When I talked with Anna and Tommy Emerson of FBC Siler about their experiences with Catholics, Anna told me a story about how they hired a worker for the house who had children in Mexico. One day, he asked Anna how to say a prayer in English before a meal. She said that she told him how to pray, as Baptists do. But he was confused. Later, she learned he was Catholic. So when their son-in-law, who is a Catholic, came to town, he taught him the proper prayer in English. Tommy and Anna Emerson, interview with the author, February 9, 2006.

47. The fact that Father Daniel had never seen the ritual performance in a parish setting suggests that his North American Catholic experience was disconnected from Spanish Catholic traditions. The arrival of Good Friday processions was just as new for some white Catholics as it was for white Protestants in Siler. The Franciscan order that Father Daniel belonged to was typically responsible for holy sites and played a historical role in the development of Good Friday processions. Good Friday processions developed in early Christianity, emerging out of Western Europe as an alternative for Christians who could not make the journey to the Holy Land. Franciscan priests, who were in charge of Roman Catholic holy sites, simulated the pilgrimage markers of Jerusalem in European fields or towns, making present a distant sacred place through the ritual performance of that sacred space. The Protestant Reformation halted that tradition in northern Europe, as Martin Luther and other reformers opposed what they considered its material trappings. The practice persisted, however, in Spain, and Spanish colonizers and Catholic missionaries carried it with them to the Americas, where it mixed with indigenous practices to form varying processional traditions within the regions of Spanish conquest that later would become the southwest United States, Mexico, and Central America. Claire Sponsler, *Ritual Imports: Performing Medieval Drama in America* (Ithaca, NY: Cornell University Press, 2004); Jennifer Scheper Hughes, *Biography of a Mexican Crucifix: Lived Religion and Local Faith from the Conquest to the Present* (Oxford: Oxford University Press, 2010). Transnational migrants then carried these traditions with them to global cities in North America like Chicago and New York, and more recently to newer Latino destinations like Siler City. Karen Mary Davalos, "The Real Way of Praying: The Via Crucis, *Mexicano* Sacred Space, and the Architecture of Domination," in *Horizons of the Sacred: Mexican Traditions in U.S. Catholicism*, ed. Timothy and Gary Riebe-Estrella Matovina (Ithaca: Cornell University Press, 2002), 41–68. Wayne Ashley, "Christ, Politics, and Processions on New York City's Lower East Side," in *Gods of the City*, ed. Robert A. Orsi (Bloomington: Indiana University Press, 1999), 341–366.

48. Carol Hall, "Good Friday Observed in Hispanic Tradition," *News and Observer*, April 3, 1999, A1.

49. Daniel Quakenbush, phone interview with and e-mail message to author, June 22, 2011.

50. Father Daniel delivered the news to the congregation during the announcement section of Mass that the church would be moving, though there was no determined location at that point. David Kalbacker, interview with the author, April 22, 2011. Some time later, Walter and Agnes Bunton, who moved from New Jersey to Siler City and joined the church in 1975, donated ten acres of land six miles east of town on Highway 64. With a site secured, the congregation undertook the task of selecting a design and raising funds for construction. According to the church history, "The capital campaign was initiated with some parishioners making pledges of donations while other parishioners sold tacos and tamales after Masses and took up a regular collection in the Spanish Masses with the request of one hour's wage every week from each person working. The Diocese of Raleigh offered a grant of $240,000 and a no-interest loan of $240,000. A significant donation came from the estate of Miss Elizabeth Brenna of Greenville, New York, by way of her estate's executrix, Mrs. Dorothea Quackenbush." Unpublished history of St. Julia Catholic Church.

51. Spencer heard about the St. Julia project from Ingrid Rodriguez, a friend who attends the Newman Center and who has family in Nicaragua.

52. The Building Committee at St. Julia included the pastor, three white members, and two Latino members. Jim Spencer, phone interview, May 11, 2011.

53. Fieldnotes, April 14, 2006. The church design has been recognized with at least one architectural award: the 2006 Tilt-Up Achievement Award, Spiritual Building Division. Centurion Construction Company, "St. Julia's Catholic Church: 2006 Tilt-Up Achievement Award Winner, Spiritual Buildings Division," Tilt-Up website, http://www.tilt-up.org/awards/2006/julia.html.

54. "Churches Get a New Accent," *News and Record,* June 10, 2000.

55. Carol Badaracco Padgett, "Construction Options: Structural Steel," *Worship Facilities* 6 (2005): 13.

56. For an account of the role that white Protestants played in preserving "the Hispano heritage of New Mexico," particular as evidenced in the Sanctuario de Chimayó, see Michael P. Carroll, *American Catholics in the Protestant Imagination: Rethinking the Academic Study of Religion* (Baltimore: Johns Hopkins University Press, 2007), 126–127.

57. Spencer commented that, for him, the design of St. Julia Church reflects an equal amount of influence from European, Greek, Mediterranean, and early Christian Church styles. Jim Spencer, phone interview with the author, May 11, 2011.

58. David Chidester and Edward T. Linenthal have identified "sacred space as ritual space, a location for formalized, repeatable symbolic performances." Each construction of sacred space is contested within the ritual space itself and the public space

that surrounds it. When Latino Catholics in Siler City performed the Good Friday processions, for example, they constructed sacred spaces within the ritual event, such as the space around the Christ figure and cross. In terms of phenomenological form, these sacred spaces were similar to those created by ritual performances in other geographic locations, like Mexico. But the processions created—and were created by—what Chidester and Linenthal have referred to as a "politics of place." Reinterpreting the comparative work of Gerardus Van der Leeuw and Mircea Eliade in light of cultural models of contestation, Chidester and Linenthal argue that the "positioning of sacred place [is] a political act," that "every establishment of a sacred place [is] a conquest of space," and "the sacrality of place...can be directly related to a politics of property." Chidester and Lintenthal's approach to the production of sacred space within a politics of place is salient to Siler City, where a religious history of racial segregation still impacts the landscape. David Chidester and Edward T. Linenthal, eds., *American Sacred Space* (Bloomington: Indiana University Press, 1995), 7–9. Roy Rappaport, though more concerned with phenomenological patterns than cultural constructions, also argues that sacred space emerges out of liturgy and ritual performance. Roy A. Rappaport, "The Obvious Aspects of Ritual," in *Ecology, Meaning, and Religion* (Richmond, CA: North Atlantic Books, 1979), 211. John Eade and Michael Sallnow describe ritual as "above all an arena for competing religious and secular discourses." John Eade and Michael J. Sallnow, eds. *Contesting the Sacred: The Anthropology of Christian Pilgrimage* (London: Routledge, 1991), 2.

59. The epitaph on the grave marker of John Joseph Alston, Jr., reads, "Alas that the fair and young The beautiful and good Should be called in the spring of earthly joy To the graves' [*sic*] dark solitude. The clod's [*sic*] of the valley lie, In courses o'er thy bed, But my soul doth oft in the shadowy hour, Commune with the sainted dead. And when thy vision comes, As now, in that magestick [*sic*] train, A voice like thine whispers oft and low, That we shall meet again." Chatham County Historical Association Cemetery Census, http://cemeterycensus.com/nc/chat/cem207.htm.

60. Federal Writers' Project (NC), *North Carolina: A Guide to the Old State* (Chapel Hill: University of North Carolina Press, 1939), 498.

61. David Meinig has argued, "Landscapes are symbolic expressions of cultural values, social behavior, and individual actions worked upon particular localities over a span of time." David W. Meinig, ed., *The Interpretation of Ordinary Landscapes* (New York: Oxford University Press, 1979), 4. Michael Conzen has proposed that much of the landscape in America appears relatively homogenous and uniform, as particularly evidenced in housing, despite the fact that a central theme in American history has been ethnic immigration. However, Conzen objects to a conformist view of American landscape evolution, citing the widespread evidence of pluralism found in many localities. This "imprint is muted by ravages of time, as modernization and the cycle of replacement have substituted mass-produced buildings and other landscape features for the more ethnically distinct accoutrements of the

past. He notes that forty or fifty years ago the American landscape was far more richly endowed with local ethnic flavor than is apparent today." A tension exists then between standardization and cultural homogenization (mass production) and ethnic particularity. That tension is evident in the contrast between the architectural display of St. Julia Catholic Church and the surrounding relatively homogenous southern rural landscape. Michael P. Conzen, "Ethnicity on the Land," in *The Making of the American Landscape*, ed. Michael P. Conzen (Boston: Unwin Hyman, 1990), 247.

62. The material presence of St. Julia Church and the public performance of Good Friday processions connect that space to a broader and more layered Nuevo South landscape in the surrounding area. In the nearby town of Pittsboro, for example, Latino Catholics processed with Our Lady of Guadalupe in front of the Confederate memorial that stands outside of Town Hall—the same memorial that Colonel John Randolph Lane had visisted in the early twentieth century. For a discussion of such emergent religious diversity in the South, see Thomas A. Tweed, "Our Lady of Guadalupe Visits the Confederate Memorial," *Southern Cultures* 8 (Summer 2002), 72–93. The ritual transformation of southern Protestant space to Latino Catholic place at St. Julia was a public performance. Belden C. Lane, *Landscapes of the Sacred: Geography and Narrative in American Spirituality* (Baltimore: Johns Hopkins University Press, 2002). David W. Meinig, ed., *The Interpretation of Ordinary Landscapes* (New York: Oxford University Press, 1979); Yi-Fu Tuan, *Space and Place: The Perspective of Experience* (Minneapolis: University of Minnesota Press, 1977).

63. For a discussion of the public display of religion, see Sally M. Promey, "The Public Display of Religion" in *The Visual Culture of American Religions* (Berkeley: University of California Press, 2001), 27–48.

64. Fieldnotes, January 15, 2006.

65. On the political changes in the Southern Baptist Convention, see Nancy Tatom Ammerman, *Baptist Battles: Social Change and Religious Conflict in the Southern Baptist Convention* (New Brunswick: Rutgers University Press, 1990).

66. Fieldnotes, April 23, 2011.

67. Resident F, interview with the author, October 6, 2006.

68. Willis Whitehead, interview with the author, January 30, 2004.

69. Carol Hall, "Good Friday Observed in Hispanic Tradition," *News and Observer*, April 3, 1999, A1.

70. Joyce Clark, "Headline: Newcomers Re-Create Christ's Passion in Siler City: Holy Drama the Latino Way," *News and Observer*, April 6, 1996, B1.

71. Ibid. For more information on the Hispanic Task force, see Milburn Gibbs, "Hispanic Task Force Meets," *Chatham News*, July 6, 1995, B1, B14.

72. David Kalbacker, interview with the author, April 22, 2011.

73. "A New Country, A New Life," *Greensboro News and Record*, May 4, 1997, A13.

74. Dorothy C. Holland, *Local Democracy Under Siege: Activism, Public Interest, and Private Politics* (New York: New York University Press, 2007), 71.

75. The arrival of new migrants to Siler City was "new" in the sense that long-term residents did not remember a time in their town's history that was comparable to the rapid changes of the 1990s. Siler residents, both black and white, were shaped by the racial and religious patterns of the South, by segregation, civil rights, and Protestant churches. Prior to their arrival, the presence of Latino laborers, particular those who were Catholic, was not a significant part of their collective experience. In a broader historical sense, though, "new" migration was not new at all. Mexican workers have been present in the Mississippi Delta since the early twentieth century. Julie M. Weise, "Mexican Nationalisms, Southern Racisms: Mexicans and Mexican Americans in the U.S. South, 1908–1939," *American Quarterly* 60 (September 2008): 749–777. For evidence of legacies of Mexican material cultures in the Mississippi Delta, see the description of the "Tamale Trail" as part of the University of Mississippi Southern Foodways Alliance project, http://www.tamaletrail.com. In addition to migrant arrivals, many Mexican Americans never physically moved but were annexed into the United States under the Treaty of Guadalupe Hidalgo in 1848. The US annexation of southwest territories placed an arbitrary national border across a region with familial and cultural ties on both sides of that dividing line. Those patterns later contributed to multiple migration trajectories, from both Mexico and the southwest United States to other parts of the United States, including southern towns like Siler City. For a demographic and historical survey of Hispanic presence in the United States, see Ana Maria Diaz-Stevens, "Colonization Versus Immigration," in *Religion and Immigration: Christian, Jewish, and Muslim Experiences in the United States*, ed. Yvonne Yazbeck Haddad, Jane I. Smith, and John L. Esposito (Walnut Creek, CA: AltaMira Press, 2003), 61–84.) For an account of migrant arrival from Central America through Texas to Siler City, see "Hispanic Immigrants Find Plenty of Job Openings in a Business Climate Eager for New Workers," *Greensboro News and Record,* May 5, 1997, A-1.

76. The demographic changes in Siler City were part of a larger phenomenon of migrant arrival to the global South. For a discussion of those migrant arrivals, see Marie Friedmann Marquardt and Manuel Vasquez, "A Continuum of Hybridity: Latino Churches in the New South," in *Globalizing the Sacred: Religion Across the Americas* (New Brunswick, NJ: Rutgers University Press, 2003), 145–170.

POSTSCRIPT

1. Richard S. Levy, *Antisemitism: A Historical Encyclopedia of Prejudice and Persecution* (Santa Barbara, CA: ABC-CLIO, 2005), 194.

2. For a description of local reaction to David Duke, see "Residents of Siler City Responded to David Duke's Visit With a Call for Unity," *Southern Exposure* 28 (2000): 13.

3. Ben Stocking, "Siler City Leaders Deny Brochure for Latino Newcomers Is Racist," *News and Observer,* June 30, 1996, B1.

4. "What Does the Future Hold? Piedmont Communities Experience Growing Pains as Population Becomes More Diverse," *Greensboro News and Record*, May 7, 1997, A10.

5. Ibid.

6. Cuadros, *A Home on the Field*, 2007.

7. To get a sense of the range of research studies conducted in Siler City, in addition to those cited throughout this book, see the study by Wolfram, Carter, and Moriello (2004) that "found that Spanish speakers in rural Siler City had more Southern-sounding dipthongs than the Hispanic speakers in urban Raleigh." Cited in Hugh Douglas Adamson, *Interlanguage Variation in Theoretical and Pedagogical Perspective* (New York: Routledge, 2009), 54.

8. John J. Valadez, *Matters of Race*.

9. See accompanying essay by David Nieves posted on the PBS website. David Nieves, "Latino/a USA: Redefining Race and Nation in a Post-Industrial America," http://www.pbs.org/mattersofrace/essays/essay1_latino_usa.html.

10. Fieldnotes, Jordan-Matthews High School Auditorium, March 6, 2006.

11. Academic interpretations and media accounts often depict rural southerners as religious anti-moderns and southern white men as prone to violence. Anthropologist Donald Nonini generalizes what he labels the categorical group of "poor rural white males" by leaping from the macro level of the state and global economic forces to the local level of human agency with little regard for what is in-between. In his words, "American neoliberalism…has reality effects that generate violence across differentially successful market 'performers'—such as the violence by white rural Southern men against Latino migrants in Siler City." Donald Macon Nonini, "American Neoliberalism, 'Globalization,' and Violence: Reflections from the United States and Southeast Asia," in *Globalization, the State, and Violence*, ed. Jonathan Friedman (Walnut Creek, CA: Altamira Press, 2002), 175.

12. City officials often were members of white Methodist and Baptist congregations. For example, former mayor Earl Fitts was a longtime member of First Baptist Church in Siler City, acting as deacon at least once in 1960. Murray M. Andrew, *First Baptist Church*, 38.

13. Milburn Gibbs, "First Rag Top Parade Big Success," *Chatham News*, July 10, 1997.

14. Phone interview with the author, June 23, 2011.

15. It also is significant that the cars in the Rag Top Parade were not restored in the same way as customized lowriders, like those that Mexican Americans display in parking lots in Austin, Texas to produce what Ben Chappell has argued is "an event in the production of social space." As far as I can tell, the renewed parade did not attempt to engage or challenge that or any other competing car restoration tradition. Rather, it attempted to ignore all signs of Latino presence, to exclude that group from its field of vision. Ben Chappell, *Lowrider Space: Aesthetics and Politics of Mexican American Custom Cars* (Austin: University of Texas Press, 2012), 7.

16. Milburn Gibbs, "First Rag Top Parade Big Success"; Milburn Gibbs, "Independence Days Past Are Remembered," *Chatham News*, July 10, 1997.

17. Gibbs, "First Rag Top Parade Big Success."

18. Robert Ronald White, Sr., was a member of First United Methodist Church and was president of the Siler City Lions Club. He served in World War II and received a Purple Heart. He passed away in 2011 at the age of eighty-seven. "Obituaries and Memoriams," *News and Record*, September 28, 2011.

19. Hobbs passed away in 2006 at the age of eighty-one. Reverend Jim Wall, pastor of FBC Siler City and friend of Hobbs, officiated the funeral. He remembered meeting Hobbs at the Rotary Club and said, "Of course, I found out real quickly that he was involved in a number of activities in the community. That's why people in this part of the county say, 'If you need to get anything done, call Pem Hobbs.'" Joseph Pardington, "Civic Leader Hobbs Dies at Age 81," *Chatham News*, February 2, 2006. Janell Ross, "Siler City Go-to Person Hobbs, 81," *News and Observer*, January 30, 2006.

20. "'Rag Top' Parade Saturday in Siler City," *Chatham News,* July 2, 1998; "Rag Top Parade Big Success in Siler City," *Chatham News,* July 9, 1998.

21. In 1999, the local paper asked, "What's more American than a Fourth of July parade?" That same year, the commissioners brought back the rodeo to the festivities. Jeanne Pierce, "Parade, Bull Ride Highlight Fourth of July Activities," *Chatham News,* July 8, 1999.

22. "July 4 Parade Set for July 1," *Chatham News,* June 29, 2000; "July Fourth Holiday Returns with Parade, Rodeo, Fireworks," *Chatham News,* July 6, 2000.

23. *Chatham News,* July 5, 2001.

24. "No July 4th Activities Set," *Chatham News,* June 27, 2002.

25. "Lake Placid Mural Society," Local Legacies, the American Folklife Center, the Library of Congress, http://lcweb2.loc.gov/diglib/legacies/FL/200002864.html.

26. Angela Delp, "New Mural Depicts Old Lifestyle," *Chatham News*, August 31, 2006, A1, A11.

27. Phone interview with the author, June 21, 2011.

28. "Chatham County Observes Quiet 4th of July Holiday" and "Photographs of First Union Bank Torn Down Over the Chatham Bank," *Chatham News*, July 6, 1978. Another marker of that lost history, the First United Methodist Church on Chatham Avenue, burned down in 1995. Rather than rebuild the church downtown, members voted to relocate to West Raleigh Street, between the Palestine neighborhood and the Siler City Country Club. Remnants of the downtown church building later were used for Hispanic Missions of the United Methodist Church.

29. Hadley, *The Town of Siler City,* photo insert between pages 27 and 28.

30. Nancy Tysor, interview with the author, Farmers' Alliance store, July 6, 2011.

31. Stayce Leanza, interview with the author, Farmers' Alliance store, August 25, 2006. Blue Heron Farm Intentional Living Community was organized in 1982 and is

located on sixty-four acres just outside of Pittsboro, North Carolina. According to their website, residents include "families, couples, and individuals who share some common values: environmentally sustainable living, celebrating life through the arts and play, closeness and connection across the generations, and a reverence for nature." Blue Heron Farm Intentional Living Community website, http://www. bhfarm.org/sustainable.htm. One of the community members told me she was a graduate student in the School of Education at UNC. She said that their community consists of artists, teachers, and others of kindred spirit. At the dedication, community members played folk songs on acoustic guitar and shouted, "Yeah, Siler City" in front of the mural. Fieldnotes, August 25, 2006.

32. J. Heath Atchley, *Encountering the Secular: Philosophical Endeavors in Religion and Culture* (Charlottesville: University of Virginia Press, 2009), 28–29.

33. On the "currency of secrets," see Paul Christopher Johnson, *Secrets, Gossip, and Gods: The Transformation of Brazilian Candomblé* (New York: Oxford University Press, 2005), 6.

34. Johnson, *Secrets, Gossip, and Gods*, 4.

35. These are the spaces where modern religion speaks, where it "interrupts," as Kathryn Lofton writes of Oprah, who "supplies the way to survive the thronged silence." Kathryn Lofton, *Oprah: The Gospel of an Icon* (Berkeley: University of California Press), 6–7.

36. Nancy L. Eiesland, *A Particular Place: Urban Restructuring and Religious Ecology in a Southern Exurb* (New Brunswick, NJ: Rutgers University Press, 2000), 16.

37. Friedrich Nietzsche, *"On the Genealogy of Morality" and Other Writings* (Cambridge: Cambridge University Press, 2006), 35.

38. Ibid.

39. Johnson, *Secrets, Gossip, and Gods*, 4.

40. Ibid., 28.

41. Willard Bohn, *Modern Visual Poetry* (Cranbury, NJ: Associated University Presses, 2001).

42. Alina Kwiatkowska, "Silence Across Modalities," in *Silence: Interdisciplinary Perspectives*, ed. Adam Jaworski (Berlin: Mouton de Gruyter, 1997), 334.

43. Ibid.

44. The predecessor to the Siler City drugstore opened in 1888 on the corner of West Raleigh Street and South Birch Avenue. Hadley, *The Town of Siler City*, 18.

45. Nietzsche, *"On the Genealogy of Morality,"* 36.

46. Ibid., 40.

47. Ibid., 35.

48. When asked if Hispanics shop at the Farmers' Alliance store, Nancy Tysor said, "We have a few. Not too many. But they're nice when they come in. We can't complain about their conduct or anything. They're real nice." Nancy Brown Tysor, interview with Bruce E. Baker, October 19, 1999. Interview K-0811. Southern Oral

History Program Collection (#4007), Documenting the South, University of North Carolina at Chapel Hill.

49. In the midst of demographic and religious changes to the local landscape, longtime Protestants drew on familiar narratives and practices inscribed into the material culture of southern place to reposition themselves within white-controlled spaces. Visual cultures of public display in the murals were a key component of Protestant historical narration as spatial claim. Anthropologists Terry Rey and Alex Stepick have argued that, "visual culture is indispensable to religion" because it provides a "chain of memory." Visual culture connects viewers to sacred spaces past, present, and future. But these are contested spaces. As historian David Morgan has suggested, viewers inscribe visual artifacts with meaning. Just as there are many viewers, there are multiple meanings. In Siler City, visual culture has been a critical component of Latino Catholic and white Protestant productions of sacred space. Both groups have attributed varied meanings to similar visual artifacts, such as the American flag and the Christian cross. In Siler City, those artifacts were connected to visual "chains of memory." The Farmers' Alliance mural connected those chains of memory to Chatham Avenue and its surrounding streets. Residents located themselves in relation to that place, and that place was firmly rooted in the American South. As I noted in the previous chapter, the visual cultures displayed in the material artifacts of Good Friday processions also connected Latino Catholics to place, but that place crossed over to Mexico, El Salvador, California, and New York. On the streets of Siler City, those "chains of memory" tangled together. For a use of Danièle Hervieu-Léger's phrase "chain of memory," in terms of visual cultures and migrant religions, see Terry Rey and Alex Stepick, "Visual Culture and Visual Piety in Little Haiti: The Sea, the Tree, and the Refuge," in *Art in the Lives of Immigrant Communities in the United States*, ed. Paul DiMaggio and Patricia Fernández-Kelly (Piscataway, NJ: Rutgers University Press, 2010), 230.

50. On competing or multiple meanings of visual display, see Thomas. A Tweed, "America's Church: Roman Catholicism and Civic Space in the Nations Capital," in *The Visual Culture of American Religion*, ed. David Morgan and Sally Promey (Berkeley: University of California Press, 2001), 72.

51. Delp, "New Mural Depicts Old Lifestyle."

Index